BIPARTITE NEGATION AND THE FINE STRUCTURE OF THE NEGATIVE PHRASE

A Dissertation

Presented to the Faculty of the Graduate School

of Cornell University

in Partial Fulfillment of the Requirements for the Degree of

Doctor of Philosophy

by

Arthur James Bell

August 2004

© 2004 Arthur James Bell

ALL RIGHTS RESERVED

BIOGRAPHICAL SKETCH

Arthur Bell was born in Cambridge, MA but grew up in Southern California. In 1988 he enrolled as an undergraduate at U.C. Santa Barbara, and, yes, his dormitory room actually had an ocean view. Initially an aquatic biology major, he quickly succumbed to the hardships of introductory chemistry. Following a junior year abroad in France, he made the switch to humanities and never looked back. He earned his B.A. (1992) and his M.A. (1994) in French, both from UCSB. Arthur spent two years as a U.S. Peace Corps volunteer in Guinea-Bissau, West Africa (1994-1996). Upon his return to the U.S., he taught French for two years at a private elementary and middle school in San José, California, before entering the Ph.D. program in linguistics at Cornell University in the fall of 1998.

To my Mother and Father

ACKNOWLEDGEMENTS

Many thanks to my graduate committee, Wayne Harbert, Carol Rosen, and John Whitman, for all of their help and encouragement. Also thanks to Abby Cohn for serving as a member on my A-exam committee, and for all of her help in the research workshop. John Bowers was my virtual fifth committee member, and I thank him for his comments and encouragement. Finally, if I can claim to be any sort of scholar at all, it would not be without the help of my committee chair, Chris Collins, whose tireless devotion to the intellectual growth of his students was a great inspiration to me. Many thanks to the following colleagues who I met and knew along the way, and who were always ready to talk shop, especially: J. Clancy Clements, Michel DeGraff, Ana Deumert, Yoshi Dobashi, Tjerk Hagemeijer, Rachel Hastings, Marek Przezdziecki, Paul Washburn, and Jiahong Yuan, (too few remembered, too many forgotten). Finally, thanks to my Ithaca crew for getting me through the hard times. Eric Gilbertson, Brendan Jackson, and Ellert "Thor" Johannsson: Good times, good times . . . keep on truckin'.

TABLE OF CONTENTS

1 Introduction **1**
    1.1   The Topic and the Data 3
    1.2   Syntactic Framework 8

2 The Syntax of Negation in Afrikaans **12**
    2.1   Negation in Afrikaans: The Data 15
        2.1.1   Matrix Clauses 16
        2.1.2   Embedded and Relative Clauses 19
        2.1.3   *Because*-Clauses 22
        2.1.4   Negative Words and *Nie*$_1$ 23
    2.2   Categorial Status and Optionality of *Nie*$_2$ 26
    2.3   Previous Analyses 28
        2.3.1   NegP and PolP 28
        2.3.2   Oosthuizen (1998) 31
        2.3.3   Molnárfi (2002) 33
        2.3.4   The NEG Criterion (Haegeman 1995) 35
    2.4   Negation in Afrikaans: The Analysis 39
        2.4.1   Movement of N-words 39
        2.4.2   *Nie*$_2$ 41
            2.4.2.1 The Category Containing *Nie*$_2$ 43
            2.4.2.2 *Nie*$_2$ and Uninterpretable Features 45
            2.4.2.3 NegP$_1$ Moves to [Spec,NegP$_2$] 47
            2.4.2.4 Prepositional Phrases and *Nie*$_2$ 50
            2.4.2.5 *Because*-Clauses and *Nie*$_2$ 53
        2.4.3   *Nie*$_1$ 57

		2.4.3.1 Categorial Status *Nie$_1$* 58

          2.4.3.2 The Expanded NegP and *Nie$_1$* Fronting 60

          2.4.3.3 Optional *Nie$_1$* with N-words 64

2.5   The Syntax of Negation in Afrikaans: a Derivation 66

      2.5.1   Negative Heads and the HMC 67

2.6   Chapter Summary 67

3   Properties of Bipartite Negation with Final NEG (BNF)   71

3.1   Bukusu, Hausa, Nweh and Dagara: The Data 72

      3.1.1   Bukusu 73

          3.1.1.1 Matrix Clauses. 74

          3.1.1.2 Embedded and Relative Clauses 77

          3.1.1.3 *Because*-Clauses 79

      3.1.2   Hausa 80

          3.1.2.1 Matrix Clauses. 81

          3.1.2.2 Embedded and Relative Clauses 86

          3.1.2.3 Clause-initial *bàa* in Hausa 91

          3.1.2.4 *Because*-Clauses 93

      3.1.3   Nweh 94

          3.1.3.1 Matrix Clauses. 95

          3.1.3.2 Embedded and Relative Clauses 97

          3.1.3.3 *Because*-Clauses 98

      3.1.4   Dagara 100

          3.1.4.1 Matrix Clauses. 100

          3.1.4.2 Embedded and Relative Clauses 102

          3.1.4.3 *Because*-Clauses 102

      3.2   Shared Properties of BNF Languages 104

4	**Parameters of BNF**			**108**

    4.1   Typological Overview of BNF Languages 109

    4.2   The Position of NEG_1 in BNF 110

    4.3   Relative Clause Negation in BNF 114

    4.4   Verb Movement in BNF 123

    4.5   Post-NEG_2 Stranding in BNF 129

            4.5.1   Afrikaans 130

                     4.5.1.1 Post-*Nie₂* versus Post-verbal: Afrikaans and Dutch . 131

                     4.5.1.2 Scope Effects of Post-NEG_2 Stranding 139

            4.5.2   Hausa 142

                     4.5.2.1 Post-Stabilizer Stranding in Hausa 147

    4.6   Negation in West Flemish 151

            4.6.1   West Flemish Negation: The Data 151

            4.6.2   Haegeman (2002). 154

            4.6.3   Categorial Status of N-words, *nie*, and *en* 157

            4.6.4   BNF analysis of West Flemish Negation 161

    4.7   Chapter Summary 164

5	**The Historical Development of BNF in Afrikaans**		**166**

    5.1   History of the Cape Colony from 1590 169

            5.1.1   Early Years 169

            5.1.2   Contact with the Khoekhoe 170

            5.1.3   From Dutch to Afrikaans 170

            5.1.4   Varieties of Dutch 171

    5.2   The Genesis of Afrikaans 173

    5.3   The History of *Nie₂* in Afrikaans 177

	5.4	Structural Origins of *Nie₂* in Afrikaans	184
		5.4.1 Negative Tags in Germanic	185
		5.4.2 Negation in Dutch	186
		5.4.3 Negation in Khoekhoe	190
		5.4.4 Negation in !Korana	193
		5.4.5 The Syntax of Negation in Khoekhoe and !Korana	196
	5.5	Borrowing and Expansion: a UG-Based Account	198
6	**The Syntax and Development of BNF in Creoles and Contact Languages**		**204**
	6.1	Creoles and Contact Languages with Mixed Systems	206
		6.1.1 Negation in Santome	208
		6.1.2 Negation in Palenquero	213
		6.1.3 Negation in Vernacular Brazilian Portuguese	224
		6.1.4 Summary of Shared Properties and Parametric Variation	233
	6.2	Diachrony of Negation in VBP, Palenquero and Santome	235
		6.2.1 African Substrates	236
		6.2.2 A UG-Based Scenario	239
	6.3	Creoles without BNF	240
	6.4	Chapter Conclusions	243
7	**Extending the Proposal**		**244**
	7.1	Negation in French	245
	7.2	A BNF Analysis of French	248
	7.3	Advantages of the Analysis	251
	7.4	Conclusions	256
References			**257**

LIST OF TABLES

Table 1. Hausa Negation Strategies 78

Table 2. Properties of BNF Languages 105

Table 3. Post-verbal constituents in Dutch and Post-nie_2 constituents in Afrikaans 138

Table 4. Nie_2 in Cape Dutch and Creole Dutch, 1826-1844 177

Table 5. Negation in a corpus of !Korana texts 192

Table 6. Five Stages of Development of BNF in Afrikaans 203

Table 7. Properties of BNF Languages 226

LIST OF FIGURES

Figure 1. Model of Afrikaans genesis, adapted from den Besten (1989) 174

Figure 2. Model of Afrikaans genesis with stages of BNF development 203

LIST OF ABBREVIATIONS AND SYMBOLS

1	first person
2	second person
3	third person
ACC	accusative
ASP	aspect
AUX	auxiliary
BN	bipartite negation
BNF	bipartite negation with final NEG
CAUS	causative
CCLs	creole and contact languages
COMP	complementizer
CP	complementizer phrase
DAT	dative
DET	determiner
DP	determiner phrase
FUT	future
HAB	habitual
LOC	locative
NC	negative concord
NEG	negative particle
NEG_1	leftmost negative particle
NEG_2	rightmost negative particle
O	object
OCC	occurrence feature

PP	prepositional phrase
PST	past tense
PL	plural
PRES	present
REL	relative clause marker
S	subject
SG	singular
uNeg	uninterpretable negative feature
V	verb

CHAPTER ONE

INTRODUCTION

Languages employ a number of distinct sentential negation strategies. However, as Zanuttini (2000:511) points out, "it is clear even from a superficial investigation of the world's languages that sentential negation is not expressed in as many ways as there are languages." Zanuttini (2000) goes on to detail four main negation strategies across languages, one of which is the main focus of her work, and also the focus of this dissertation: the use of one or more (invariant) particles to mark sentential negation. Indeed, dating back at least as far as Jespersen's (1917) seminal work, linguists have attempted to provide adequate empirical descriptions and theoretic analyses of the syntax, semantics, and historical development of negation in languages that employ negative particles. The main goal of this dissertation is to make a substantive contribution to this tradition.

The major works on the syntax of negation draw their data by and large from a handful of Indo-European languages, including English (Jespersen 1917, Horn 1989), French (Pollock 1989, Moritz and Valois 1994), (dialects of) Italian (Zanuttini 1991, Cinque 1999), and West Flemish (Haegeman and Zanuttini 1991, Haegeman 1995)- notable exceptions being Laka's (1990) thesis on Basque, Kato (1994, 1999) and Watanabe (2004) on Japanese, and the recent study by Benmamoun (2000) on negation in Arabic. Thus, another goal of this dissertation is to add to the empirical base of negation data by examining languages "unrelated to those languages that have been used to shape current theories on the syntax of negation" (Nkemnji 1995:112).

As I will discuss in greater detail in §2.3.1, these theories are built around the notion that two negative particles in a single negative clause are housed in a single projection, termed the Negative Phrase or NegP (Pollock 1989, Ouhalla 1990). The syntactic relationship between the two particles is one of specifier to head. This approach to the syntax of particle negation is nicely summarized by Ouhalla (1990), as follows:

> [...] sentence negation is expressed in terms of a NegP category which consists of a head element and a specifier. **Variation among languages is restricted to whether both or either of the two elements of NegP is realized lexically**. In languages like Turkish and Berber the head is realized lexically while the specifier is realized as an empty operator. In languages like German, Swedish and Colloquial French it is the specifier which is realized lexically, while the head is realized as an abstract morpheme. Finally, in languages like Standard French both the head and the specifier are realized lexically (Ouhalla 1990:191, my emphasis).

In the chapters that follow, I will examine languages that, like Standard French, use two separate particles to express sentential negation. However, I will explicitly argue against the approach outlined by Ouhalla (1990) above. Instead, I will propose an "articulated" or "expanded" NegP that can house two separate negative heads, as well as other projections that I show to be internal to the NegP complex. In support of this proposal, I will present data on negation from a number of languages, including Afrikaans, Bukusu, Dagara, Hausa, Nweh, Palenquero, Vernacular Brazilian Portuguese, and Santome. These relatively diverse languages show a striking similarity in their sentential negation strategies: all use a pre-verbal negative particle in conjunction with a normally phrase-final negative particle, as in (1).

(1)   Subject   **NEG**   Verb   XP   **NEG**

In this dissertation, I will cover four broad areas relating to the negation strategy in (1). First, I propose a detailed syntactic account of the negation strategy in (1), using both language-specific and cross-linguistic data. I argue that a single, unified analysis can elegantly capture the shared properties of sentential negation in the above-mentioned languages. Second, I show that the variation encountered across the negation strategies in these languages can be explained in terms of parameters made available under UG. Third, I look at the historical development of the negation strategy in (1), and propose an account for the rise of this negation strategy in certain creole and contact languages. Fourth, I explore to what extent the proposed analysis of the negation strategy in (1) can be adapted to account for a broader group of bipartite negation languages, including West Flemish and French.

The dissertation is organized as follows. In next section, I provide a brief introduction to the topic and the data. Then in §1.2, I present my background assumptions and discuss the theoretical framework of the dissertation. In Chapter Two, I present data from Afrikaans, and develop the core of the syntactic analysis. Chapter Three brings data from other languages to bear, and presents a more detailed picture of the unifying properties of the negation strategy in (1). Chapter Four is a discussion of the parameters observed across the languages that negate as in (1). In Chapter Five, I move to a discussion of the historical development of negation in Afrikaans. In Chapter Six, I present data from a number of creole and contact languages. I argue that these languages represent intermediate stages in the development of the negation strategy shown in (1). Finally, in Chapter Seven, I entertain the possibility that the articulated NegP can account for a broader range of bipartite negation languages. Having examined West Flemish in Chapter Four, I turn to a discussion and analysis of French in Chapter Seven. I argue that the articluated NegP can indeed accommodate French, and has several distinct advantages over the 'single NegP' analysis of Pollock (1989), Ouhalla (1990), Haegeman (1995), and others.

1.1   The Topic and the Data

The negation strategy in (1) can be loosely described as a subtype of *bipartite negation* (henceforth BN), since it uses two separate morphemes in a single clause to mark a single instance of sentential negation. Standard French provides a paradigmatic example of BN.

(2) Jean **ne** connais **pas** Marie.   **STANDARD FRENCH**
     John NEG know NEG Mary
     'John doesn't know Mary.'

In Standard French, and the French widely spoken in the 18th and 19th centuries, sentential negation is normally expressed by the use of two separate particles, the preverbal *ne* (optional in most spoken dialects of modern French) and the post-verbal *pas*. I gloss such particles as NEG throughout the introduction so as not to impose a particular analysis: for example, assuming that *pas* is the equivalent of English *not* by glossing *pas* as *not*. Note that the two particles in French give a single negative meaning to the sentence, rather than the double negative reading we might expect if each of the two particles were interpreted as a separate instance of negation. This strategy is fairly widely attested. Consider three more examples, from Moroccan Arabic, West Flemish, and Tarifit Berber.

(3) a. Nadia **ma**-ža-t-**š**.   **MOROCCAN ARABIC**
       Nadia NEG come.past.3fs-NEG
       'Nadia didn't come.'   (Benmamoun 2000:69)

    b. ...da Valère **nie** nor us (**en**)-goat.   **WEST FLEMISH**
       that Valère NEG to home NEG-goes
       '...that Valère does not go home.' (Haegeman 1995a:126)

    c. **Ur**   izri   **shi**   immas   **TARIFIT BERBER**
       NEG$_1$ see.past.3s NEG$_2$ mother-his
       "He didn't see his mother" (Ouali 2002)

The data in (3) illustrate bipartite negation in Moroccan Arabic, West Flemish, and Tarifit Berber. All three languages, like French, employ two separate particles to express a single instance of sentential negation. In Moroccan Arabic and Berber, there is a pre-verbal negative particle accompanied by a post-verbal negative particle. The post-verbal particle precedes direct and indirect objects and complement clauses, and is only found in phrase-final position when such elements are not present, or in the presence of object clitics. Given these similarities, the negation strategies of French, West Flemish and Berber have often received similar treatments in the literature (Cf. Pollock 1989, Haegeman 1995, and Ouali 2002, respectively).

Pollock (1989) proposes that the negative particles *ne* and *pas* in French are in a relationship of head to specifier, arguing that a single negative projection, NegP, houses both. Hageman and Zanuttini (1991) and Haegeman (1995) refine this idea and, building on Rizzi (1991), propose the NEG Criterion. Essentially a well-formedness condition on syntactic structure, the NEG Criterion requires a spec-head relation to obtain between a negative head and one or more negative words – be they negative adverbs, quantifiers, or negative polarity items – at some point in the derivation.

A number of other languages employ two separate particles in sentential negation. Unlike French, West Flemish and Moroccan Arabic, these languages generally take the form illustrated in (1) above, and repeated, with some examples, in (4)a-i below.

(4) a. Subject **NEG** Verb XP **NEG**

b. Piet het **nie** 'n appel by die mark geëet **nie**.　　　　　　**AFRIKAANS**
　Peter has NEG an apple at the market eaten NEG
　'Peter didn't eat an apple at the market.'

c. Peter **se**-a-la-ba　a-kula sitabu **ta**.　　　　　　　　　　　**BUKUSU**
　Peter NEG-SA-TNS-be SA-buy book NEG
　'Peter will not be buying a book.' (Bell & Wasike 2003)

d. Lāmî **bà** tà ci àbinci à　kāsuwā **ba**.　　　　　　　　　　**HAUSA**
　Lami NEG he eat food PREP market NEG
　'Lami didn't eat food at the market.' (Newman 2000:358)

e. Njikèm à kè **te** fiá nkāp anbó Atem əjúa **bɔ́**.　　**NWEH**
   Njikem AGR P-2 NEG give money to Atem yesterday NEG
   'Njikem did not give money to Atem yesterday.' (Nkemnji 1995:112)

f. Ɂʊ **bɛ́** kɔ́ Ɂa pɔ́g kámáànd Ɂadián **ɛ́**.　　**DAGARA**
   he NEG give the woman corn today NEG
   'He didn't give corn to his wife today.' (Delplanque 1990:52)

g. Ê **na** ka bila konsê xitu ku kwa sa nê **fa**.　　**SANTOME**
   3SG NEG ASP turn know place that thing be in-3SG NEG
   'He doesn't recognize the place where the thing is.' (Hagemeijer 2004)

h. Kolómbá **na** tá methé pa no tá zunto 'ne **wa**.　　**ANGOLAR**
   whites NEG TA want for us be near them NEG
   'The whites don't want us (living) near them.' (Dieck 2000)

i. **Não** sei se você está mentindo **não**.　　**VERNACULAR BRAZILIAN**
   NEG know if you are lying NEG　　**PORTUGUESE**
   'I don't know whether you are lying.' (Schwegler 1985-7:199)

The data in (4)b-i also illustrate bipartite negation, following the loose definition adopted above. In each case, sentential negation is expressed with two separate negative particles. However, unlike French, West Flemish and Moroccan Arabic, the second negative particle appears in sentence-final position across the languages in (4)b-i, following objects, prepositional phrases, complement clauses and adverbials. It is by all measures, given the data in (4)b-i, a radically sentence-final particle. In addition to the sentence-final position of the second negative particle, the languages illustrated in (4)b-i share a number of morpho-syntactic properties related to negation. I therefore propose in this dissertation that the negation strategy schematized in (4)a, and attested in (4)b-i, can be captured by a unified analysis. To distinguish the bipartite negation strategy in (4)a from bipartite negation in French, West Flemish and Moroccan Arabic, I will term the former *bipartite negation with final NEG*, or BNF. In the chapters that follow, I provide an account of BNF from both a synchronic and a diachronic perspective.

I build up the analysis in the following manner. First, in Chapter Two, I look in detail at negation in Afrikaans, examining data from the literature as well as my own field data. I propose that the standard NEG Criterion analysis, in addition to being theoretically undesirable, cannot account for the BNF data in (4)b-i. I propose instead an 'expanded NegP', housing the two negative morphemes in BNF, both of which have the status of functional heads. I argue that the word-order facts in BNF result from XP-movement of the lower NegP into the specifier of the higher NegP. Furthermore, I propose that the expanded NegP also contains one or more intermediate projections that serve as landing sites for phrases and constituents that can be stranded to the right of the final NEG particle. XP-movement followed by remnant movement accounts for this stranding.

In Chapter Three, I examine data from four other languages that exhibit what I argue to be the defining properties of BNF. I discuss these properties in detail, thereby solidifying the analysis of what I argue to be a unique negation strategy made available under UG, namely, BNF. Then, in Chapter Four, I look at the main areas of syntactic variation across BNF languages. I propose several parameters within the BNF system, and discuss their particular cross-linguistic instantiations. In Chapter Five I depart from the synchronic analysis to discuss the historical development of BNF in Afrikaans. I argue, *contra* previous accounts, that neither language contact nor superstrate influence can fully account for the development of BNF. I propose that language universals played a crucial role. Furthermore, I propose a five-stage development model for the growth of BNF in Afrikaans. In Chapter Six, I look at negation in three creole/contact languages. One of the three, Santome, appears to exhibit all of the core properties of BNF. The other two, Palenquero and Vernacular Brazilian Portuguese (VBP), present many similarities with BNF, but also contain data that fall outside the properties and parameters of BNF defined in Chapters Two, Three and Four. I propose a synchronic analysis of the Palenquero and VBP data. Furthermore, I argue that, VBP and Palenquero represent an intermediate stage in the development of BNF, and thus can inform us about the precise stages of the growth of BNF across languages. I extend the proposal to French in Chapter Seven, where I argue that the expanded NegP analysis can account for bipartite negation as well as BNF.

1.2 Syntactic Framework

In this dissertation I adopt Minimalism (Chomsky 1995, 2000, 2001) as my theoretical framework. I assume a lexicon composed of lexical items or LIs – the lexicon of a given speaker of English being roughly equivalent to the "words" that speaker knows. LIs are used to form a *numeration,* which is a list of the LIs to be combined by a given derivation. *Merge* is taken to be the fundamental syntactic operation combining two (or more) LIs or constituents. *External Merge* (also *set Merge*) combines two LIs to form a set $\{\alpha,\beta\}$.[1] *Internal Merge* (the operation we normally conceive of as "movement") is identical to *External Merge* except that it operates on already-existing structure, effectively "moving" one piece of structure (an LI or a whole phrase or constituent) to another position. *Agree* is the relation established between a probe with uninterpretable features (e.g. ϕ-features) and a goal with matching interpretable features. *Internal Merge* is licensed under *Agree*, and is triggered by the need to eliminate the uninterpretable feature(s) of the probe and the occurrence feature *OCC* (also known as *EPP*), also on the probe.

Agree is established when the probe encounters the nearest matching goal, with the concept of "nearest matching goal" being defined by the Minimal Link Condition (MLC). The MLC in turn is crucially dependent on the concept of C-Command, both of which I define in (5) and (6).

---

[1] Or, more strictly, $\{\gamma, \{\alpha, \beta\}\}$, with γ serving as the label of α.

(5) **Minimal Link Condition (MLC)**: An *Agree* relation can be established between a probe (P) and a goal (G) with matching φ-features iff there is no intervening category α such that P C-commands α, α C-commands G, and the same uninterpretable features of P also match the features of α.

(6) **C-Command**: α C-commands β iff every node of the tree that dominates α also dominates β, but α neither dominates β nor β dominates α.

In addition to the MLC and C-command, I assume that *Merge* operates in accordance with the *Extension Condition,* which I state in (7).

(7) **Extension Condition**: The operation *Merge* can only target root syntactic objects.

I assume the widespread availability of XP-movement and remnant movement. Consider a schematic representation of remnant movement in (8).

(8)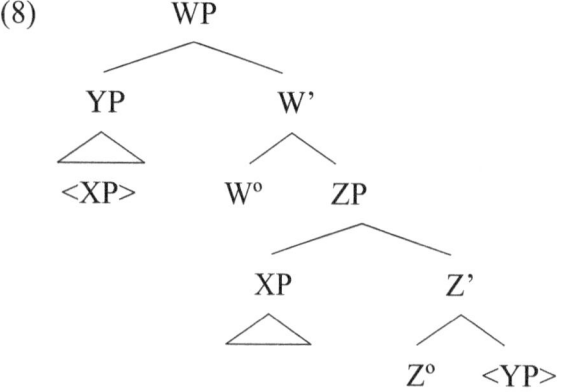

The derivation in (8) illustrates remnant movement. XP has moved out of YP to Spec,ZP, leaving behind the "remnant" YP. The remnant-YP then moves to Spec,WP. I make very specific use of the mechanism of remnant movement to account for certain cases of stranding in the context of negation (cf. den Besten & Webelhuth 1990; Pearson 1999, 2001; Müller 2000; Koopman & Szabolcsi 2000; Haegeman 2000; Nilsen 2003; and Aldridge 2003 for various other applications of remnant movement).

I adopt the Linear Correspondence Axiom (LCA) of Kayne (1994), and assume that the order Specifier-Head-Complement is universal. According to Kayne (1994), branching is unidirectional to the right, movement is invariably leftward, and all languages are underlyingly head-initial. This proposal has particular relevance to the questions at hand, since it has led to a re-evaluation of traditional analyses of SOV languages like Dutch. While earlier work on Dutch syntax proposed that the SOV word-order of Dutch was reflected in embedded clauses, Koster (1994), Zwart (1997), Haegeman (2002) and others argue convincingly that Dutch is underlyingly SVO, and that both SOV (embedded) and SVO (matrix) orders are derived from this order. Robbers (1997) argues much the same for Afrikaans. In this dissertation, I follow Kayne (1994) and the specific proposal of Robbers (1997) in claiming that Afrikaans has underlying SVO word order.

I also adopt the basic structure of the articulated left periphery as set forth by Rizzi (1997). This is in line with the general tendency in much recent work to break up the core projections CP, IP and *v*P into a number of separate functional projections (cf. Pollock 1989, Rizzi 1997, Cinque 1999). Adopting the notion that IP and *v*P are *fields*, and not simply single projections, allows for much greater flexibility in capturing a large variety of cross-linguistic data. I argue below, along these lines, that the traditional negative projection NegP should also be considered a field, since it appears to house multiple negative functional categories as well as other functional projections, at least in certain languages.

In the historical chapters, I draw by and large on the theory of language contact and change developed in Harris & Campbell (1995), which assumes that the basic mechanism of contact-induced change is structure borrowing, straight forwardly defined as follows:

> Borrowing is a mechanism of change in which a replication of the syntactic pattern is incorporated into the borrowing language through the influence of a host pattern found in a contact language (Harris & Campbell 1995:51).

Although borrowing doubtless played an important role in the development of the negation strategy in question here, I also argue, in relation to creole and contact languages, that there is a universal component at work. In so doing, I assume the view of creolization put forth in recent work by DeGraff (1999, 2001, 2003), who argues that creolization reduces to first- and second-language acquisition processes working in concert with the basic principles of language change put forth, for example, in Harris & Campbell. DeGraff argues pointedly against the theory of relexification (Lefebvre 1998), which holds that creole grammars, and Haitian Creole in particular, are entirely the result of structure borrowing and transfer. Rather, DeGraff proposes a theory in which both borrowing and language universals play a role, and this simply because the theory reduces to language acquisition. The historical context of creolization is unique, but the linguistic mechanisms that led to the birth of these new languages are not.

CHAPTER TWO

NEGATION IN AFRIKAANS: SYNTACTIC ANALYSIS

Bipartite negation, as we defined it in Chapter One, is the use of two separate morphemes in a single clause to mark a single instance of sentential negation. We have seen examples of BN in a number of languages, Bukusu, Dagara, French, Hausa, Moroccan Arabic, Nweh, Palenquero, Santome, and West Flemish. As is apparent from these data, the syntax of BN differs markedly across languages. In French and Moroccan Arabic, for example, the two negative morphemes bracket the verb, and object clitics, if present. The leftmost negative morpheme appears before the verb, while the rightmost negative marker appears after the verb but before full NP objects, prepositional phrases, and embedded clauses. In Bukusu, Hausa and Nweh, we observed that the leftmost negative morpheme precedes the verb, while the rightmost negative can appear in sentence-final position, following objects, prepositional phrases, and embedded clauses. As I will show in Chapter Three, Afrikaans negation patterns by and large with Bukusu, Hausa and Nweh, raising the interesting possibility that a unified analysis can account for negation across these languages. An even more interesting possibility, that the proposed analysis can be extended to French, is discussed in detail in Chapter Seven.

Afrikaans employs a BN[1] strategy in most contexts. The leftmost negative morpheme can be either a negative word (*nooit* 'never,' *niks* 'nothing,' etc.), or, in simple sentential negation, the particle *nie*. It is traditionally analyzed in the literature as the locus of negative force, that is, the syntactic position that yields the negative meaning to the sentence (den Besten 1977, 1985; Robbers 1992; Donaldson 1993;

---

[1] I continue to employ the term *bipartite negation* while I present the analysis of Afrikaans. At the beginning of Chapter Three, I put forth the general proposal that negation in Afrikaans and a number of other languages can receive a unified analysis. I then adopt the rubric *bipartite negation with final NEG*, or BNF, throughout the remainder of the dissertation.

Ponelis 1993; Oosthuizen 1998; Bell 2001, 2004; Molnárfi 2002). In Minimalist terms, this corresponds to the notion of interpretable features: the leftmost negative in Afrikaans possesses an interpretable negative feature.

The rightmost negative morpheme, which is spelled out as the invariant particle *nie*, is somewhat more mysterious. As I will show below, it cannot be the sole marker of sentential negation. Yet its (normally obligatory) presence is clearly triggered by the presence of negation, as its morphology would suggest. Also, in certain cases, its syntactic position appears to perform an important semantic function, disambiguating *because*-clauses. Consider the pattern of negation in Afrikaans as illustrated in (1), where **NEG$_1$** represents the leftmost negative particle and NEG$_2$ the normally phrase-final negative particle.[2]

(1)   a.   *Negative simple intransitive:*
                  Subject Verb **NEG$_1$**

        b.   *Negative complex intransitive*:
                  Subject AUX **NEG$_1$** Verb **NEG$_2$**

        c.   *Negative transitive*:
                  Subject Verb **NEG$_1$** Object (Prepositional Phrase) **NEG$_2$**

        d.   *Negative embedded clause (intransitive or transitive):*
                  ... Complementizer Subject **NEG$_1$** (Object) Verb **NEG$_2$**

In (1)a-d I schematize, in broad fashion, the negation paradigm in Afrikaans. As we can see in (1)a, simple (single verb) intransitives allow a single negative morpheme. In most other contexts, a single instance of sentential negation receives two overt markers, as in (1)b-d. I will provide examples, and discuss the fact that the

---

[2] Den Besten (1977), Ponelis (1993) and Donaldson (1993) all gloss the rightmost negative particle *nie* as 'not'. Oosthuizen (1998) prefers the gloss *NIE*, while Robbers (1992) glosses the rightmost *nie* as 'Neg.' Throughout the dissertation, I will gloss this particle as either *nie$_2$* or NEG$_2$.

rightmost negative morpheme can precede certain constituents and clauses, in the sections below.

Some aspects of negation in Afrikaans are unsurprising, given a Germanic – or indeed Indo-European – model of sentential negation with negative particles (Cf. Pollock 1989; Haegeman & Zanutinni 1991; Haegeman 1995, 2002). First, the position of the leftmost negative morpheme in the verbal field is consistent with that of negative morphemes in many languages using particle negation, including those showing BN. Second, like many Germanic languages, Afrikaans shows verb-second effects (the verb moves to the second position in matrix clauses, Cf. Wackernagel's law). This accounts for the fact that NEG_1 follows the verb in matrix clauses (1)a-c. Third, as in West Flemish, negative words such as *niks* 'nothing', *nooit* 'never' – presumably generated as *v*P complements or adjuncts – undergo displacement to a higher position.

The rightmost negative particle NEG_2, unlike BN systems in Romance or other Germanic languages, can follow almost any complement or adjunct, including heavy complement clauses and adverbial adjuncts (Donaldson 1993:401-417). Thus, the position of NEG_2 is at variance with that of the rightmost negative particle in many other languages with bipartite systems, in particular Arabic, French, and, most interestingly from an historical perspective, closely related Germanic languages with BN such as West Flemish (see chapters 4-6). In addition to its position, there are certain morpho-syntactic properties associated with NEG_2 in Afrikaans. Again, these properties are not attested in Arabic, French, or West Flemish – three languages that form the core data for theories on the syntax of negation in Benmamoun (2000), Pollock (1989) and Haegeman (1995, 2002), respectively. As I argue below, the theories just mentioned cannot fully account for the position and behavior of NEG_2 in Afrikaans.

As we shall see, there are certain constituents and phrases that can appear either to the left or to the right of nie_2 – in particular, prepositional phrases (PPs) and complement clauses (CPs). Other complements, such as determiner phrases (DPs) and adverbs, can never appear to the right of nie_2. I propose an analysis of these facts based on XP-movement followed by remnant movement. As I show, the behavior of post-nie_2 constituents in Afrikaans appears to be closely related to the behavior of post-verbal constituents in Dutch. I argue that similar movement operations are involved in both cases. In Chapter Three, I discuss the fact that other languages also employ a similar strategy to strand constituents to the right of NEG_2, and also to strand elements to the right of other phrase-final functional categories – for example, Hausa uses remnant movement to strand constituents to the right of the stabilizer particle. Interestingly, the constituents are by and large identical to those that follow NEG_2 in Hausa.

The chapter is organized as follows. In §2.1, I examine the data on Afrikaans negation in detail. In §2.2, I consider the categorial status of the rightmost negative morpheme nie_2. In §2.3, I present and critique previous syntactic analyses of Afrikaans negation, including Oosthuizen (1998) and Molnárfi (2002). I also discuss a NEG Criterion analysis of the Afrikaans data. Then, in §2.4, I present my analysis. I offer a summary of the arguments presented in the chapter, and some concluding remarks, in §2.5. To begin, consider the data on Afrikaans negation in §2.1.

2.1 Negation in Afrikaans: The Data

The data in this chapter come from six main sources: Oosthuizen (1998) Donaldson (1993, 2000), Robbers (1992, 1997), and my own fieldword on Afrikaans. Each of the authors mentioned employs a slightly different scheme in glossing their examples. For the sake of clarity and consistency, I modify their glosses when necessary, in particular for the final negative morpheme *nie*, which I gloss as nie_2 or NEG_2.

Donaldson (1993) gives only translations, and thus all glosses of his data are my own, and follow the same pattern as my glosses of the other data.

The first goal of this chapter is to provide a syntactic analysis of the position and function of the rightmost negative morpheme nie_2. Therefore, the following subsections focus primarily on the distribution of nie_2 in various clause types. The second goal of the chapter is to provide an analysis of displacement of negative words (*nooit* 'never', *niks* 'nothing', *nêrens*, 'nobody,' henceforth *N-words*). Throughout the section we will see numerous examples of the distribution of N-words in Afrikaans, and I devote §2.1.4 to an in-depth presentation of N-word data. In §2.1.1, I illustrate the position of nie_2 in matrix clauses. In §2.1.2, I show how nie_2 functions in the context of embedded and relative clauses. Then in §2.1.3 I look at the behavior of nie_2 in *because*-clauses. Finally, I examine the syntactic behavior of N-words in §2.1.4.

2.1.1 Negation in Matrix Clauses

In this section I discuss negation in matrix clauses, with particular attention paid to the position of nie_2. Sentential negation in Afrikaans is normally realized with at least two morphemes: a phrase-internal particle *nie* and a phrase-final or post-verbal invariant particle *nie*. Consider the data in (2).

(2) a. Hulle was **nie** betrokke **nie**.   **AFRIKAANS**
they were nie_1 involved nie_2
'They were not involved.' (Oosthuizen 1998)

b. Sy sluit **nooit** die deur **nie**.
she locks never the door nie_2
'She never locks the door.' (ibid.)

c. Hulle is **g'n** so arm **nie**.
they are not so poor nie_2
'They aren't all that poor.' (ibid.)

The data in (2) illustrate the general distribution of the two negative morphemes in declarative sentences in Afrikaans. Nie_1 directly follows the tensed verb in matrix clauses, owing to verb movement to second position. The rightmost negative particle *nie₂* follows main verbs (2)a, direct objects (2)b, and adjectival complements (2)c. Next, consider the data in (3).

(3) a. Jy praat **nie** duidelik **nie**.
 you speak *nie₁* clearly *nie₂*
 'You're not speaking clearly.' (Donaldson 1993)

 b. Hy het **nie** gedink aan die ernstige gevolge **nie**.
 he has *nie₁* think of the serious consequences *nie₂*
 'He didn't think of the serious consequences.' (ibid.)

 c. Wie het **nie** opgedaag **nie**?
 Who has *nie₁* arrived *nie₂*
 'Who hasn't arrived?' (Oosthuizen 1998)

In (3) we observe *nie₁* in its unmarked position immediately following the tensed verb in matrix clauses. As we can see above, *nie₂* can follow adverbs (3)a and prepositional phrases (3)b. The bipartite negation strategy in Afrikaans also occurs in other clause types, such as *Wh*-questions (3)c. According to Donaldson (1993:402-419), *nie₂* must always follow direct and indirect nominal object complements. However, he points out that the position of prepositional phrases vis-à-vis *nie₂* is variable in Afrikaans (Cf. also Robbers 1997:81-82). Indeed, prepositional phrase adjuncts can occur before or after *nie₂* – although there appears to be a difference in grammaticality between post-*nie₂* PP adjuncts and post-*nie₂* PP complements, to which I return in Chapter 4. While it is more natural for a heavy prepositional phrase to follow *nie₂*, there are no absolute restrictions related to heaviness, and light prepositional phrases can follow *nie₂* as easily as heavy ones can precede it (Donaldson 1993:406). Consider the data in (4).

(4) a. Sy het **niks** gesê op die vergadering **nie**.
 she has nothing said at the meeing *nie₂*
 'She said nothing at the meeting.' (Oosthuizen 1998)

b. Sy het **niks** gesê **nie** op die vergadering.
she has nothing said *nie₂* at the meeing
'She said nothing at the meeting.' (ibid.)

c. Hoekom word daar **nie meer** ingegaan op die direkte invloed van
how come is there no more delve into the direct influence of

die bruin Afrikaanssprekendes **nie**?
the colored Afrikaans-speakers *nie₂*

'How come one isn't delving any more into the influence of coloured speakers of Afrikaans?' (Donaldson 1993)

d. Hoekom word daar **nie meer** ingegaan **nie** op die direkte invloed
how come is there no more delve *nie₂* into the direct influence

van die bruin Afrikaanssprekendes?
of the colored Afrikaans-speakers

'How come one isn't delving any more into the influence of coloured speakers of Afrikaans?' (ibid.)

Placing the prepositional phrase after *nie₂* in (4)b and (4)d does not trigger a change in meaning. However, some speakers find that placing the prepositional phrase after *nie₂* gives it some type of contrastive focus, or that a contrastive focus intonation is more easily associated with a prepositional phrase that follows *nie₂*. I discuss these facts in greater detail in Chapter Four below.

Next, consider the data in (5), which show that *nie₂* cannot appear alone as the sole marker of sentential negation.

(5) Sy sluit *(**nooit**) die deur **nie**.
she locks never the door *nie₂* (Oosthuizen 1998)

Nie₂ cannot appear as the sole marker of sentential negation in Afrikaans. Below in §2.4.2.2, I argue that this fact is one piece of evidence that *nie₂* does not possess interpretable negative features, but rather has an uninterpretable [uNeg] feature that enters into an *Agree* relation with the [+neg] feature associated with *nie₁*. The particle *nie₂* is obligatory in most environments in Afrikaans, and licensed by the presence of sentential negation. It is not enough that a clause contain some negative element to license *nie₂*. Consider the following data in (6).

(6) a. Hulle kan iets uit **niks** maak
     they can something out nothing make
     'They can make something out of nothing.' (Robbers 1997:35)

   b. **Nie**-lede is ook welkom.
     non-members is also welcome
     'People who are not members are also welcome.' (ibid.)

The sentences in (6) both contain words with inherent negative force, i.e. with interpretable negative features. Yet in neither case is the presence of *nie₂* licensed. As I will discuss in detail in my analysis below, *nie₂* is present only in case the sentence expresses sentential negation, or particular types of constituent negation. In structural terms this will reduce to *nie₂* being licensed just in case the sentence contains an (expanded) NegP.

Ponelis (1993:455) states that "clause-final *nie* is for the most part obligatory in the standard language and most varieties of Afrikaans." Donaldson (2000:61) states that in all contexts besides simple intransitives, "a second *nie* is required," while Oosthuizen (1998:61) states that "a negative sentence contains, as a general rule, a second 'negation word' in final position, viz. the item *nie*."

In the next subsection, I present data on negation in the context of embedded and relative clauses.

2.1.2 Negation in the Context of Embedded and Relative Clauses

Negation of an embedded clause is also normally accomplished with two separate particles, an N-word or *nie₁*, and *nie₂*. As in matrix clauses, *nie₂* appears at the end of the clause. The N-word or *nie₁* in embedded clauses appears to the left of the verb, as there are no verb-second effects in embedded clauses in Afrikaans (de Kleine 1997; Robbers 1997). Consider the data in (7).

(7) Ek het geweet dat hy **nie** sou kom **nie**.
 I AUX know that he *nie*₁ would come *nie*₂
 'I knew that he wouldn't come.' (Donaldson 1993)

A negative relative inside an affirmative clause is negated with *nie*₂ immediately following the relative, not at the end of the sentence. Consider (8).

(8) Mense wat **nie** rook **nie** lewe langer.
 people who *nie*₁ smoke *nie*₂ live longer
 'People who don't smoke live longer. (ibid.)

In cases where the matrix clause is negated, but the embedded clause, (9)a-b, or relative clause, (9)c-d, is not, the position of *nie*₂ in Afrikaans is variable. Consider the data in (9).

(9) a. Ek het **nie** geweet dat hy sou kom **nie.**
 I AUX *nie*₁ know that he would come *nie*₂
 'I didn't know that he would be coming.' (Donaldson 1993)

 b. Ek het **nie** geweet **nie** dat hy sou kom.
 I AUX *nie*₁ know *nie*₂ that he would come
 'I didn't know that he would be coming.' (ibid.)

 c. Ons het **nooit** die mense geken wat in hierdie huis gebly het **nie**.
 we AUX never the people know who in this house live AUX *nie*₂
 'We never knew the people who lived in this house.' (ibid.)

 d. Ons het **nooit** die mense geken **nie** wat in hierdie huis gebly het.
 we AUX never the people know *nie*₂ who in this house live AUX
 'We never knew the people who lived in this house.' (ibid.)

As we see in (9), the *nie*₂ particle associated with a negative matrix clause can appear either at the end of the sentence, following a non-negative embedded clause (9)a, or immediately following the matrix clause (9)b. Similar facts hold for relative clauses, as I show in (9)c-d. According to Donaldson (1993:404), the sentences in (9)a and (9)c, where nie_2 is sentence-final, illustrate the unmarked position for nie_2, although (9)b and (9)d are perfectly acceptable.[3] Any theory of negation in Afrikaans must account for both of these possible positions for nie_2.

When the matrix and the embedded clause are both negative, there are of course two nie_1 particles, one associated with the matrix clause, and one with the embedded clause. The position of nie_2 is again variable. Consider the data in (10).

(10) a. Ek het **nie** geweet dat hy **nie** sou kom **nie**.
I AUX nie_1 know that he nie_1 would come nie_2
'I didn't know that he wouldn't come.' (Donaldson 1993)

b. Ek het **nie** geweet **nie** dat hy **nie** sou kom **nie**.
I AUX nie_1 know nie_2 that he nie_1 would come nie_2
'I didn't know that he wouldn't come.' (ibid.)

c. *Ek het **nie** geweet dat hy **nie** sou kom **nie nie**.
I AUX nie_1 know that he nie_1 would come nie_2 nie_2

d. *Ek het **nie** geweet **nie** dat hy **nie** sou kom.
I AUX nie_1 know nie_2 that he nie_1 would come

In cases where both the matrix and the embedded clause are negative, we observe either two separate instantiations of nie_2 (10)b, or a single nie_2 at the end of the sentence (10)a. Native speaker judgments confirm that both (10)c, with a double nie_2 in sentence-final position, and (10)d, where the embedded clause lacks nie_2, are ungrammatical.

As with nie_2 variation around prepositional phrases, native speakers report no change in meaning when nie_2 associated with a negative matrix clause appears either before or after an affirmative embedded clause. Unlike the prepositional phrase facts, however, native speakers report no focusing effects related to the position of nie_2 in

---

[3] Note that both (9)c and (9)d involve extraposition of the relative clause. For simplicity's sake, I ignore this fact throughout my analysis.

the context of relative or embedded clauses. As I mentioned above, there is a specific context in which the position of *nie₂* triggers a change in meaning. I consider these data in subsection 2.1.3.

2.1.3 Negation in *Because*-Clauses

The particle *nie₂* in Afrikaans has a privileged role in the disambiguation of *because*-clauses in negative environments. Consider the sentence in English shown below in (11). Depending on intonation and stress, (11) can have either the reading shown in (a), in which Peter did not leave, or the reading in (b), in which Peter did leave, but not due to the fact that it was raining.

(11) Peter didn't leave because it was raining.
    a. ¬leave(Peter)
    b. leave(Peter) ¬because it was raining

Now consider the data in (12)a-d below. In Afrikaans, the reading in (11)a, in which the *because*-clause is outside the scope of negation, is available when *nie₂* appears to the left of the *because*-clause, as in (12)a and (12)c. The reading in (11)b, where the *because*-clause is inside the scope of negation, is available when *nie₂* appears to the right of the *because*-clause, as in (12)b and (12)d.

(12)   a.   Hy het dit **nie** gedoen **nie** omdat hy betaal is.
                  he have it *nie₁* done *nie₂* because he paid is
                  'He did not do it, because he was paid.' (Robbers 1997:40)

       b.   Hy het dit **nie** gedoen omdat hy betaal is **nie.**
                  he have it *nie₁* done because he paid is *nie₂*
                  'He did not do it because he was paid (but for another reason)' (ibid.)

       c.   Piet het **nie** vertrek **nie**, omdat dit gereën het.
                  Peter has *nie₁* left *nie₂* because it raining has
                  'Peter didn't leave, because it was raining.'

       d.   Piet het **nie** vertrek omdat dit gereën het **nie**, (maar het vetrek omdat ...)
                  Peter has *nie₁* left because it raining has *nie₂* (but has left because)
                  'Peter left not because it was raining, (but because ...)'

The position of *nie₂* is variable in embedded and relative clauses, but affects no change in meaning, as we saw in §2.1.2 above. However, the position of *nie₂* relative to *because*-clauses in the context of negation determines the relative scope of negation over the *because*-clause. As Donaldson (1993) points out, this property is unique to *because*-clauses with *omdat* 'because.' Consider the sentence in (13).

(13)   Hy kan **nie** kom **nie** want hy is siek.
       he can *nie₁* come *nie₂* because he is sick
       'He won't be coming because he's sick.' (Donaldson 1993:407)

Unlike the sentences in (12), the only available position for *nie₂* in (13) is to the left of the *because*-clause. Note that (13) has *want* 'because' rather than *omdat*. Compare this fact to the behavior of *since* in English, where a similar restriction on the possible readings in negative environments holds. Consider for example "Peter is not going since he is sick," where the only possible interpretation is that Peter is not going.

In the final subsection of §2.1, I will consider in greater detail the data on negative words in Afrikaans.

2.1.4   Negative Words and *Nie₁*

The locus of negative force in Afrikaans – defined as the morpheme containing the interpretable negative feature – is the leftmost negative. Donaldson (1993) terms any morpheme associated the *negator*. In some cases, the negator is an N-word – that is, a lexical category that carries inherent negative force. Note that using an N-word in an elliptical answer is one of the principle tests for a negative concord item – that is, a lexical item with an interpretable negative feature [+neg] (Cf. Ladusaw 1992; Kato 1994; Haegeman 1995; Déprez 1999; and especially Watanabe 2004 for a detailed discussion of N-words and negative concord). Indeed, Afrikaans *niks* 'nothing', *nooit* 'never', *nêrens* 'nowhere', *niemand* 'nobody', and *geen* 'none' can all be used as elliptical answers. Consider the data in (14).

(14) Q: Hoeveel geld het jy?   **AFRIKAANS**
      How much money have you
      'How much money do you have?'

    A: **Geen**.
      'None.' (Donaldson 1993:413)

The N-words just mentioned contrast to negative polarity items (NPIs), which must be licensed by the overt presence of negation to be interpreted as negative. We have seen above that the canonical position of N-words in a negative sentence in Afrikaans is immediately following the tensed verb in matrix clauses, and preceding the tensed verb in embedded clauses. However, N-words, as lexical categories, can also occur as subjects, and undergo topicalization and leftward displacement (focus movement). Consider the data in (15).

(15) a. **Geen** mens weet **nie**.
      no person knows *nie$_2$*
      'No-one knows.' (Donaldson 1993)

   b. **Niemand** kom **nie**.
      nobody come *nie$_2$*
      'Nobody is coming.' (ibid.)

   c. **Niks** gebeur **nie**.
      nothing happen *nie$_2$*
      'Nothing is happening.' (ibid.)

As we would expect, negative quantifiers in Afrikaans can appear in subject position. This confirms the general intuition that they are lexical categories. Note that in all cases the presence of negation in subject position licenses the presence of *nie$_2$* in sentence-final position. Now consider the data in (16).

(16)   a.   Ons voel **nêrens** veilig **nie**.
we feel nowhere safe nie_2
'We don't feel safe anywhere.' (Oosthuizen 1998)

        b.   **Nêrens** voel sy veilig **nie**.
nowhere feels she safe nie_2.
'Nowhere does she feel safe.' (ibid.)

We observed in (15) that N-words can appear in subject position. However, the sentences in (16)a and (16)b already contain a subject, namely *sy* 'she.' In (16)b, *nêrens* 'nowhere' undergoes displacement, most probably to Spec,CP. Note that *nêrens* in this position triggers verb-second.

As we have seen above, in simple sentential negation Afrikaans employs nie_1 in the pre-verbal position, and nie_2 in sentence-final position. One important issue in an analysis of Afrikaans negation, to which I shall return presently in §2.2, is the categorial status of nie_1. In some ways nie_1 patterns with other N-words. Consider the data in (17).

(17)   a.   Hy het **nie** gekom **nie**.
he has nie_1 come nie_2
'He didn't come/hasn't come.' (Donaldson 1993)

        b.   **Nie** hy het gekom **nie.**
nie_1 he has come nie_2
'**He** is not coming.' (Molnárfi 2002, *my gloss*)

        c.   ***Nie** het hy gekom **nie**.
nie_1 has he come nie_2 (ibid.)

The example in (18a) illustrates simple sentential negation in Afrikaans. As in (16)b above, nie_1 can be fronted, as in (17)b. The result, according to Donaldson (1993), is a contrastive focus interpretation on *hy* 'he,' as suggested by the boldface type in the translation. First, note that, while fronting *nêrens* focuses *nêrens*, fronting nie_1 focuses the subject. Second, note that fronting *nie* in (17)b does not trigger verb-second, unlike fronting *nêrens* above. Indeed, employing verb-second with fronted *nie₁* results in ungrammaticality (18c), as pointed out by Molnárfi (2002). This suggests that (17)b and (16)b have rather different syntactic structures. I return to these data in §2.4.3 below.

Oosthuizen (1998) provides data on co-occurrence of an N-word with *nie₁*. Consider the data in (18).

(18) a. Ek sal jou **nooit** (**nie**) vergeet ***nie.***
I will you never *nie₁* forget *nie₂*
'I will never forget you.' (Oosthuizen 1998)

b. Dit blyk dat sy absoluut **niks** (**nie**) het opgedaag **nie**.
it seems that she absolutely nothing *nie₁* can remember *nie₂*
'It seems that she can remember absolutely nothing.' (ibid.)

In (18)a-b, we see a leftmost negative morpheme *nie₁* occurring optionally in the presence of N-words *nooit* 'never' and *niks* 'nothing.' One native-speaker consultant with whom I worked found such examples as (18)a-b ungrammatical with *nie₁* spelled out. However, other speakers find these examples grammatical, or only slightly degraded, with overt *nie₁*. Therefore, any theory of negation in Afrikaans must account for these data as well.

In the remainder of the chapter, I will provide a comprehensive theory of the syntax of negation in Afrikaans. I will focus on four main issues: i) the categorial status and syntactic function of the negative morpheme *nie₂*; ii) the syntactic structure, features and operations that capture the position and behavior of *nie₂*; iii) the specific mechanisms by which N-words undergo displacement in Afrikaans; iv) the categorial status and syntactic function of *nie₁*.

2.2 Categorial Status of *Nie₂*

Unlike N-words, *nie₂* is an invariant particle. Its phonological shape never changes, and it can appear in a very limited number of positions. It cannot be fronted, nor can it appear as a topic or in a focus position. Also, as Molnárfi (2002) points out, phonologically *nie*$_2$ cannot receive any focus stress. Based on these facts, and following I will argue that *nie*$_2$ is a clausal functional head, following Oosthuizen (1998).

One clear piece of evidence that *nie*$_2$ is of a different category than N-words comes from adverbial modification facts. Consider the data in (19).

(19) a. Dit blyk dat sy **absoluut niks** (**nie**) kan onthou **nie**.
it seems that she absolutely nothing *nie*$_1$ can remember *nie*$_2$
'It seems that she can remember absolutely nothing.' (Oosthuizen 1998)

   b. *Dit blyk dat sy **niks** (**nie**) kan onthou **absoluut nie**. (ibid.)

   c. *Dit blyk dat sy **niks absoluut** (**nie**) kan onthou **nie**. (ibid.)

The adverb *absoluut* 'absolutely' can modify the N-word *niks* 'nothing' in (19)a. However, *absoluut* cannot modify *nie*$_2$ in (19)b. The resulting sentence is ungrammatical. Were *nie*$_2$ of the same category as *niks*, we might expect it to be modifiable by adverbs. This is contrary to fact. *Nie*$_2$ is a clausal functional category. Note in addition that the leftmost, optional *nie*$_1$ in (19)c cannot be modified in this context. I argue below that this is due to the absence of a structural position between the N-word and *nie*$_1$. Note that *nie*$_1$ can be modified by adverbs when it is the sole negator. Consider the sentences in (20).

(20) a. Hulle was **nie** betrokke **nie**.
they were *nie*$_1$ involved *nie*$_2$
'They weren't involved.' (Oosthuizen 1998)

   b. Hulle was **glad nie** betrokke **nie**.
they were entirely *nie*$_1$ involved *nie*$_2$
'They weren't involved at all.' (ibid.)

Before moving into the analysis, I discuss two previous analyses of Afrikaans negation in the next section. As we will see, both of these analyses have serious empirical and theoretic shortcomings.

2.3 Previous Analyses of *Nie$_2$*

In this section I briefly review some of the main literature on the syntax of negation, and discuss proposals for a Negative Phrase (NegP) and a Polarity Phrase (PolP), in §2.3.1. I then critique two recent analyses of negation in Afrikaans, both of which make specific proposals with regards to the syntax and distribution of the final particle *nie$_2$*. I look first at the analysis of Oosthuizen (1998), in §2.3.2. I then examine the analysis of Molnárfi (2002) in §2.3.3. I will show that the predictions of both theories are straightforwardly disconfirmed by the data. In addition, as I will argue, they are theoretically problematic. Finally, I discuss how to handle the Afrikaans data using the NEG Criterion (Haegeman 1995) in §2.3.4. First, consider the proposals for NegP and PolP.

2.3.1 NegP and PolP

In the early generative literature, negative particles such as English *not* were normally assumed to be adverbs, housed in some type of adverbial phrase. More recently, several authors have proposed that negative particles, and also negative quantifiers (such as *nobody*) and negative adverbs (such as *never*) are housed in a separate projection NegP. The proposal for NegP projection is most fully developed in the literature in Pollock (1989), Ouhalla (1990), and Haegeman & Zanuttini (1991). In particular, Ouhalla (1990) argues that the NegP projection is part of UG, and is always licensed in the presence of sentential negation. Pollock (1989) and Haegeman & Zanuttini (1991) put forth specific proposals for sentential negation involving two negative morphemes – Standard French and West Flemish, respectively. In languages such as Standard French, Pollock (1989) argues that the discontinuous negative *ne...pas* is housed in NegP. *Ne* is the head of NegP, while *pas* is the specifier. I will argue against this proposal in Chapter Seven.

Recall the basic claim made by Ouhalla (1990), presented in Chapter One of the dissertation and repeated below:

> [...] sentence negation is expressed in terms of a NegP category which consists of a head element and a specifier. Variation among languages is restricted to whether both or either of the two elements of NegP is realized lexically. In languages like Turkish and Berber the head is realized lexically while the specifier is realized as an empty operator. In languages like German, Swedish and Colloquial French it is the specifier which is realized lexically, while the head is realized as an abstract morpheme. Finally, in languages like Standard French both the head and the specifier are realized lexically (Ouhalla 1990:191).

According to Ouhalla (1990), the single NegP hypothesis can accommodate a wide range of cross-linguistic data, given the availability of two positions inside the single NegP. As I discuss in Chapter Seven, Ouhalla (1990) also argues that the single NegP hypothesis can capture the cyclic effects of particle negation in historical perspective – often referred to as the Jespersen cycle.

The notion of a Polarity Phrase "PolP" as separate and distinct from NegP first appears in the literature in Culicover (1990), who in turn cites an unpublished (1989) manuscript by Kyle Johnson. Culicover's (1990) basic pre-Rizzian idea is that there are two functional projections in the left periphery, CP, and PolP. CP is argued to be the traditional position housing complementizers (*that* in English), while PolP is taken to house negative and *Wh* elements, as well as English *so*.

This basic proposal is explored in much greater detail in Laka (1990, 1994), who proposes that "natural languages do not have a separate syntactic category for negation, but rather include this element in a broader, more abstract category" (Laka 1994:74). She terms this projection Σ-phrase. It houses both negative elements and emphatic affirmative elements such as English *so* and Basque *ba*. Consider the data in (21).

(21)   a. Jon **ez** da etorri.   **BASQUE**
            Jon not has arrived
            'Jon hasn't arrived.'

          b. Jon **ba** da etorri.
            Jon so has arrived
            'Jon has so arrived.'   (Laka 1990:101)

Laka (1990) uncovers the surprising parallels between Basque and English both in terms of negation and in terms of emphatic affirmation, realized in English with the morhpeme *so* and in Basque with the morpheme *ba*. Note that, both in English and Basque, the negative and emphatic affirmative particles are in complementary distribution. These data, Laka argues, are strong support for her proposal that negation and affirmation are housed in the same projection, namely ΣP.

In more recent work, both Oosthuizen (1998) and Haegeman (2002) posit the existence of a Polarity Phrase in the context of sentential negation in Afrikaans and West Flemish, respectively. I discuss these accounts in turn in the next section, and in Chapter Four. The basic argument in the two papers is that Afrikaans and West Flemish have both a negative particle (for Oosthuizen it is a head, nie_1, while for Haegeman it is a maximal projection, WF *nie*) **and** a polarity head (Afrikaans nie_2 and WF *en*). In the case of Afrikaans, I argue that the PolP projection, as conceived by Culicover (1990) and extended as ΣP by Laka (1990, 1994), does not effectively capture the data. Unlike English and Basque, there are no affirmative or emphatic particles that occur in complementary distribution with the final negative particle *nie*. This fact renders meaningless the notion of *polarity* as related to Afrikaans nie_2, since nie_2 has no positive counterpart and thus cannot be part of a more abstract projection that shifts a sentence from a negative to a positive 'pole' or vice-versa. As I discuss in greater detail in Chapter Four, Haegeman (2002) puts much weight on the fact that WF *en* adds negative emphasis to a sentence, making it somewhat like a negative version of English *so* in sentences such as (21)b above. Again, however, there is no positive counterpart to WF *en*, making the polarity proposal less than convincing. In the next section, I consider Oosthuizen's (1998) analysis of Afrikaans negation in more detail.

2.3.2 Oosthuizen (1998)

Oosthuizen (1998) proposes an analysis of *nie$_2$* in the Minimalist framework of Chomsky (1995). He argues that *nie$_2$* heads a Polarity Phrase, PolP, projected in the left periphery, above CP. In his account, feature-checking drives movement of the entire CP to [Spec,PolP], pied-piping the whole clause and accounting for the phrase-final position of *nie$_2$*. As Oosthuizen (1998) points out, such phrase structures are not in line with minimalist operations, and violate Kayne's (1994) LCA. Consider the derivation in (22), abstracted from Oosthuizen's (1998) analysis.

(22)

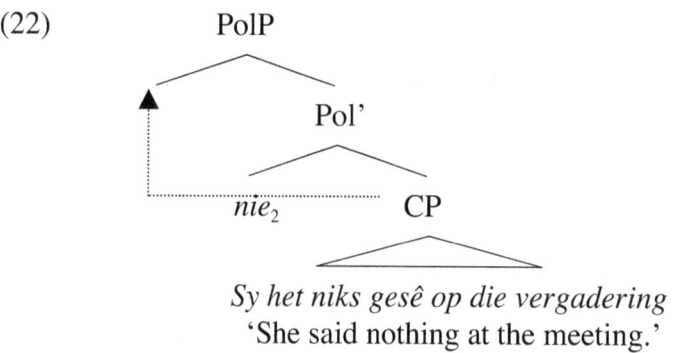

Sy het niks gesê op die vergadering
'She said nothing at the meeting.'

Oosthuizen's (1998) analysis makes the strong prediction that *nie$_2$* is a radically final particle in Afrikaans. Because PolP dominates CP, and the entire CP moves to [Spec,PolP], it follows necessarily that *nie$_2$* occur only sentence-finally. As we have seen above, this is not borne out in the data. While *nie$_2$* can appear in sentence-final position, it very often occurs to the left of prepositional phrases and embedded clauses, and can also be non-final when following an embedded relative clause. Oosthuizen (1998:88) notes that postposed prepositional phrases are "clearly problematical" for his analysis of *nie₂*, but proposes no solution. In addition, we have seen that *nie₂* can appear to the left of *because*-clauses, and that this positional difference triggers a change in meaning. Again, the analysis proposed by Oosthuizen (1998) cannot, without modification, account for the PP stranding data.

We could propose a modified version of Oosthuizen's (1998) analysis in an attempt to overcome some of these problems. Under this account, which I will call modified-Oosthuizen, *nie₂* is the head of PolP, which is projected in the left-periphery above CP. However, we have noted that certain constituents and phrases can appear to the right of *nie₂*, including prepositional phrases, embedded clauses, and *because*-clauses. This suggests a position intermediate between PolP and CP – an XP-level category of some indeterminate type (to be defined in greater detail below). Under the proposed modified-Oosthuizen account, PolP dominates XP, which in turn dominates CP. Consider the derivation in (23).

(23)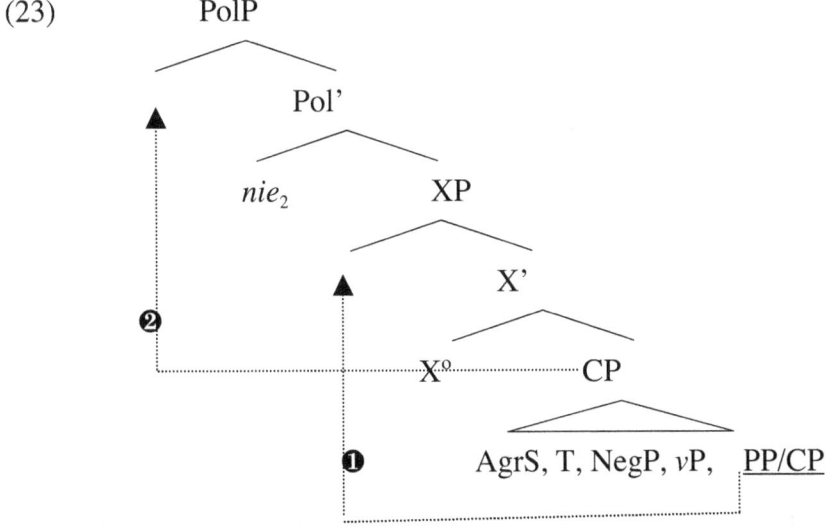

The derivation in (23) represents the modified-Oosthuizen analysis that I propose as a potential solution to the overly-powerful prediction of Oosthuizen (1998), namely that

nie_2 is radically final. In (23), a PP or CP can move to [Spec,XP] in a first part of the derivation. The CP-remnant is then free to move to [Spec,PolP], pied-piping the entire clause. This account can easily capture the variable position of nie_2. I return to a detailed discussion of PP and CP stranding in Chapter 3, and explore whether or not such an account has cross-linguistic applicability. Overall, I adopt several key aspects of Oosthuizen's (1998) analysis, while making certain adjustments and modifications to accommodate a wider group of languages.

2.3.3 Molnárfi (2002)

Molnárfi (2002) argues that the rightmost negative morpheme nie_2 is a phonologically reduced copy of nie_1, and an overt manifestation of the end of negative scope. The notion of *copy* employed by Molnárfi (2002) should be distinguished from the minimalist "copy theory of movement" (Chomsky 1995, Fox 2000). A deleted copy in the minimalist sense corresponds roughly to a trace in older principles-and-parameters work. A copy in Molnárfi's (2002) sense is a phonologically-reduced homophonous particle, but does not relate to displacement. Rather, the copy of *nie* is due to a process of "percolation" of NEG throughout the VP, and "the post-verbal negator is in this respect only a phonetically reduced copy of nie_1," and in fact a non-projecting element. (Molnárfi 2002:224).[4] The result of negative "percolation" is a negative doubling (*Negationsklammer*) effect, i.e. a copy of *nie* which surfaces at the end of the domain of negative scope. I will argue against Molnárfi's account on both empirical and theoretic grounds.

Molnárfi's (2002) theory predicts that the copy of nie_1, nie_2, should be phonologically reduced. This prediction is borne out in the data, since nie_2 cannot receive contrastive stress. Following this chain of reasoning, I argue that Molnárfi's

---

[4] "Der postverbale Negator ist in diesem Sinne nur eine phonetisch reduzierte Kopie von nie_1 und kein projektionsfähiges Element" (Molnárfi 2002:224).

(2002) theory makes a further prediction, namely that nie_2 should not have a separate syntactic function as a negative head, since it is merely a copy of nie_1. This prediction is straightforwardly disconfirmed by the data on *because*-clauses, which show that nie_2, as a separate syntactic head, plays a very important role in XP-movement.

In general, it is difficult to reconcile Molnárfi's (2002) account with the theoretical assumptions adopted in this paper. For example, Molnárfi posits the availability of a mechanism allowing a copy of a syntactic head to be spelled out to the right of its base position. Translating this into principles-and-parameters or minimalist terms, we would be forced to appeal to rightward head movement, or a right-branching structure, allowing nie_1 to move to some rightward position. Yet such movement operations and such structures are universally ruled-out since Kayne (1994); thus, adopting a minimalist version of Molnárfi's (2002) theory would require some radical shifts in assumptions about the nature of displacement and syntactic structure.

Even assuming we could adapt Molnárfi's account to minimalist syntax, there are further empirical arguments against his theory of a cross-linguistic nature. The leftmost morpheme nie_1 and the rightmost morpheme nie_2 in Afrikaans are homophonous. This is a key component of Molnárfi's theory, since we would not expect an unstressed, syntactically inactive copy of a syntactic head to differ in phonological shape. However, as I show in §4 three below, there are several languages whose negation strategies parallel the negation strategy of Afrikaans in which the leftmost and rightmost negative morphemes are not homophonous. Furthermore, it appears to be a general fact about these languages that the rightmost negative morpheme is phonologically reduced. Rather than isolate Afrikaans as a separate case governed by a unique process of copying, I argue that a unified syntactic account can explain how negation functions in all of these languages.

Finally, as I argue in Bell (2003), the fact that the *nie* morphemes are homophonous (as are the *não* morphemes in Vernacular Brazilian Portuguese, the *no* morphemes in contact varieties of Spanish, etc.) has much more to do with the particular historical development of Afrikaans than with its syntax. Strong evidence for this fact comes in Chapter Three, where I will show that several other languages (Bukusu, Dagara, Hausa, Nweh) employ a highly similar negation strategy to Afrikaans, but with two non-homophonous morphemes.

In the next section I turn to a brief discussion of the NEG Criterion.

2.3.4 The NEG Criterion and Afrikaans

Perhaps the most well-known theory of the syntax of negation within the wider Principles and Parameters framework is the NEG Criterion (Haegeman and Zanuttini 1991, Haegeman 1995), which deals in particular with negation strategies where more than one (overt) negative morpheme is employed. Essentially a well-formedness condition on syntactic structure, the NEG Criterion requires two negative morphemes to have a specific structural relation with one another: in particular, a relation of specifier to head, (henceforth *spec-head*)[5]. I give the NEG Criterion in (24).

(24) **The NEG Criterion** (Haegeman 1995)
 a. A NEG operator must be in a spec-head configuration with an X^o [+NEG];
 b. An X^o [+NEG] must be in a spec-head configuration with a NEG-operator.

Consider a specific implementation of the NEG Criterion in West Flemish. In negative sentences such as (25)a, Haegeman (1995) argues that West Flemish *nie* is a lexical (i.e. non-functional) category, alongside other "inherently negative" N-words equivalent to English *nobody* and *never*. The particle *en* is argued to head a negative projection NegP. The derivation for (25)a is sketched in (25)b. Under Haegeman's

---

[5] Note that this relation holds in languages where two negative morphemes normally give a *single negative interpretation* to a clause, and not in cases of double negatives such as English "John didn't *not* go to the store."

(1995) analysis, Agr selects NegP, which in turn selects TP. Note that both TP and AgrP are head-final (right branching) in Haegeman's analysis. This allows Haegeman to derive the phrase-final position of the verb, which undergoes multiple head movement to Agr°. The particle *en*, which is optional in West Flemish, heads NegP but undergoes clitic movement to adjoin to the verb.

(25) a. ...da Valère **nie** nor us **(en)**-goat.　　　　　　　　**WEST FLEMISH**
　　　　 that Valère NEG to home NEG-goes
　　　　 '...that Valère does not go home.' (Haegeman 1995:126)

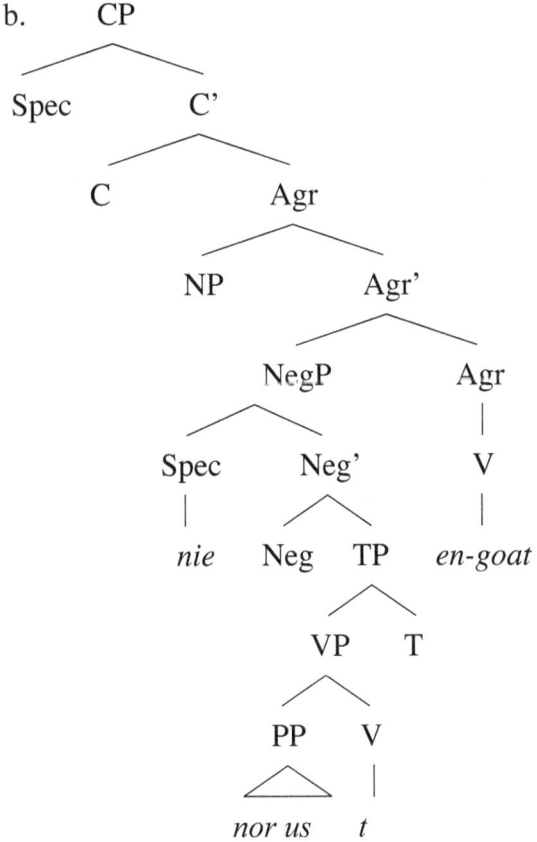

b.

The NEG Criterion, and specifically (24)a, requires some N-word (or, presumably, a null operator) to be in the specifier of the projection headed by *en*. (24)b requires *en* to be in the head of the phrase of which the operator is the specifier. Interestingly, the NEG Criterion makes no reference to NegP. *En* heads NegP by stipulation. As we will see, Haegeman (2002) modifies her analysis of *en*, arguing that it heads a polarity phrase PolP not unlike that proposed for Afrikaans in Oosthuizen (1998). By proposing what she terms an 'extended' NegP, Haegeman (2002) is able to derive West Flemish word order while bringing her analysis in line with Kayne (1994) and, more specifically, the analysis of Zwart (1997) proposing that underlying word order in Dutch is SVO. I will discuss Haegeman (2002) in greater detail in the following section.

Returning to the NEG Criterion, consider its implementation in an Afrikaans sentence such as (26)a below, structurally very similar to West Flemish. Recall that Haegeman (1995) argues that West Flemish *nie* is a lexical category, while *en* is a functional category. We could assume, *contra* what I have argued above, that Afrikaans nie_1 is a lexical category, while nie_2 is a functional category. A NEG Criterion analysis of (26)a would appear as in (26)b. The only major structural problem to solve -- although it is certainly a difficult issue – would be why nie_2 cliticizes to the right of the verb in Afrikaans, but to the left of the verb in West Flemish.

(26) a. ... dat die kinders **nie** in die huis praat **nie**.   **AFRIKAANS**
        that the children nie_1 in the house talk nie_2
        '...that the children don't talk in the house'

b.

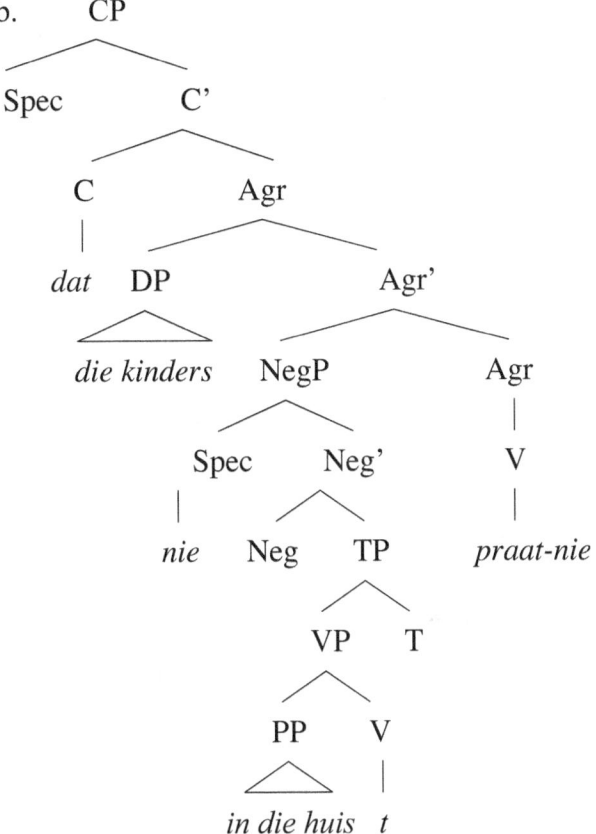

I will reject the NEG Criterion analysis of Afrikaans in (26)b for several reasons. From an empirical point of view there are several undesirable aspects to (26)b. First, as I show in sections 2.1 and 2.2 above, both nie_1 and nie_2 in Afrikaans are functional categories. In particular, as I will show in my analysis below, they are *clausal* functional heads. This fact about Afrikaans is immediately at variance with a straight-forward implementation of the NEG Criterion, parallel to West Flemish, in which nie_1 is in Spec,NegP and nie_2 heads NegP. Second, the analysis in (26)b is unable to capture the PP- and CP-stranding data. There is no available landing site for PPs and CPs that are stranded to the right of nie_2. Third, the analysis in (26)b cannot accommodate the *because*-clause data in Afrikaans. Again, there is no available landing site for *because*-clauses to the right of nie_2. Fourth, as I will show in Chapter Three, the NEG Criterion analysis also fails to capture the negation strategies of several other languages that behave in a similar fashion to Afrikaans. From a theoretical perspective there are also several reasons for rejecting the NEG Criterion as a viable option for Afrikaans. First, we cannot adopt Kayne (1994). Second, we must rely on an external criterion to trigger the movement(s) that yield the correct word order. This is contrary to the Minimalist approach I have adopted here, in which movement is triggered by the need to eliminate uninterpretable features. As I will show in a moment, it is in fact possible to derive some aspects of the NEG Criterion within Minimalism, and without reliance on well-formedness conditions on syntactic structure. I now turn to a presentation of the analysis.

2.4 Negation in Afrikaans: The Analysis

In this section, I propose an alternative to the analyses of Oosthuizen (1998) and Molnárfi (2002), and also the NEG Criterion, all of which, I have argued, have important shortcomings. In my analysis, I take into account not only the general position of *nie*$_2$, but also certain syntactic properties of negation in Afrikaans, such as the behavior of *because*-clauses and the position of stranded PPs and CPs. Furthermore, I propose a unified account of the triggers for displacement, both of N-words, and of the phrase-level categories that move to the left of *nie*$_2$. I will build my analysis from the bottom up, following the derivational cycle. I begin with a general proposal for N-word displacement in §2.4.1. Then in §2.4.2, I offer an analysis of the position and behavior of *nie*$_2$, including the placement of prepositional phrases, complement clauses, and *because*-clauses vis-à-vis *nie*$_2$. I offer some concluding remarks on the analysis in §2.4.3.

2.4.1 Movement of N-words

In this section I discuss the movement of N-words in Afrikaans, and propose an account of N-word displacement that shows the NEG Criterion can be reduced to feature-deletion and *Internal Merge*. To begin, consider the sentence in (27).

(27) Sy sluit **nooit** die deur **nie**.
      she locks never the door nie_2
      'She never locks the door.'   (Oosthuizen 1998)

Following standard assumptions, I posit a Negative Phrase NegP dominated by T and dominating vP. NegP houses N-words and nie_1, but not nie_2. Furthermore, following standard assumptions and the specific analyses of Pollock (1989), Haegeman (1995), and Zanuttini (1997), I argue that N-words such as *nooit* 'never', *nêrens* 'nowhere' and *niemand* 'nobody' are externally-merged into a position below $NegP_1$ and subsequently move to [Spec,nie_1] before Spell-Out. The base position of negative adverbs like *nooit* 'never' is most likely an adverbial adjunct position. Negative quantifiers such as *niemand* 'nobody' are assumed to move from argument positions such as [Spec, vP] and [Spec,VP]. In this section I explore the triggers for the movement of N-words to [Spec,$NegP_1$].

As we observed above, an N-word normally occurs without nie_1, although nie_1 and an N-word can also co-occur for some speakers. I will discuss the latter case below. In cases where an N-word occurs without nie_1, I assume a null head on $NegP_1$ with an uninterpretable feature [uNeg] that must be eliminated before Spell-Out.[6] The N-word *nooit* has an interpretable [+neg] feature that values the unvalued [uNeg] on nie_1. In addition, I argue that the head of $NegP_1$, Neg°, has an OCC feature that must be eliminated.[7] The presence of OCC licenses Internal Merge. I give the operations in (28) and the derivation and structure in (29) and (30).

(28) a. Agree(Neg°, N-word)
      b. OCC(Neg°, N-word); Merge(N-word, $NegP_1$)

---

[6] I assume the goal to be inherently active, as in Ndayiragije (2003).
[7] See McClosky (2002) on complementizer agreement in Irish in terms of uninterpretable features for some parallels to the analysis I develop here.

(29) a. [NegP1 Neg° ... [AdvP *nooit*]]
         [uNeg][OCC]   **[+Neg][UF]**

   b. [NegP1 Neg° ...[AdvP *nooit*]]
         ~~[uNeg][OCC]~~

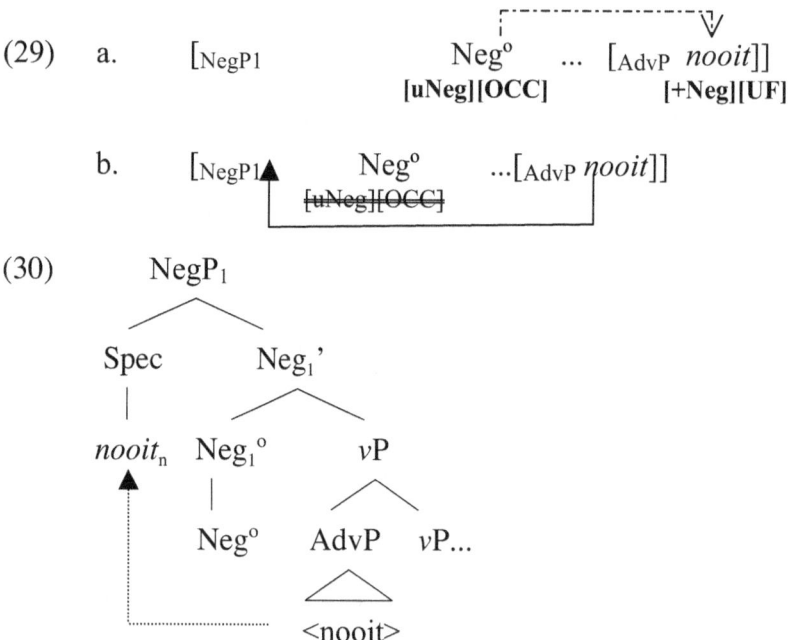

(30) NegP₁ tree with Spec *nooit*ₙ, Neg₁′ → Neg₁°, vP → Neg°, AdvP ⟨nooit⟩, vP...

In addition to accounting for surface word order, this analysis results in a spec-head relation between the N-word *nooit* and the negative head Neg°. This relation is a key component of the standard principles-and-parameters analysis of negation, the NEG Criterion (Haegeman 1995). By positing that the structure in (30) is obtained via *Agree* and *Merge*, we have derived a core principle of the NEG Criterion within Minimalism. Now we must account for the position and behavior of *nie₂*, in the next section.

2.4.2 *Nie₂*

In this section I propose a syntactic analysis of the position of *nie₂*. We have seen that *nie₂* is a functional category, and I will argue that it occupies the position of a syntactic head. The presence of *nie₂* is licensed by the presence negation, i.e. some word with an interpretable negative feature [+neg]. However, there are empirical and theoretic reasons to believe that *nie₂* is not contained within the CP-domain in a PolP-type projection, but rather within the IP domain.

Nie₂ normally occurs in sentence-final position, yet prepositional phrases (PPs) and complement clauses (CPs) can also occur to the right of *nie₂*, so *nie₂* is not radically sentence-final. Consider the schematics below.

(31)   a. S *nie* PP O V *nie*
       b. S *nie* O PP V *nie*
       c. S *nie* O V *nie* PP
       d. S *nie* O V CP *nie*
       e. S *nie* O V *nie* CP

In (31)a-d I show the variation allowed for PPs and CP in negative contexts in Afrikaans. The position of PPs, especially adjunct PPs, is highly variable. I will return to a detailed discussion of these facts, as they relate to post-verbal constituents and scrambling in Dutch, in Chapter 4.

Assuming the category housing *nie₂* is dominated by IP, and that it in turn dominates vP, we have two options for deriving its position. First, the verb and direct object could move, and PPs and CPs could move in a separate operation to a position left of *nie₂*. This would explain why *nie₂* is not always radically final: PPs and CPs can be left stranded below *nie₂*. A second possibility would be that some phrase containing the verb, object, and the PP/CP moves leftward in a single operation. Considering the fact that the unmarked position for PPs and CPs is to the left of *nie₂*, and also based on the behavior of *because*-clauses, I will opt for the latter analysis, and propose that $NegP_1$ and everything contained in it moves to the specifier of *nie₂*. This analysis leaves several questions open. First, what is the nature of the category containing *nie₂*? Second, what are the triggers for movement? And finally, what can account for PPs ad CPs following *nie₂*? I will look at these three question in turn in the next three subsections.

2.4.2.1 The Category Containing *Nie₂*

Based on the discussion thus far, and on data from *because*-clauses that I will analyze below, I argue that *nie₂* is housed in a projection NegP₂, which is part of an expanded NegP complex. The notion of an expanded NegP is based on the development of other expanded functional projections, including the expanded IP (Pollock 1989), VP/*v*P (Chomsky 1995) and the articulated CP-domain (Rizzi 1997). As we would expect given the nature of other expanded projections, the functional heads contained inside the expanded NegP each have somewhat different featural content, and perform somewhat different functions – although they are still related to sentential negation, just as tense and agreement are related to verbal inflection in the expanded IP projection, and so forth.

Given the data from Afrikaans, we know that the expanded NegP contains at least two overt functional categories, *nie₁* and *nie₂*, both of which I argue to be syntactic heads. In terms of linear order, we observe that *nie₁* always precedes *nie₂* in the clause. Thus it would be natural to assume that the projection housing *nie₁* dominates the projection housing *nie₂*, yielding a structure as in (32).

(32)
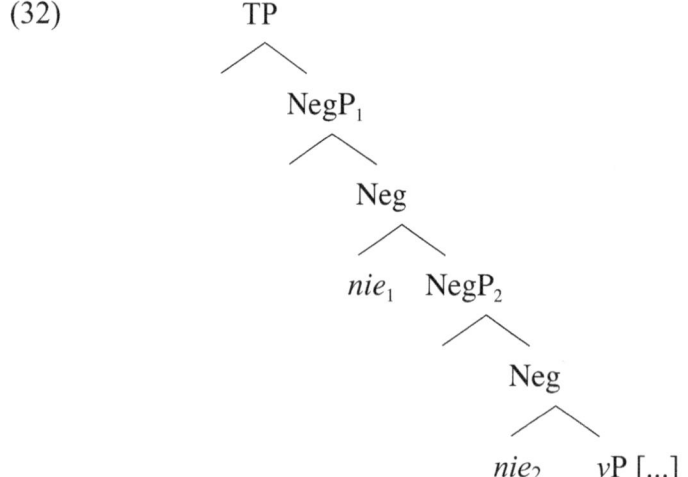

Consider the structure in (32) above.[8] The hierarchical ordering of *nie*$_1$ and *nie*$_2$ mirrors the surface-observed order of the morphemes. To derive the position of *nie*$_2$, *v*P must move to [Spec,NegP$_2$], pied-piping everything contained in *v*P. To explain post-posed PPs, there must be a position dominated by NegP$_2$ but dominating *v*P, to which PPs and CPs move. However, the structure proposed in (32) immediately encounters several important theoretic and empirical problems.

First, it is unclear what the trigger for *v*P-movement to [Spec,NegP$_2$] might be. One possibility is that an uninterpretable negative feature on *nie*$_2$ is valued by an interpretable [+neg] feature on the verb, establishing a probe-goal relation and licensing internal merge (driven by and OCC feature). Indeed, this is similar to the proposal of Oosthuizen (1998) for CP-movement to [Spec,PolP], who argues in effect that verbs in negative environments in Afrikaans have an interpretable [+neg] feature. As I have argued in Bell (2004), languages with so-called *negative verbs* may be examples of overt manifestation of a negative verbal feature. These languages include Samoyedic, Permic and Mordvin languages (Hajdu 1963), as well as Turkish, Finnish, Hungarian and Korean (Dahl 1979, Payne 1985). However, no such overt manifestation is visible in Afrikaans. Thus we would be left to stipulate the presence of an interpretable [+neg] feature associated with the verb.

Second, consider the distribution of features in Afrikaans negation proposed thus far. I have argued that the locus of sentential negation in Afrikaans is the NEG$_1$ position, spelled-out as either an N-word or *nie*$_1$. The LI in this position contains an interpretable negative feature. I posit that *nie*$_2$ is a clausal functional head containing some *uninterpretable* features – an analysis that I justify in the next section. Consider again the ordering in (32). We see that the category containing the interpretable

---

[8] Throughout this chapter I assume a fixed ordering of TP dominating NegP and thus a derivational approach, following Chomsky (1995) but *contra* for example Ouhalla (1991), who argues for a configurational approach. I will return to this issue in Chapter Three and Chapter Four.

feature, NegP$_1$, dominates the category containing the uninterpretable feature, NegP$_2$. This runs counter to other examples of interpretable-uninterpretable feature pairs. For example, the uniniterpretable φ-features on T dominates the interpretable [φ] feature on *v*P-internal subjects. Therefore, we might expect the expanded NegP to follow the same pattern, with *nie*$_2$ dominating *nie*$_1$, as in (33).

(33)
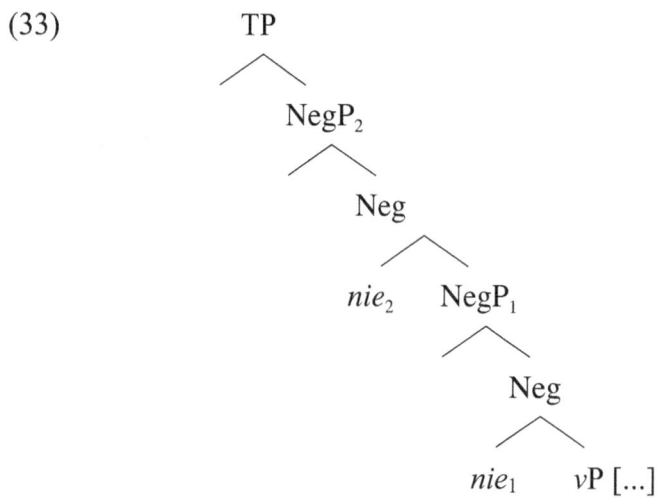

The structure in (33), which is minimally different from (32), has the distinct advantage of allowing the uninterpretable negative feature on *nie*$_2$ to dominate the interpretable negative feature on *nie*$_1$, making this case parallel to other cases of interpretable-uniniterpretable feature pairs. As I show in the next section, there is in fact a very natural reason to posit the structure in (33), since it allows us to easily explain the triggers for movement of NegP$_1$ to Spec,NegP$_2$, accounting for the phrase-final position of *nie*$_2$.

2.4.2.2   Nie$_2$ and Uninterpretable Features

A crucial part of the proposed analysis of Afrikaans involves the featural content of the negative particles *nie*$_1$ and *nie*$_2$. For mainly theory-internal reasons, I have argued that *nie*$_2$ contains uninterpretable negative features [uNeg] that are valued by the interpretable negative feature [+neg] associated with *nie*$_1$. This proposal, as we shall see, allows for an *Agree* relation to obtain between nie_2 and nie_1, straight-forwardly explaining the phrase-final order of nie_2 as derived by XP-movement of the category containing nie_1 to the specifier of nie_2. It also corresponds to the general assumption in Minimalism (Chomsky 2001) that the need to eliminate uninterpretable features drives Internal Merge. However, an alternative proposal could argue that both nie_1 and nie_2 contain interpretable features. After all, both are spelled out as separate negative morphemes. Why should nie_2 not also contain an interpretable negative feature? This argument is especially attractive in light of the fact that some dialects of Afrikaans allow negative concord (NC), where more than one N-word can appear in a single sentence containing a single instance of sentential negation. Consider the following data.

(34) a. **Niemand** het **niks** gedoen **nie**
nobody has nothing done nie_2
'Nobody did anything.' (Robbers 1997:37)

b. Pop sê hy't **nie meer** krag vir **niks** **nie**
Pop say he-have no more strength for nothing nie_2
'Pop says that he does not have any strength for anything.' (ibid.)

The data in (34) show that (some dialects of) Afrikaans allow NC. Although both (34)a and (34)b contain two N-words, the sentences do not receive a double-negative interpretation. If NC is possible with multiple N-words, then we can easily justify both nie_1 and nie_2 containing interpretable features as another instance of NC.

As a first argument against this proposal, consider the fact that not all speakers of Afrikaans accept the sentences in (34)a-b as grammatical. Indeed, one Afrikaans native-speaker consultant judged both (34)a and (34)b as highly degraded, and provided further examples of multiple instances of N-words where only a double negative reading is possible (or which are ungrammatical altogether). Consider the following example.

(35) a. Johan sien **nooit** vir Maria op enige plek **nie**.⁹
John sees never *vir* Mary in any place *nie₂*
'John never sees Mary anywhere.'

b. *Johan sien **nooit** vir Maria op geen plek **nie**.
John sees never *vir* Mary in no place *nie₂*

Some speakers of Afrikaans do not allow NC interpretations of the sentences in (34)a-b or (35)b. Rather, a single N-word is accompanied by an NPI, as in (35)a. However, we see that these speakers still employ *nie₂* in sentences such as (35)a. If *nie₂* contained interpretable features, we might expect dialects that do not allow NC in the context of N-words to block *nie₂* in general, unless we propose that NC operates separately in the case of *nie₁*-*nie₂* – a seemingly undesirable stipulation.

As further evidence, we will see in Chapter Three that other languages employing a similar negation strategy to Afrikaans do not contain N-words at all, but rather NPIs. These languages also employ a phrase-final particle highly similar in position and function to *nie₂*. We could stipulate an NC relation between NEG₁ and NEG₂ in these languages. Yet they clearly do not allow NC in any other context, since they do not even contain inherently negative lexical categories that could enter into an NC relation. Given these facts, I continue to argue that *nie₂* contains uninterpretable [uNeg] features while *nie₁* contains an interpretable [+neg] feature.

2.4.2.3 NegP₁ moves to [Spec,NegP₂]

To begin, assume the structure in (33) above to be correct. As discussed in §2.3.1 above, I argue that NegP occurs in the domain of IP in Afrikaans. We have seen for example that Oosthuizen proposes a higher position for the phrase containing *nie₂* in Afrikaans, which he labels PolP. However, I assume here that the negation strategy in Afrikaans does not consist of two entirely separate functional projections, such as PolP in the CP-domain and NegP in the IP domain. Rather, I posit that TP in Afrikaans

---

⁹ See den Besten (2000) for a rich discussion of the Afrikaans particle *vir*.

selects a single, expanded NegP complex containing both negative heads nie_1 and nie_2. As I will show, there is a close syntactic relationship between these two functional categories, and, I argue, a strict (universal) hierarchical ordering relation in which $NegP_2$ dominates $NegP_1$. This proposal is akin in certain ways to the strict hierarchy of functional categories proposed in the CP-domain by Rizzi (1997). I wish to put forth a similar proposal for the Neg domain.

As just discussed, I propose that nie_2, the head of $NegP_2$, has an uninterpretable feature [uNeg] that must be eliminated before Spell-Out. As I argued above, it is problematic to stipulate that an interpretable negative feature on the verb values the uninterpretable negative feature on nie_2. However, since nie_2 dominates nie_1 in (33), we need not search for interpretable negative features on the verb. Rather, we can simply state that the interpretable negative feature on nie_1 (i.e. the head of $NegP_1$), values the uninterpretable negative feature on nie_2. In the presence of an N-word, the interpretable feature will be associated with the N-word, yielding similar results, as I show below.

The N-word or nie_1 has an interpretable [+neg] feature that values the unvalued [uNeg] on nie_2. The elimination of uninterpretable features is achieved via the operation *Agree* (Chomsky 2000:122), which is established between a *probe* (P) and a *goal* (G) ; in this case nie_2 (P) and the nie_1 (G).[10] In addition, I argue that nie_2 has an OCC feature that must be eliminated (Chomsky 2001). The presence of OCC licenses the operation *Merge* – movement of the lexical category associated with the goal into the specifier of the probe. In this case, the movement operation is $NegP_1$ to [Spec,$NegP_2$]. For ease of presentation, I assume an *Agree* relation between nie_2 and the category containing the interpretable negative feature, which I represent below as

---

[10] I assume that goals are inherently *active* by virtue of the fact that they contain the relevant interpretable feature, such as [+neg] in the case of an N-word. Thus I do not stipulate an uninterpretable feature to activate the goal. (Cf. Ndayiragije 2003).

nie_1. The *Agree* relation can be established between nie_2 and an N-word, or nie_2 and nie_1, yielding identical results. I provide the steps in the derivation in (36) and a partial derivation in (37).

(36) a. Agree(nie_2, nie_1)
b. OCC(nie_2, nie_1); Merge($NegP_1$, $NegP_2$)

(37) $NegP_1$ movement to [Spec,$NegP_2$]

a. [$_{NegP2}$ nie_2 [$_{NegP1}$ nie_1 [$_{vP}$]]]
       [uNeg][OCC]   [+neg]
       ⟵———Agree———⟶

b. [$_{NegP2}$ nie_2 [$_{NegP1}$ nie_1 [$_{vP}$]]]
       [uNeg][OCC]
       Merge

Derivations are cyclic and obey the extension condition. The first relation established is *Agree*, between nie_2 and nie_1 (36)a. The [uNeg] feature on nie_2 is eliminated under the *Agree* relation (Chomsky 2000). An OCC feature on nie_2 requires some XP-level category to move to [Spec,$NegP_2$], licensing the operation *Merge* (36)b. $NegP_1$ merges with [Spec,$NegP_2$] (36)c.

Now consider the sentence in (38)a below. Here, the N-word *niks* contains the interpretable negative feature. We know that *niks* possesses an interpretable negative feature, since, for example, it can be used as a single-word negative reply to a question. Under the account developed here, nie_2 attracts *niks*, and the entire *v*P is pied-piped along with $NegP_1$ to [Spec,$NegP_2$]. Consider the sentence in (38)a and the derivation in (38)b.

(38) a. Sy het **niks** gesê op die vergadering **nie**.
she has nothing said at the meeting nie_2
'She said nothing at the meeting.' (Oosthuizen 1998)

b.

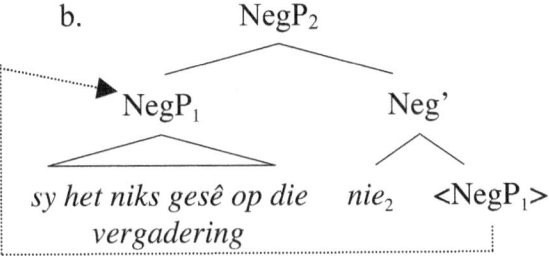

At this point, my analysis yields exactly the same results as the unmodified version of Oosthuizen (1998) described in §2.3 above. It also makes the same strong prediction that *nie₂* is radically final, contrary to fact. In the next two subsections, I examine the data on postposed prepositional phrases, complement clauses, and *because*-clauses. Then, in Chapter 4, I return to a more detailed discussion of post-*nie₂* stranding as it relates to post-verbal constituents and scrambling in Dutch.

2.4.2.4 Post-*Nie₂* Stranding

As discussed above, one serious shortcoming of the account offered by Oosthuizen (1998), and of the NEG Criterion analysis of Afrikaans, is their inability to accommodate data such as (39), repeated from above.

(39) a. Sy het **niks** gesê **nie** op die vergadering.
         she has nothing said at the meeing   *nie₂*
         'She said nothing at the meeting.' (Oosthuizen 1998)

   b. Ek het **nie** geweet **nie** dat hy sou kom.
       I AUX *nie₁* know *nie₂* that he would come
       'I didn't know that he would be coming.' (Donaldson 1993)

   c. Ons het **nooit** die mense geken **nie** wat in hierdie huis gebly het.
       we AUX never the people know *nie₂* who in this house live AUX
       'We never knew the people who lived in this house.' (ibid.)

I have argued above that NegP₁ moves to [Spec,NegP₂], pied-piping everything contained in it to this position as well. Yet certain constituents and clauses can be left behind, stranded below *nie₂*. To account for this, I propose a functional projection inside the expanded NegP, dominated by NegP$_2$ but dominating NegP$_1$. Call this projection XP. The expanded NegP now appears as in (40).

(40)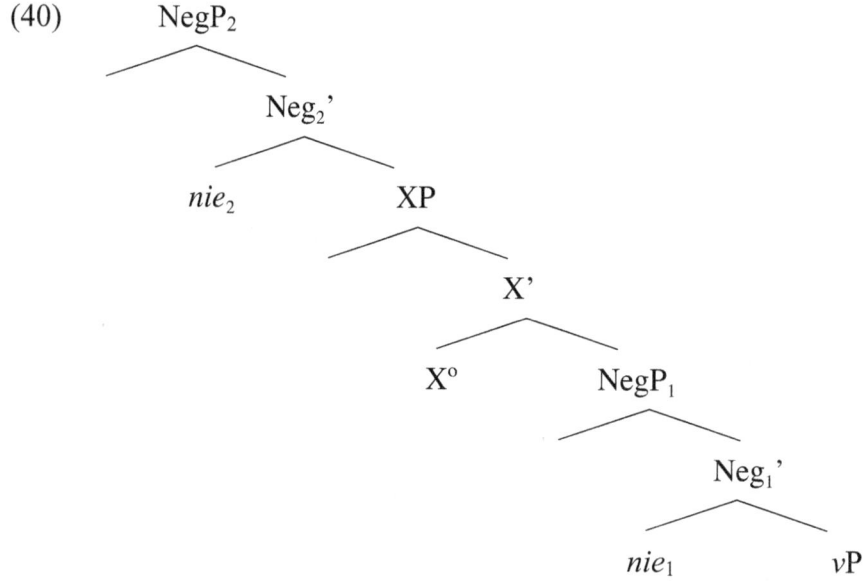

Given this structure, we can now develop an analysis to account for post-posing of prepositional phrases and CP-complements after *nie$_2$*. To begin, consider the example of a postposed PP in (41). I return to the very interesting question of NPIs in post-posed PPs in Chapter 4, §4.5.1.3 below.

(41) Sy het **niks** gesê **nie** op die vergadering.
      she has nothing said *nie$_2$* at the meeing
      'She said nothing at the meeting.' (Oosthuizen 1998)

The expanded NegP structure proposed in (40) accommodates the data in (41) as follows. First, the prepositional phrase merges with [Spec,XP], as in (42)a below. Second, the NegP$_1$-remnant merges with [Spec,NegP$_2$] in (42)b, via mechanisms described in §2.4.1.2 above.

(42) a. [$_{NegP2}$ Neg *nie$_2$* [$_{XP}$ [$_{NegP1}$ *nie$_1$* [$_{vP}$ S [$_{VP}$ O V [$_{PP}$ *op die vergadering*]]]]]

      b. ... [$_{NegP2}$ NegP$_1$ [*nie$_2$* [$_{XP}$ [$_{PP}$ *op die vergadering* [$_{<NegP1>}$]]]]]

(42)a shows that the PP evacuates from its *v*P-internal position to Spec-XP. Following this movement, the NegP$_1$ remnant moves to Spec,NegP$_2$, effectively strands the PP behind *nie$_2$* and yielding the correct word order. The operations in (42) are represented in the structure in (43)b.

(43)   a.   ... gesê **nie** op die vergadering.
            ... say *nie$_2$* at the meeting.

    b.

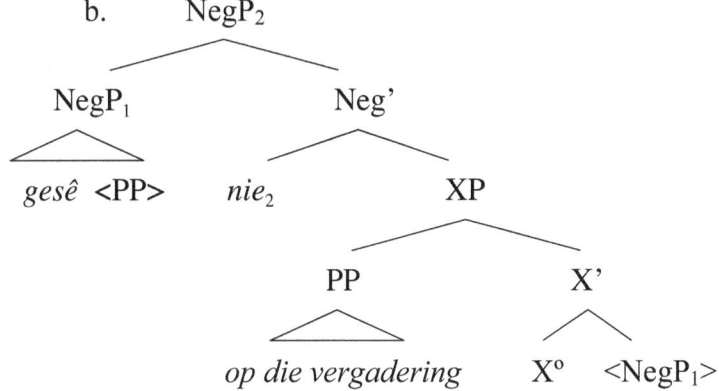

The structure in (43)b illustrates the derivation of a postposed PP in sentential negation. The PP has moved out of *v*P to [Spec,XP] prior to NegP$_1$-remnant movement to [Spec,NegP$_2$]. I assume that a similar operation can account for postposed complement clauses, including the data on embedded clauses given above.

While PPs and CPs can be stranded to the right of *nie$_2$*, other constituents cannot, as a general rule. Consider the data in (44)a-d.

(44)   a.   ...dat hy **nie** *die werk* gedoen het **nie**.
                that he *nie$_1$* the work done has *nie$_2$*
                '...that he hasn't done the work.'

    b.   *...dat hy **nie** gedoen het **nie** *die werk*.
               that he *nie$_1$* done has *nie$_2$* the work

    c.   ... dat hy **nie** *siek* is **nie**.
               that he *nie$_1$* sick is *nie$_2$*
               '...that he isn't sick.'

d. ... dat hy **nie** is **nie** *siek*.
   that he *nie₁* is *nie₂* sick

Neither DPs nor adverbial complements (APs) can be stranded to the right of *nie₂*, as we observe in (44)b and (44)d respectively. As I show in Chapter 4, this fact is closely related to the fact that DPs and APs cannot generally appear in post-verbal position in either Dutch or Afrikaans. Indeed, as I will show, there is a close correlation between scrambling and post-verbal constituents in Dutch on the one hand, and scrambling and post-*nie₂* constituents in Afrikaans on the other. The argument is further strengthened by cross-linguistic data showing that languages allowing post-NEG₂ constituents are more likely to allow scrambling, or to contain structures in other (non-negative) contexts that show similar movement operations to be available (i.e. stranding via XP-movement followed by remnant-movement).

2.4.2.5   *Because*-Clauses and *nie₂*

Consider again the very interesting case of *because*-clauses in Afrikaans. As we saw in §2.1 above, *because*-clauses can either precede or follow *nie₂*. Unlike the position of prepositional phrases and CP-complements, however, the position of the *because*-clause relative to *nie₂* results in a change in meaning. If the *because*-clause occurs to the right of *nie₂*, negation takes scope only over the matrix clause. If, on the other hand, the *because*-clause occurs to the left of *nie₂*, negation appears to take wide scope over the whole clause. I repeat the relevant data in (45).

(45) a.   Hy het dit **nie** gedoen **nie** omdat hy betaal is.
         he have it *nie₁* done *nie₂* because he paid is
         'He did not do it, because he was paid.' (Robbers 1997:40)

    b.   Hy het dit **nie** gedoen omdat hy betaal is **nie**.
         he have it *nie₁* done because he paid is *nie₂*
         'He did not do it because he was paid (but for another reason)' (ibid.)

First, let us assume that *because*-clauses in Afrikaans are PP-adjuncts, and that *omdat* 'because' is composed of a preposition *om* and a complementizer *dat* (see Veld 1993:155 on *omdat* in Dutch for a similar approach. Note that the sentence in (45)a can also be rendered in English by fronting the entire *because*-clause, yielding, "because he was paid, he didn't do it." This is the correct interpretation of the Afrikaans sentence in (45)a. In Afrikaans, a potential ambiguity (either, "he didn't do it, the reason being because he was paid" as in (45)a, or, "he did it, not because he was paid" as in (45)b) is resolved by the position of nie_2 relative to the *because*-clause. Essentially, what can be achieved in English by fronting of the *because*-clause, or intonation (a pause before the *because*-clause), is achieved via syntactic means in Afrikaans.[11] In what follows, I offer an analysis of *because*-clauses in negative environments in Afrikaans which is consistent with my analysis in sections 2.4.2.2 and 2.4.2.3 above, and which can clearly explain the different interpretations of (45).

The core of my proposal involves the notion that there is an expanded Negative Phrase containing various functional heads that are normally associated in some way with negation. One of these heads is nie_1, which, as we have seen, contains an interpretable negative feature. Another NegP head is nie_2, which appears, in the case of *because*-clauses, to mark the end of negative scope. Thus in (45)a, it seems that the *because*-clause has somehow moved outside the scope of negation. I argue that this fact reflects actual syntactic movement to a position internal to expanded NegP, i.e. to the left of nie_1.

When nie_2 occurs to the right of the *because*-clause, the *because*-clause is inside the scope of negation, as in (45)b. I propose that one movement operation,

---

[11] There are also intonational differences between (45)a and (45)b. However, the position of nie_2 is the crucial factor in disambiguation between the two sentences.

NegP$_1$ to [Spec,NegP$_2$], accounts elegantly and economically for the position of *nie$_2$* in this case. Consider the abbreviated derivation in (46).

(46) [$_{NegP2}$ SPEC *nie$_2$* [$_{NegP1}$ *nie$_1$* [$_{vP}$ [$_{PP}$ *omdat hy betaal is*]]]]

In the case of sentences such as (45)a, the derivation is slightly more complex. First, assume a functional projection intermediate between NegP$_2$ and NegP$_1$. I will call this projection YP to distinguish it from the XP projection proposed above for scrambling PPs. The head of YP, Y°, has an uninterpretable feature [uF] that must be eliminated. A corresponding interpretable feature [+F] on *omdat* 'because' in (45)b values the unvalued feature on Y°. This proposal immediately explains the difference between *omdat* 'because' and *want* 'since.' Only *omdat* allows the alternation described in this section. The LI *want* 'since, because' does not have a [+F] feature and cannot merge with YP. If *omdat* is [+F], an *Agree* relation is established between the scope head and *omdat*. Subsequently an OCC feature on the scope head licenses internal merge of the PP *omdat*-clause and [Spec,YP]. I provide the relations in (47), a derivation in (48), and a partial structure in (49).

(47) a. Agree(Y°,PP)
b. OCC(Y°,PP); Merge(PP,Spec-YP)

(48) a. ... [$_{NegP2}$ Neg *nie$_2$* [$_{YP}$ [$_{NegP1}$ *nie$_1$* [$_{vP}$ [$_{PP}$ *omdat hy betaal is*]]]]

b. ... [$_{NegP2}$ *nie$_2$* [$_{YP}$ PP [$_{NegP1}$ *nie$_1$* [$_{vP}$ [<CP>]]]]

(49)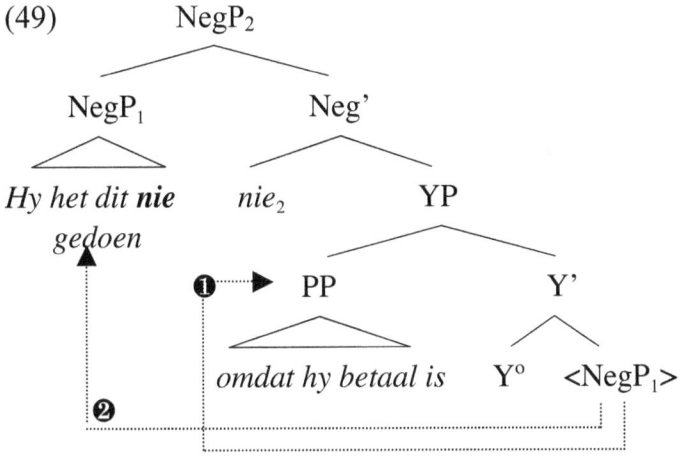

The partial structure in (49) illustrates *because*-clause movement to YP, and subsequent remnant movement of NegP₁ to [Spec,NegP₂]. What is the nature of YP? Is it a different category from the XP proposed above for PP and CP scrambling? As we will see in Chapter Four, cross-linguistic evidence suggests that they are different categories, since all BNF languages have postposed *because*-clauses, while not all have postposed PPs or CPs. Note that in Afrikaans, as in other BNF languages, we observe a concrete change in meaning. When a *because*-clause moves to [Spec,YP], it is removed from the scope of negation. This predicts that, whether the categories are the same or not, we may observe this scopal elsewhere. Most postposed PPs show no difference in meaning, except for an 'afterthought' interpretation on the PP. However, consider the following data involving an NPI embedded in a PP.

(50) a. ?Sy het niks gesê **nie** *vir haar suster.*
 she has nothing said *nie₂* to her sister
 'She said nothing to her sister.'

 b. * Sy het niks gesê **nie** vir enige iemand.
 she has nothing said *nie₂* to any someone

As we have seen above, most PPs can be stranded following *nie₂*, as in (50)a. However, when the PP contains a negative polarity item, the sentence is ungrammatical. NPIs in Afrikaans, as in English, must be inside the scope of negation. Placing the PP containing the NPI to the right of nie_2 appears to place the NPI outside the scope of negation, resulting in ungrammaticality. I return to these data in Chapter 4, §4.5.1.3.[12]

This analysis of *because*-clauses has several other advantages. First, it clearly shows how the *because*-clause receives its interpretation when it follows nie_2. A *because*-clause that moves into YP is effectively moving outside the scope of negation, i.e. to a position not c-commanded by nie_1 or and N-word. Note that nie_1 still c-commands N-words inside $NegP_1$, but that given the remnant $NegP_1$ movement to [Spec,$NegP_2$], nie_1 no longer c-commands the *because*-clause. Therefore, it is outside the scope of negation, thus remaining outside the scope of negation. This predicts that NPIs in post-NEG_2 position should be degraded or ungrammatical: a fact borne out in the discussion of post-NEG_2 constituents in Chapter 4, §4.5.1.3. Second, as I discuss in chapter three, this analysis has broad cross-linguistic applicability. Several languages with similar negation strategies to Afrikaans also exhibit similar *because*-clause behavior. Crucially, however, not all of these languages allow for postposed PPs and CPs, again illustrating that the category housing these elements is distinct from the *because*-clause YP.

Having considered movement of N-words and the expanded NegP, let us return to a discussion of nie_1.

2.4.3 Nie_1

In this section I return to the question of the categorial status and function of the leftmost negative particle nie_1, and the syntactic relationship between nie_1 and nie_2. As we have seen, simple sentential negation in Afrikaans involves the use of two

---

[12] It would also be possible to argue that the *because*-clause is base generated in YP when it appears in post-verbal position. Because the results of such an analysis are identical to the one proposed here, and there are no strong arguments in favor of a base generated analysis of postposed *because*-clauses, I pursue the movement analysis in order to draw out the parallels between postposed PPs and CPs and postposed *because*-clauses.

negative morphemes, *nie₁* and *nie₂*. There are many similarities between *nie₁* and *nie₂*, not the least of which is their identical, and invariant, phonetic shape. Both *nie₁* and *nie₂* occupy relatively fixed positions in the clause, certainly as compared with CPs and PPs, and to a lesser extent DPs, which can undergo focus- or topic-movement and/or scrambling (Robbers 1997). Indeed, according to Molnárfi (2002), *nie₂* is simply an overtly-realized copy of *nie₁*; the two instantiations correspond to a single functional head. I argue that this analysis fails to account for the behavior of *nie₂* in *because*-clauses, where it has a clear syntactic function. Also, as I will show in Chapter Three, languages with very similar negation strategies to Afrikaans do not employ homophonous particles, but rather have particles with unique phonetic shapes that nonetheless correspond in clausal position, syntactic function and, I argue, syntactic features, to *nie₁* and *nie₂*. Thus there is convincing cross-linguistic evidence that *nie₂* is not a copy of *nie₁*.

Putting these issues aside for the moment, let us turn to a detailed discussion of the categorial status of *nie₁*.

2.4.3.1 Categorial Status of *Nie₁*

Following Oosthuizen (1998) and Molnárfi (2002), I argue that *nie₁* is a functional head, i.e. and X° category, that heads a negative projection NegP within the proposed "expanded NegP." One convincing piece of evidence for the status of *nie₁* as a functional head comes from adverb modification facts. When standing on its own, *nie₁* can be modified by adverbs. Consider the sentences in (51).

(51) a. Hulle was **nie** betrokke **nie**.
 they were *nie₁* involved *nie₂*
 'They weren't involved.' (Oosthuizen 1998)

 b. Hulle was **glad nie** betrokke **nie**.
 they were entirely *nie₁* involved *nie₂*
 'They weren't involved at all.' (ibid.)

(51)a shows simple sentential negation, with nie_1 and nie_2. In (51)b, the adverb *glad* stands in the standard structural relationship to nie_1, adjunction to NegP, indicating modification in Afrikaans, and, as we would expect, the negation is qualitatively modified, from *not* to *not at all*, by the emphatic adverbial *glad*. However, these data do not conclusively show whether nie_1 is a functional or lexical category. Now consider the data in (52).

(52)   a. Dit blyk dat sy **absoluut niks** (**nie**) kan onthou **nie**.
            it   seems that she absolutely nothing *nie* can   remember nie_2
            'It seems that she can remember absolutely nothing.'   (Oosthuizen 1998)

       b. *Dit blyk dat sy **niks** (**nie**) kan onthou **absoluut nie**. (ibid.)

       c. *Dit blyk dat sy **niks absoluut** (**nie**) kan onthou **nie**. (ibid.)

As in (52)b above, we see that the N-word *niks* can be modified by an adverb such as *absoluut* in Afrikaans. However, note that the optional nie_1 that can occur following *niks* cannot be modified, nor, as we have seen above, can the rightmost functional head nie_2. If *niks* and nie_1 were housed in multiple specifiers of $NegP_1$, it would be easy to imagine that an adverbial adjunct could adjoin between the specifiers. What would prevent such a structure? However, if nie_1 is a clausal functional head, as I argue here, then we can easily show that there is in fact no structural position for *absoluut* in (52)b. The adverb adjoins to $NegP_1$ in (52)a as in the structure in (53)a. But there is no position available in (52)b, as I show in (53)b.

(53)

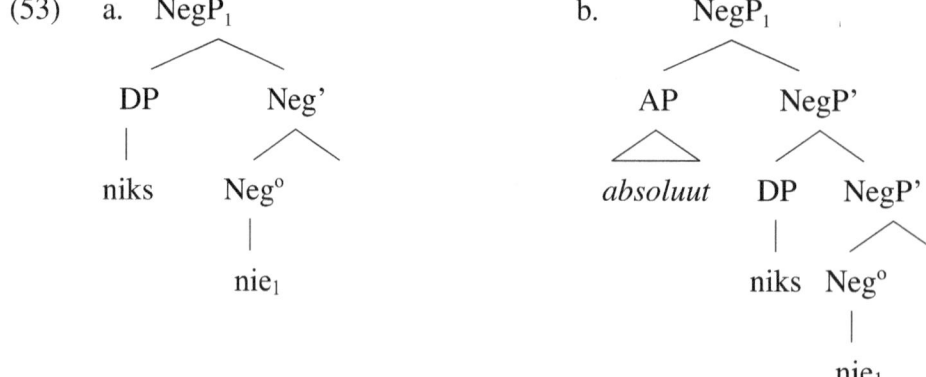

In (53), there is no available position between [Spec,NegP$_1$] and Neg° for an adverb. Therefore, a clear structural constraint explains why *nie$_1$* cannot be modified in this case, and shows that *nie$_1$* is a clausal functional head. There is even stronger evidence concerning the functional status of *nie$_1$*, however, involving data on N-word and *nie$_1$* fronting. I turn to this in the next section.

2.4.3.2   The Expanded NegP and *Nie$_1$*-Fronting

I have argued for an expanded Negative Phrase housing at least two negative heads in Afrikaans, *nie$_1$* and *nie$_2$*. As I showed above in §2.4.2, the rightmost negative *nie$_2$* occupies certain highly predictable positions in clause structure, and appears to play a role in a limited but important syntactic operations, such as disambiguating *because*-clauses, and triggering internal merge of NegP$_1$ with [Spec,NegP$_2$].

Nie$_1$ plays its own, very different role in sentential negation. *Nie$_1$* is similar to N-words in being the locus of negative force, that is, the morpheme containing the interpretable negative feature. *Nie$_1$* possesses an interpretable [+neg] feature, as do N-words. Unlike N-words, which are clearly lexical categories, I argue that *nie$_1$* is a functional category. In addition to the evidence from adverb modification given above, another piece of evidence for this fact comes from left-displacement of N-words and *nie$_1$* respectively. Although the position of *nie$_1$* is by and large invariant in the clause, there are cases in which *nie$_1$*, like N-words, can appear in clause-initial position, as in (54)b.

(54) a. **Nêrens** voel sy veilig **nie**.
nowhere feels she safe *nie$_2$*.
'Nowhere does she feel safe.'   (Oosthuizen 1998)

b. **Nie** hy het gekom **nie.**
nie$_1$ he has come *nie$_2$*
'**He** is not coming.'   (Molnárfi 2002, *my gloss*)

c. *__Nie__ het hy gekom **nie**.
nie$_1$ has he come *nie$_2$*   (ibid.)

Like *nêrens* in (54)a, *nie*$_1$ in (54)b can appear at the front of the clause. However, fronting *nêrens* gives a focus interpretation to *nêrens*, while moving *nie*$_1$ to the front of the clause gives contrastive focus to the subject (Donaldson 1993). Furthermore, note that moving *nie*$_1$ does not trigger verb-second, while fronting *nêrens* does. Both of these facts strongly suggest dissimilar syntactic structures for (54)a and (54)b. If *nie*$_1$ and *nêrens* were both lexical categories, housed in the specifier position of NegP$_1$, we would expect them to undergo exactly the same types of focus- or topic-movement. Indeed, all N-words can undergo movement similar to *nêrens* in (54)a, yet *nie*$_1$ never can. Any theory in which *nie*$_1$ is a SPEC of NegP must have an explanation for this asymmetry. If *nie*$_1$ is a clausal functional head, the asymmetry is easily explained.

Following standard assumptions, I argue that fronting of N-words in examples such as (54)a is a type of focus-movement to a focus phrase in the left-periphery. The N-word *nêrens* in (54)a has undergone an initial movement from a *v*P-internal position to [Spec,NegP$_1$] (Cf. Déprez 1999). It then undergoes a further movement to [Spec,CP], presumably to eliminate both the uninterpretable [foc] feature and the OCC feature associated with a phonologically-null focus head. Verb-second requires the verb to appear in second position, crucially, within the clause. This serves to illustrate that focus-movement of *nêrens* to [Spec,CP] is a movement within the clause containing the verb. I provide an abbreviated structure for (54)a in (55) below.

(55)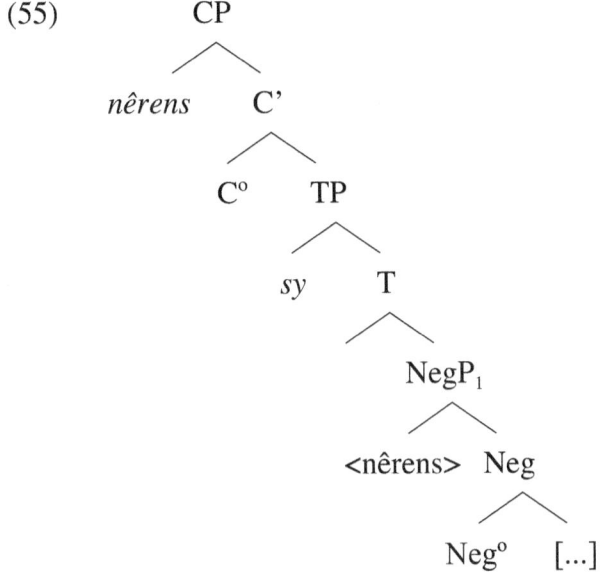

Verb-second is licensed when an N-word is fronted, because there is a specifier position to which the N-word can move, and an available head position to which the verb can move. We could argue that verb-second is blocked in the case of *nie*$_1$-fronting. Imagine for example that *nie*$_1$ moves to the head of the focus phrase in (55), or alternatively to the head of CP. This would leave no head position above TP to which the verb could move, effectively blocking verb-second in this case, and accounting for the ungrammatical sentence in (54)c.

A second possibility is the following. We know that the inflected verb must occupy the second position in matrix clauses. Crucially, this ordering requirement is only active within the clause-level. A verb from inside an embedded clause (where verb-second is not attested) does not jump a CP-barrier into second position of the matrix clause. Rather, the verb-second ordering holds within the domain of the matrix CP. Since *nie*$_1$-fronting in (54)b does not trigger verb-second, we may simply argue that the projection housing *nie*$_1$ in this contexts takes a CP-complement, that is, *nie*$_1$ is outside the domain of CP and thus not active in the verb-second calculation. What projection could house *nie*$_1$ in this case? One real possibility is some sort of polarity phrase such as that proposed by Oosthuizen (1998). Although I have not adopted his analysis for various empirical and theoretic reasons outlined above, the existence of a polarity phrase that dominates CP neatly explains the distributional facts and absence of verb-second in *nie₁*-fronting. Consider the abbreviated structure in (56).

(56)
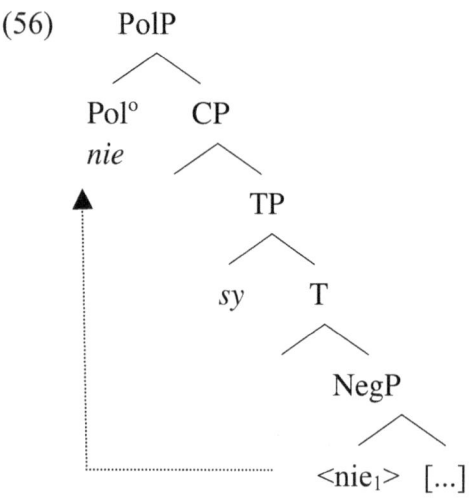

In the structure represented in (56), *nie₁* has undergone head movement to PolP. Note that, to effect this movement, *nie₁* has either moved through, or skipped over at least one intervening head, *viz.* T, in apparent violation of the Head Movement Constraint (HMC). I will return to this point below. Alternatively, we could propose that *nie₁* has several possible complements, but always projects a NegP₁. Under this scenario, NegP₁ would be projected above CP just in case *nie₁* occurs in sentence-initial position. However, assuming a head movement analysis, if PolP takes CP as a complement, then the verb in (56), which moves to T, will be in second position within the domain of CP despite the presence of *nie₁*. Finally, since *nie₁* moves to Pol° and not a focus position, as does *nêrens* in (55) above, we have a convincing explanation of the difference in interpretation between these two sentences based on the structural differences outlined in (55) and (56). Next, consider the optional *nie₁* that can co-occur with and N-word.

2.4.3.3 Optional *Nie₁* with N-word(s)

In this section I consider the status of the optional *nie₁* observed alongside N-words in certain contexts. Recall the examples in (57) from above.

(57) a. Hulle was **nie** betrokke **nie**. AFRIKAANS
 they were *nie₁* involved *nie₂*
 'They were not involved.' (Oosthuizen 1998

 b. Ek weet **nie**.
 I know *nie₁*
 'I don't know.' (Donaldson 1993)

 c. Ek sal jou **nooit** (**nie**) vergeet ***nie***.
 I will you never *nie₁* forget *nie₂*
 'I will never forget you.' (ibid.)

In (57)a we see a case of what I have been calling simple sentential negation. No N-words are present, only *nie₁* and *nie₂*. As we know, this sentence is ungrammatical or not interpreted as negative if either one of these particles is absent. However, there are cases in which *nie₁* can appear alone (57)b, suggesting that *nie₁* is the locus of negative force, i.e. possesses an interpretable negative feature [+neg], in this context. I argue that the morpheme *nie* in (57)b is indeed *nie₁* based in part on examples of pleonastic *nie₂* such as shown below in (58)a-b. Here, we see a phrase-final *nie* morpheme. Yet the sentences are not interpreted as negative. If the *nie* morpheme in (58)a-b were identical in feature content to that in (57)b, we would expect (58)a-b to have a negative interpretation.

(58) a. Jy joef my mouliks daarvan te oortuig **nie**.
  you have-to me hardly it-of to convince *nie₂*
 'You hardly have to convince me of that.' (Oosthuizen 1998)

 b. ?Ek sou dit kwalik sonder sy julp kon regkry **nie**.
  I would it hardly without his help could right-get *nie₂*
 'I would hardly have been able to manage it without his assistance.' (ibid.)

Oosthuizen (1998) illustrates some cases of optional nie_1 co-occurring with N-words, in sentences such as (57)c.[13] As I argued above, N-words have an interpretable [+neg] feature, as does nie_1. If the nie_1 in (57)c is the same nie_1 as (57)a-b – certainly the default assumption – then we must first explain why (57)c does not receive a double-negative interpretation, given that it possesses at least two separate [+neg] features. The most straight-forward explanation, and the one I will opt for, is to claim that sentences such as (57)c are simply illustrations of negative concord in Afrikaans, along the lines of (59), repeated from above.

(59)   **Niemand** het **niks**   gedoen **nie**
       nobody   has nothing done nie_2
       'Nobody did anything.'   (Robbers 1997:37)

The sentence in (59) has two N-words, each possessing an interpretable [+neg] feature. Yet the sentence has a single negative interpretation. This is the standard definition of negative concord in the literature on negation (Horn 1989, Haegeman 1995, Déprez 1999, Watanabe 2004). If we assume that one of the two negative features in both (57)c and (59) are factorized (see Watanabe 2004) or otherwise made unavailable to SEM for interpretation, then these may both be cases of negative concord. Interestingly, some speakers of Afrikaans judge examples of negative concord such as (59) to be highly marked or of marginal acceptability, exactly as for (57)c. Likening the absence of a double negative reading in (57)c to that in (59), and calling both "negative concord," is of course merely giving a name to the phenomenon, while not explaining the phenomenon in any detailed way. However, it is important to note that Afrikaans allows negative concord in other contexts, and,

---

[13] It should be noted that many speakers of Afrikaans find these sentences highly marked, although they do occur in both standard and non-standard dialects of Afrikaans and are at least marginally acceptable to the speakers I have consulted.

interestingly, that sentences with NC, including those with an optional overt *nie*₁, are judged unacceptable or highly marked by some speakers.

In the next section, I consider derivation of a negative sentence in Afrikaans.

2.5　The Syntax of Negation in Afrikaans: a Derivation

I have proposed a number of steps in the derivation of a negative sentence in Afrikaans. Now, consider the complete derivation in (60)b of the sentence in (60)a. In cyclic fashion, the steps are as follows: ❶ the N-word merges with NegP₁; ❷ NegP₁ merges with NegP₂; ❸ the verb merges with T; and, ❹ the subject merges with TP.

(60)　a. Sy sluit **nooit** die deur **nie**.
　　　　she locks never the door *nie*₂
　　　　'She never locks the door.'　(Oosthuizen 1998)

b.

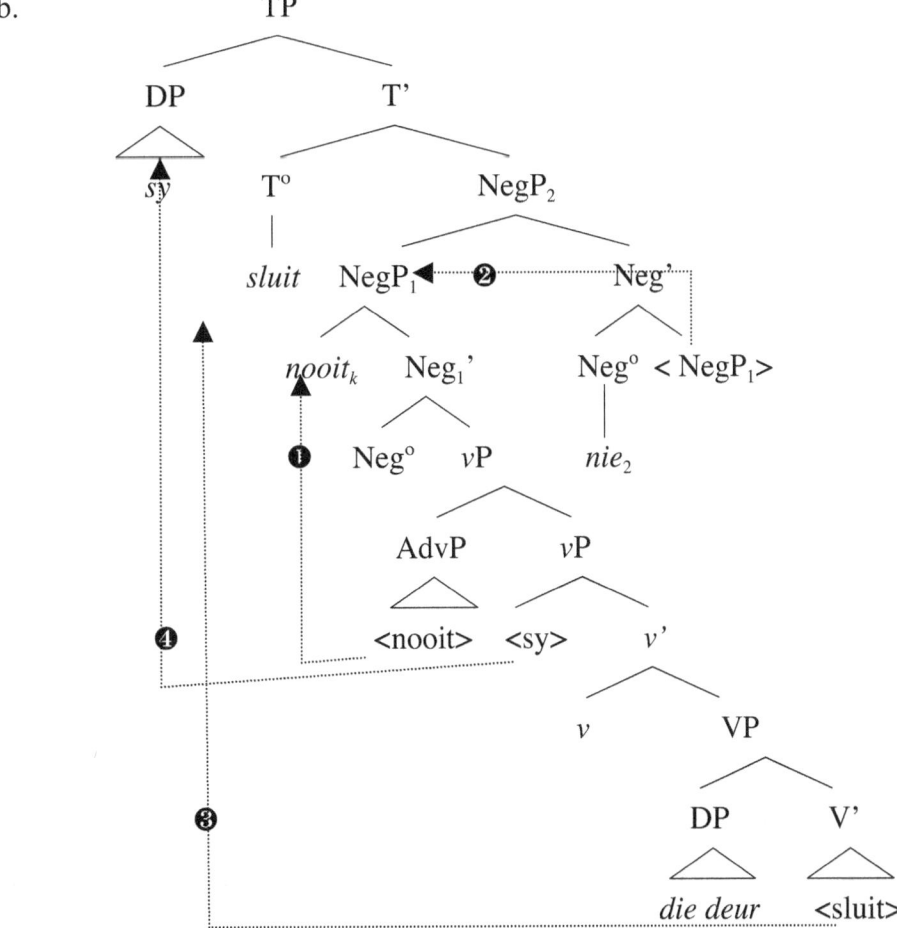

The representation in (60) is a complete derivation of a negative sentence in Afrikaans. The N-word merges with NegP$_1$. Subsequently NegP$_1$ merges with [Spec,NegP$_2$]. The verb moves to T, and the subject to TP, following standard assumptions (den Besten 1990, Koster 1994, Zwart 1997). This derivation raises one final important question: in case *nie*$_1$ is overt, is the movement of the verb over the negative head *nie*$_1$ a violation of the Head Movement Constraint? I discuss this question in the next section.

2.5.1 Negative Heads and the Head Movement Constraint

One remaining question concerns negative heads and the Head Movement Constraint (HMC). As we just saw, movement of the verb to T is of concern since it is an apparent violation of the HMC. Consider the abbreviated structure in (61).

(61)

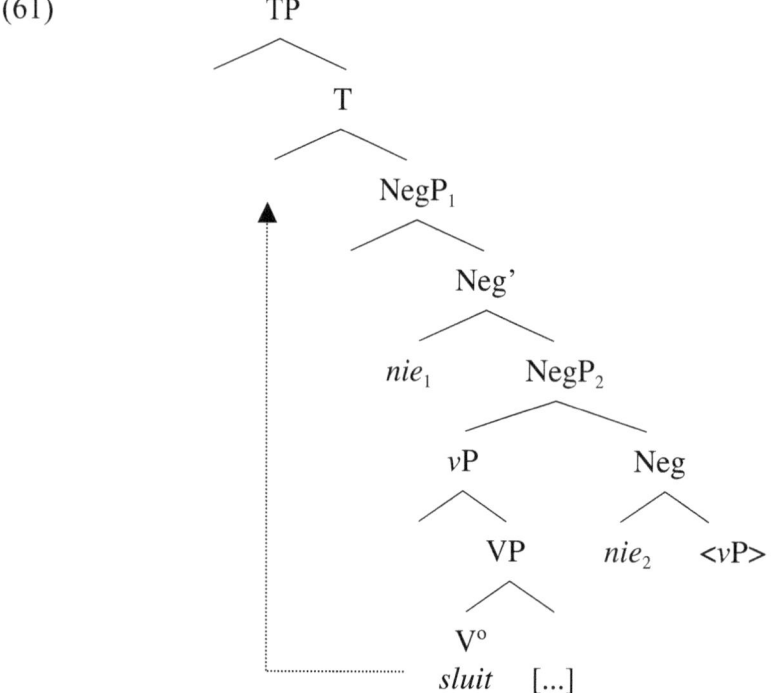

A staunch defender of the HMC could take the apparent violation of the HMC in (61) as evidence that *nie*$_1$ is in a specifier position, and is therefore not a clausal functional head, *contra* the wealth of evidence, given in this dissertation and in Oosthuizen (1998) and Molnárfi (2002) that *nie*$_1$ is indeed a clausal functional category. If *nie*$_1$ were a specifier in (61), there would be no violation of the HMC, since no overt head would intervene between V° and T°. I argue that there is no HMC violation here, on the grounds that all negative heads are opaque to the HMC computation. Thus, I argue that a negative head cannot intervene and block verb movement to T.[14] Indeed, there are cross-linguistic data to confirm this hypothesis about negative heads. Consider negation in French. Following the standard analysis for French (Pollock 1989), *ne* in French is the head of NegP and also a clitic. NegP intervenes between TP and VP. Updating the theory proposed in Pollock (1989) to include the HMC, as well as notions of branching and adjunction from Kayne (1994), we see that verb movement from V° to T° is in clear violation of the HMC. Consider the structure in (62), adapted from Pollock (1989:127).

(62)
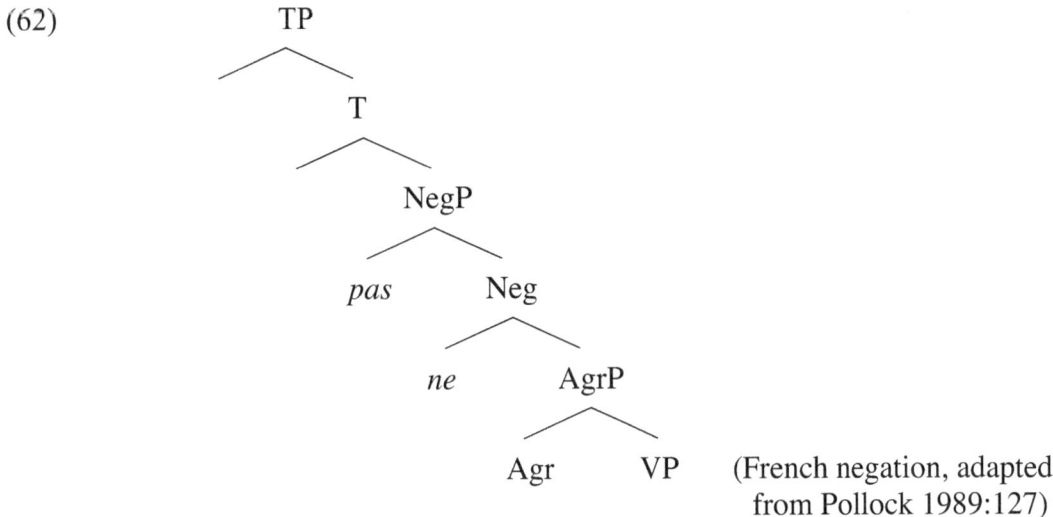

(French negation, adapted from Pollock 1989:127)

Movement of the verb from V° to T° should be blocked, given the HMC, by the intervening head *ne*. We might claim that the verb moves through Neg° on its way

---

[14] Cf. Zwart (1997) and Collins (2003) for other examples of apparent HMC violations.

to T°. However, given that head-adjunction is to the left (Kayne 1994), this would yield the ungrammatical order (for French) of Verb-*ne*, rather than *ne*-Verb. Instead, it appears that the negative head *ne* is opaque to the HMC computation, and that the verb moves to T, after which the clitic *ne* undergoes head movement and left-adjoins to the verb. We will see further examples of this fact in chapter three.

In the final section, I offer a summary of the chapter and some concluding remarks.

2.6 Chapter Summary and Conclusions

In this chapter I have presented data on, and developed an analysis of, the syntax of negation in Afrikaans. In the case of simple sentential negation, I argue that the negative morphemes nie_1 and nie_2 are both clausal functional heads, based on their behavior and distribution. I propose an expanded Negative Phrase housing both nie_1 and nie_2, which are syntactic heads of separate projections $NegP_1$ and $NegP_2$, respectively. Movement of an N-word to [Spec,$NegP_1$] eliminates the uninterpretable features on nie_1 and accounts for the observed Spec-head relation between N-word and nie_1 (required under the NEG Criterion) in minimalist terms. I argue that, since nie_1 acts as both probe (for N-words) and goal (for nie_2), it possesses both interpretable and uninterpretable negative features, and forms an *Agree* chain. The rightmost particle nie_2 plays a role in disambiguating *because*-clauses, and marking the lower limit of the scope of negation. I argue that $NegP_2$ dominates $NegP_1$ in the expanded NegP, and that nie_2 attracts either nie_1, or an N-word, both of which possess an interpretable feature [+neg]. $NegP_1$ is pied-piped to [Spec,$NegP_2$], accounting for the phrase-final position of nie_2 and explaining the syntactic relationship between nie_2 and nie_1. The expanded NegP also contains projections intermediate between $NegP_2$ and $NegP_1$. For example, there is a position XP to which PPs and CPs can scramble. I also argue for a position YP to which *because*-clauses move, thereby removing them from the scope of negation, since they are no longer c-commanded by and N-word/nie_1.

In the next chapter, I bring cross-linguistic data to bear on this analysis. I show that there are a number of languages that appear on the surface to have a similar negation strategy to Afrikaans. In addition, I show that there is a cluster of morphosyntactic properties shared by negation in Afrikaans and these languages. Finally, the languages I look at will be of substantial help in further refining the nature of the proposed expanded NegP projection.

CHAPTER THREE

PROPERTIES OF BIPARTITE NEGATION WITH FINAL NEG (BNF)

In this chapter I consider the analysis of Afrikaans negation proposed in Chapter 2, in light of a number of other languages employing similar bipartite negation strategies with a final NEG morpheme. As we saw in Chapter 2, Afrikaans employs a negation strategy that I have shown to differ significantly from bipartite systems such as French. As we will see in this chapter, Afrikaans negation patterns in many ways with negation in Bukusu (Central Bantu), Hausa (Chadic), Nweh (Grassfields Bantu), and Dagara (Gur). The negation strategies of all five of these languages share a number of core properties which I will describe below. I argue that the expanded NegP analysis provided for Afrikaans can capture the data in Bukusu, Hausa, Nweh, and Dagara as well. In addition to allowing a unified analysis of the cross-linguistic data, I further argue that adopting the expanded NegP solves a number of problems inherent in other analyses.

The principle surface similarity between Afrikaans negation and negation in the above-mentioned languages is their use of a phrase-final negative particle, used in conjunction with a pre-verbal negative particle. Given the use of the final particle, I will refer to these languages as having *bipartite negation with final NEG*, henceforth BNF. Languages using BNF are of interest in part because, as Nkemnji (1995:112) points out for Nweh, they are "unrelated to those languages that have been used to shape current theories on the syntax of negation." Bipartite systems such as French, West Flemish, and Arabic (Moroccan, Egyptian, Sanʕaanii) have received much attention in the literature, and form the core data in current theories of the syntax of negation (cf. Pollock 1989, Haegeman 1995, Benmamoun 2000). In this chapter, I will present data from a group of languages employing a bipartite system apparently quite unlike that in French, Arabic, or West Flemish. I further develop the expanded-NegP theory to accommodate the wider range of BNF data provided in this chapter.

The chapter is organized as follows. In §3.1, I introduce negation data from Bukusu, Hausa, Nweh, and Dagara. In §3.2, I move into a presentation of the cluster of morpho-syntactic properties shared by BNF languages, while also outlining some interesting differences. In §3.3, I extend the expanded NegP analysis given for Afrikaans to the languages from §3.1. I offer some concluding remarks in §3.4.

3.1 Bukusu, Hausa Nweh, and Dagara: the Data[1]

The negation strategies of Bukusu, Hausa, Nweh, Dagara and Afrikaans exhibit a striking surface similarity. Consider the data in (1) below.

(1) a. Peter **se**-a-la-ba a-kula sitabu **ta**.   **BUKUSU**
      Peter NEG-SA-TNS-be SA-buy book NEG
      'Peter will not be buying a book.' (Bell & Wasike 2003)

    b. Lāmî **bà** tà ci àbinci à kàsuwā **ba**:   **HAUSA**
      Lami NEG he eat food PREP market NEG
      'Lami didn't eat food at the market.' (Newman 2000:358)

    c. Njikèm à kè **te** fiá nkāp anbó Atem əjúa **bɔ́**.   **NWEH**
      Njikem AGR P-2 NEG give money to Atem yesterday NEG
      'Njikem did not give money to Atem yesterday.' (Nkemnji 1995:112)

    d. ʔʊ **bɛ́** kɔ́ ʔa pɔ́g kámáànd ʔadián **ɛ́**.   **DAGARA**
      he NEG give the woman corn today NEG
      'He didn't give corn to his wife today.' (Delplanque 1990:52)

    e. Hy het **nie** gedink aan die ernstige gevolge **nie**.   **AFRIKAANS**
      he has *nie*$_1$think of the serious consequences *nie*$_2$
      'He didn't think of the serious consequences.' (Donaldson 1993)

---

[1] The languages are presented in no particular order.

In (1)b, the discontinuous *bà...ba* marks sentential negation in Hausa. Similarly, we observe *se...ta* in Bukusu in (1)a, *te...bɔ* in Nweh in (1)c, *bέ...έ* in Dagara (1)d, and *nie...nie* in Afrikaans in (1)e. The surface similarities between the negation strategies in these five languages are striking. In each case we see a leftmost negative particle associated with the verbal field, and a phrase-final negative particle that can follow adverbials (1)c,e, direct objects (1)a, and prepositional phrases (1)b,e. There are also differences immediately apparent. In Afrikaans, (1)e, verb-second effects cause the auxiliary or main verb to move around the leftmost *nie* in matrix clauses. In Hausa (1)b and Bukusu (1)a, the leftmost negative marker precedes the subject agreement marker, while in Nweh, (1)c, the leftmost negative follows tense and agreement and directly precedes the verb. The leftmost negative marker in Dagara, in (1)d, immediately precedes the verb.

The presence of these surface similarities and differences in themselves constitute interesting syntactic data. BNF languages also exhibit a small cluster of morpho-syntactic properties related to negation that I discuss in §3.2. First, let us examine the data from each language in more detail, in the following four subsections. In presenting the data, I follow the same basic pattern as in chapter two, discussing negation in matrix clauses, then embedded clauses, then *because*-clauses.

3.1.1 Bukusu

In this section I examine sentential negation in Bukusu, a Bantu language spoken by roughly 565,000 people in the Bungoma district of the Western Province of Kenya. Bukusu is an agglutinative language, and the verb is usually a complex unit that can contain as many as ten affixes, including tense, aspect, mood, and agreement markers. The unmarked ordering of affixes in matrix clauses is as follows: negative, subject agreement (SA), tense, object agreement (OA), verb root, final vowel (fv). Like many Bantu languages, Bukusu also has a rich system of noun class agreement, which I do not discuss in any detail here. All data on Bukusu presented here comes either from Bell & Wasike (2003), or from consultation with native speaker Aggrey Wasike.

Sentential negation in Bukusu is bipartite. The two particles which mark negation are not homophonous. The leftmost NEG particle, *se*, occurs to the left of the verb, before both the subject agreement marker and tense markers, in matrix clauses. If we consider *se* as a verbal prefix, then it seems to be the leftmost prefix. I argue in §3.3 that *se* is indeed a prefix, and moves to adjoin to the subject agreement marker. The rightmost NEG particle, *ta*, occurs at the end of the negated sentence.[3] To begin, consider sentential negation in matrix clauses.

3.1.1.1   Bukusu Negation in Matrix Clauses

Matrix negation in Bukusu follows a familiar pattern. The leftmost negative marker *se* appears to the left of the verbal complex, while the rightmost marker *ta* is normally found in sentence-final position, in intransitives, following adverbial complements, and direct objects. Sentences in (2) illustrate.

(2)   a. Peter **se**-a-le-ič-a **ta**.   BUKUSU
         Peter NEG-SA-TNS-come-Fv NEG
         'Peter will not come.'

      b. Peter **se**-a-le-ič-a   bwangu **ta**.
         Peter NEG-SA-TNS-come- Fv quickly NEG
         'Peter will not come quickly.'

      c. Peter **se**-a-la-kula sitabu **ta**.
         Peter NEG-SA-TNS-buy book NEG
         'Peter will not buy a book.'

      d. Peter **se**-a-la-kula   sitabu bwangu **ta**.
         Peter NEG-SA-TNS-buy book quickly NEG
         'Peter will not buy a book quickly.'

---

[3] The particle *ta* can also surface as *tawe*, seemingly in free variation with *ta*. For simplicity, all examples given here employ *ta*. There is no independent meaning to /we/ in /tawe/.

The final particle *ta* also follows prepositional phrases. Recall that in Afrikaans, the position of the rightmost negative *nie*$_2$ is variable with respect to PPs. In Bukusu, this is not the case. The final negative marker *ta* must obligatorily follow post-verbal PPs and direct objects. Consider the data in (3).

(3) a. Peter **se**-alica-ng-a-xo mu McDonald's **ta**.
 Peter NEG-SA-TNS-eat-SA-ever at McDonald's NEG
 'Peter never eats at McDonald's.'

 b. * Peter **se**-alica-ng-a-xo **ta** mu McDonald's.
 Peter NEG-SA-TNS-eat-SA-ever NEG at McDonald's
 'Peter never eats at McDonald's.'

The position of adverbs and nominals is somewhat flexible in Bukusu. For example, they can be moved to the front of the clause, creating a focus interpretation. Consider two examples in (4).

(4) a. ? Bwangu, Peter **se**-a-le-ič-a **ta**.
 quickly Peter NEG-SA-TNS-come- Fv NEG
 'Quickly, Peter will not come.'

 b. ? Sitabu, Peter **se**-a-la-kula **ta**.
 book Peter NEG-SA-TNS-buy NEG
 'A book, Peter will not buy.'

In stark contrast, the position of both *ta* and *se* is extremely rigid. Essentially, *se* must appear before the subject agreement marker, but after the subject, and *ta* must appear at the end of the clause. Again, recall from chapter two that the leftmost negative marker *nie*$_1$ in Afrikaans can appear clause-initially, before full NP subjects. In Bukusu, however, any attempt to move either *ta* or *se* to the front of the clause results in ungrammaticality, as illustrated below in (5) and (6).

(5) a. * **Ta** Peter **se**-a-le-ič-a bwangu.
 NEG Peter NEG-SA-TNS-come-fv quickly

b. * **Ta** Peter **se**-a-la-kula sitabu.
      NEG Peter NEG-SA-TNS-buy book

(6) a. * **Se** Peter-a-le-ič-a bwangu **ta**.
       NEG Peter-SA-TNS-come-fv quickly NEG

   b. * **Se** Peter a-la-kula sitabu **ta**.
      NEG Peter-SA-TNS-buy book NEG

The leftmost negator *se* can appear in sentence-initial position in case there is no overt subject. Consider (7).

(7) a. **Se**-a-le-ič-a bwangu **ta**.
       NEG-SA-TNS-come-Fv quickly NEG
       'He/she will not come quickly.'

   b. **Se** a-la-kula sitabu **ta**.
      NEG-SA-TNS-buy book NEG
      'He/she will not buy a book.'

Both *se* and *ta* are obligatory in matrix clauses in Bukusu. As shown in (8) below, omitting one or the other results in ungrammaticality.

(8) a. *Peter **se**-a-la-kula sitabu.
       Peter NEG- SA-TNS-buy book

   b. *Peter a-la-kula sitabu **ta**.
      Peter SA-TNS-buy book NEG

Unlike Afrikaans, there are no contexts in Bukusu in which the leftmost negator, *se*, can appear as the sole marker of sentential negation. I nonetheless argue that *se* is indeed the locus of sentential negation in the Bukusu clause – meaning that *se* is the morpheme associated with the interpretable NEG feature – based on data from *because*-clauses presented below.

Broadly speaking, it seems that Bukusu negation is a more restrictive version of Afrikaans negation. The negative particles *se* and *ta* are both obligatory in all negative matrix clauses, and the positions in which they can appear are extremely limited. Next, let us consider how negation functions with embedded and relative clauses in Bukusu.

3.1.1.2 Bukusu Negation in the Context of Embedded and Relative Clauses

Negation in the context of embedded and relative clauses functions much the same as negation in matrix clauses in Bukusu, with one very interesting difference. Given what we observed in matrix clauses, it comes as no surprise that the position of *se* and *ta* in embedded and relative clauses is strictly fixed in Bukusu. Consider the data in (9)-(10).

(9) a. Peter **se**-a-kula engokho niyo maayi a-a-kat-il-e omukeni **ta**.
Peter NEG-SA-buy chicken which mother SA-TNS-slaughter-APPL-Fv guest NEG
'Peter did not buy the chicken which mother slaughtered for the guest.'

b. *Peter **se**-a-kula engokho **ta** niyo maayi a-a-kat-il-e omukeni
Peter NEG-SA-buy chicken NEG which mother SA-TNS-slaughter-APPL-Fv guest

(10) a. Peter **se**-a-bolele John ali Sally a-mala ekasi **ta**.
Peter NEG-SA-tell John COMP Sally SA-finish work NEG
'Peter did not tell John that Sally finished her work.'

b. *Peter **se**-abolele John **ta** ali Sally amala ekasi
Peter NEG-tell John NEG COMP Sally finish work

Recall that in Afrikaans, the position of a non-negative embedded or relative clause is variable with respect to *nie*$_2$ (chapter two, example 11). In Bukusu, this is not the case. The final negative marker *ta* must appear following the relative (9) or embedded (10) clause. As the (b) examples show in both of these sentences, placing the embedded or relative clause after *ta* results in ungrammaticality. This fact appears to coincide with the general unavailability of post-posed PPs discussed in §3.1.1.1 above. Simply put, *ta* has one and only one position in both matrix and embedded/relative clauses: sentence-final. This includes cases in which both the matrix and the embedded clause are negative. Consider the data in (11).

(11) a. Peter **se**-abolele John ali Sally **se**-amala ekasi **ta**.
Peter NEG tell John COMP Sally NEG finish work NEG
'Peter did not tell John that Sally did not finish her work.'

b. *Peter **se**-abolele John ali Sally **se**-amala ekasi **ta ta**.

c. *Peter **se**-abolele John ali **ta** Sally **se**-amala ekasi **ta**.

Both the matrix and the embedded clause in (11)a are interpreted as negative, yet there is only one *ta*, in sentence-final position. Two contiguous *ta* morphemes are illicit, as in (11)b. The data in (11)c illustrate the general the fact that *ta* cannot occur between a matrix and an embedded clause; it is radically sentence final in Bukusu, except, as we will see, in *because*-clauses.

Finally, consider the case of negative relative clauses, illustrated in (12).

(12) a. Peter a-kula engokho niyo maayi a-**xa**-a-kat-il-e omukeni **ta**.
Peter SA-buy chicken which mother SA-NEG-TNS-slaughter-APPL-fv guest NEG
'Peter bought the chicken which mother did not slaughter for the guest.'

b. * Peter a-kula engokho niyo maayi **se**-a-a-kat-il-e omukeni **ta**.
Peter SA-buy chicken which mother NEG-SA-TNS-slaughter-APPL-fv guest NEG

c. * Peter a-kula engokho niyo maayi a-**se**-a-kat-il-e omukeni **ta**.
Peter SA-buy chicken which mother SA-NEG-TNS-slaughter-APPL-fv guest NEG

Thus far we have observed that *se* is the leftmost negative particle in Bukusu, both in matrix and embedded clauses. However, in relative clauses, the leftmost negative marker is *xa*, as in (12)a. Note that the position of *xa* differs from that of *se*. While *se* always precedes the subject agreement marker, *xa* follows the subject agreement marker but preceedes tense. I return to these data in the discussion of BNF parameters in Chapter Four. Next, consider the case of *because*-clauses.

3.1.1.3   Bukusu Negation in *Because*-Clauses

In Afrikaans we observed that the position of the rightmost negative marker *nie*$_2$ functions to disambiguate *because*-clauses in the context of negation. Recall the English sentence, given in chapter two, and repeated here in (13).

(13)   Peter didn't leave because it was raining.
   a. ¬ leave (Peter)
   b. leave (Peter), ¬ because it was raining

The sentence in (13) is ambiguous in English between the readings in (13)a and (13)b. Normally this ambiguity is resolved through intonation and stress. Now consider the Bukusu sentences in (14).

(14)   a. Peter **se**-a-rekux-a   **ta**   sikila efula   y-aba yi-pa.
          Peter NEG-SA-leave-Fv NEG because rain SA-was SA-beat
          'Peter did not leave, because it was raining.'

     b. Peter **se**-a-rekux-a sikila   efula   y-aba yi-pa **ta**,   a-rekuxa sikila ....
        Peter NEG-SA-leave-Fv because rain SA-was SA-beat NEG SA-leave because ...
        'Peter left not because it was raining, he left because ...'

In (14)a, the rightmost negative marker *ta* appears directly preceding the *because*-clause, triggering the reading suggested in (13)a. In (14)b *ta* follows the *because*-clause, triggering the reading suggested in (13)b. The same distribution and the consequent change in meaning can be seen in (15).

(15)   a. Peter **se**-a-mu-lekha-nga   **ta**   sikila   a-siima khu-khwinyaa na-ye
          Peter NEG-SA-OA-leave-habitual NEG   because SA-likes to-play   with-her
          'Peter does not usually leave her, because he likes to play with her.'

     b. Peter **se**-a-mu-lekha-nga   sikila   a-siima khu-khwinyaa na-ye **ta**.
        Peter NEG-SA-OA-leave-habitual because SA-likes to-play   with-her NEG
        'Peter usually leaves her not because he likes to play with her.'

As the data in (14) and (15) suggest, *ta* in *because*-clauses seems to mark the lower boundary of negative scope. If *ta* appears to the left of the *because*-clause, then the *because*-clause is outside the scope of negation. If *ta* is occurs sentence-finally, negation takes scope over the *because*-clause. It is clear that there are two possible positions for the second negative particle, *ta*, in (14) and (15), or, alternatively, that there are two possible positions for the *because*-clause, namely preceding or following *ta*. This is in stark contrast to the data on embedded and relative clauses, in which *ta* can only appear in sentence-final position. I return to these data in §3.3 below, where I argue that *because*-clauses can move to a dedicated position in negative environments in all BNF languages. Based on the Bukusu data, I argue that this position is distinct from the position to which PPs and CPs can scramble in Afrikaans and, as we shall see, in Hausa as well.

3.1.2 Hausa

Hausa, a Chadic language spoken by approximatey 30 million people, employs five distinct negation strategies, summarized in *Table 1* below, from Newman (2000). The most common strategy is bipartite marking with the discontinuous markers *bà(a)...ba*, used to negate all VPs of tenses/aspects/moods (TAMs) except the continuous and the subjunctive (Newman 2000:357). Consider *Table 1*.

Table 1. Hausa Negation Strategies. (from Newman 2000:357)

Marker	Goes with
(1) bà(a) ... ba	TAMs other than the continuous and subjunctive
(2) bā	negative continuous TAM
(3) bābù / bâ	existential; HAVE sentences, etc.
(4) bàa ... ba	equational (nonverbal) sentences, NPs, etc.
(5) kadà / kâr̃	subjunctive

As summarized by Newman (2000), the discontinuous negation strategy with final *ba* is used in Hausa in all TAMs other than the continuous and the subjunctive. It is also found in equational sentences, and constituent (NP) negation. Newman (1971) suggests that discontinuous *bà(a)...ba* negation was the only strategy available in proto-Hausa, and that the various secondary negation strategies observed today are recent historical developments. I return to this point in Chapters Five and Six below.

Like Afrikaans and Bukusu, the unmarked position for the rightmost negative marker *ba* is sentence-final, although, as we will see in a moment, Hausa patterns more like Afrikaans than like Bukusu in allowing certain constituents and phrases to appear after final *ba*. Hausa is analogous to Bukusu in the placement of the leftmost negative. Recall that the leftmost negative marker *se* in Bukusu matrix clauses appeared obligatorily preceding the subject agreement marker. Similarly, in Hausa, the leftmost negative *bà* occurs "immediately before the PAC, the person-aspect complex that consists of the weak subject pronoun and the TAM. If there is an overt subject, this occurs before the NEG marker" (Newman 2000:357).[4]

To begin, consider negation in Hausa matrix clauses.

3.1.2.1   Hausa Negation in Matrix Clauses

In TAMs other than subjunctive and continuous, Hausa employs two particles in sentential negation, the pre-verbal *bà(a)* and the phrase-final *ba*. It is important to note that, although these particles have similar phonetic shape, they are distinct functional particles, and are not homophonous in any sense in Hausa. The following paradigm illustrates this fact quite clearly.

(16)   a.   *bà(a)*   (leftmost negative marker)
        b.   *ba*   (rightmost negative marker)
        c.   *baa*   'to give'
        d.   *bâ*   (question particle)

---

[4] Before moving into the data, I would like to indicate that the glosses for all data from Newman (2000) and Jaggar (2001) are my own. Newman and Jaggar provide Hausa examples, and English translations, but rarely give morpheme-by-morpheme glosses. I glossed these data in consultation with a speaker of Hausa. However, minor errors may remain, although they should not bear on the rather straight-forward line of argumentation presented here, which involves the positioning of negative morphemes in the Hausa clause.

The leftmost negative marker has low tone and, in certain circumstances, a long vowel. The final negative marker has a short vowel and high tone. These can be contrasted with the verb 'to give', *baa*, with a long vowel and high tone, and the phrase-final question particle *bâ*, with a short vowel and falling tone. Given these data, Hausa is another clear example of a BNF system, like Bukusu, in which the two negative particles are not completely homophonous.

Consider the data in (17), which show that the leftmost negative *bà* occurs between an overt NP subject and the weak subject pronoun, or phrase-initially if only the weak subject pronoun is present. Note that the full NP subject can be complex, as in (17)d.

(17) a. yārinyă **bà** tà dāwō **ba**. HAUSA
  girl NEG she return NEG
  'The girl didn't return.' (Newman 2000:357)

 b. Bintà **bà** tà ga Hàawaa **ba**.

  Binta NEG she see Haawaa NEG
  'Binta didn't see Haawaa.' (Hill 1976:63)

 c. **bà** mù san sù **ba**
  NEG we know them NEG
  'We don't know them.' (Newman 2000:574)

 d. mălàmai **bà** sù ji kōmē **ba**
  teachers NEG they hear anything NEG
  'The teachers didn't hear anything.' (ibid.:357)

 e. dà nī dà kai **bà** mâ zaună tăre cikin àmānă **ba**.
  and you and I NEG we live together in peace NEG
  'You and I will not live together peacefully.' (ibid.)

The rightmost negative marker *ba* in Hausa follows direct objects (17)b,d, object pronouns, (17)c, intransitive verbs, (17)a, and prepositional phrases. Note the presence of the negative polarity item *kōmē* 'anything' in (17)d. One interesting shared property of negation in Bukusu, Hausa, and Nweh is the apparent absence of negative words, or N-words, of the type we observed in Afrikaans – words with their own inherent negative force (i.e. containing an interpretable NEG feature), such as English *nothing* and *nobody*.

Interestingly, there is some dialectal variation in the placement of direct objects in Hausa with respect to final *ba*. Newman (2000:358) reports that, in certain northern dialects of Hausa, *ba* can appear before direct objects. Consider the data in (18).

(18) a. **bà** mù kāmà ɓàrāwòn **ba**   **HAUSA**
       NEG we catch thief NEG
       'We didn't catch the thief.' (Newman 2000:358)

     b. **bà** mù kāmà **ba** ɓàrāwòn   **NORTHERN HAUSA DIALECTS**
       NEG we catch NEG thief
       'We didn't catch the thief.' (Newman 2000:358)

Clearly, we are concerned in this dissertation with the variety of Hausa represented in (18)a. Placing the final *ba* before direct objects in non-Northern Hausa, as in (18)b, is illicit. However, it is interesting to note the existence of this variation, and I will return to these facts in detail in Chapter Four.

Next, consider prepositional phrases and other post-verbal constituents. The final negative particle *ba* can follow PPs in Hausa, as the data in (19) illustrate. This is true whether the PP is relatively light, as in (19)a-b, or quite heavy, as in (19)c-d.

(19) a. **bà** mu kàn fita dà tsakař rāna **ba**.   **HAUSA**
       NEG 1pl normally go-out PREP full sun NEG
       'We don't normally go out at midday.' Newman 2000:358

     b. Lāmî **bà** tà ci àbinci à kāsuwā **ba**.
       Lami NEG he eat food PREP market NEG
       'Lami didn't eat food at the market.' Newman 2000:358

c. **bā** yâ yankà rāgō dà wukā irin wannàn **ba**.
   NEG he cut ram with knife type this NEG
   'He's not likely to slaughter a ram with a knife such as this.' (ibid.)

e. mātā tasà **bà** tâ shiryā manà kālācī dà rùɓaɓɓen nāmā **ba**.
   wife his NEG she prepare 1PL-DAT meal with rotten meat NEG
   'His wife wouldn't prepare us a meal with rotten meat.'

According to Newman (2000), there is a heaviness constraint on the post-verbal constituents that may precede *ba*. A very heavy complement clause preceding *ba* leads to a somewhat degraded sentence. Consider the data in (20).

(20) a. **bài** yi kirā gà mutānē **ba** dà sù zō dandàlī
        NEG-he make call towards people NEG COMP they come town-square
   'He did not call upon the people to come to the town square.' (Newman 2000:359)

   b. ? **bài** yi kirā gà mutānē dà sù zō dandàlī **ba**
        NEG-he make call towards people COMP they come town-square NEG
   'He did not call upon the people to come to the town square.' (ibid.)

In (20) we observe that placing the rightmost negative *ba* after a particularly heavy complement clause results in a slightly degraded sentence. This suggests that, as in Afrikaans, certain phrases and constituents can appear to the right of the rightmost negative *ba*. Again, I return to these data in detail in the discussion of BNF parameters in Chapter 4.

Unlike Afrikaans and Bukusu, Hausa has verbal constructions reminiscent of serial verbs, where two verbs occur in a single clause without the presence of a conjunction. Consider the contrast between (21)a-b and (21)c-d. When two negative sentences are conjoined, each has its own pair of negative morphemes, as in (21)a-b. However, an alternative construction, in (21)c-d, contains only one set of negative morphemes bracketing the entire clause. According to Newman (2000), negation takes scope over both verbs in (21)c-d, that is, the truth value of (21)a is identical to (21)c, and so forth. If (21)c-d are correctly analyzed as serial verb constructions, the presence of a single set of negative morphemes provides evidence that serial verb constructions are single clauses in Hausa. If there were two clauses in (21)c, for example, we would expect two sets of negative morphemes, as in (21)b. We will see similar data from Nweh in §3.1.3 below, and I will return to these data in §3.3.[5]

(21) a. **bài** kàrɓā **ba** kuma **bài** kaɾ̃àntā **ba**.
NEG-he accept-it NEG-he and NEG read-it NEG
'He didn't accept it and he didn't read it. (Newman 2000:360)

b. **bà** zā sù shā giyằ **ba** kuma **bà** zā sù yi rawā **ba**.
NEG FUT they drink beer NEG and NEG FUT they do dance NEG
'They are not going to drink beer and they are not going to dance.' (ibid.)

c. **bài** kàrɓa yā kaɾ̃àntā **ba**.
NEG-he accept-it he read-it NEG
'He did not accept it and read it.' (ibid.)

d. **bà** zā sù shā giyằ sù yi rawā **ba**.
NEG FUT they drink beer they do dance NEG
'They are not going to drink beer and dance.' (ibid.)

Thus far we have seen that the rightmost negative *ba* appears following objects, prepositional phrases, and other post-verbal complements. However, unlike Afrikaans, PPs cannot normally appear to the right of *ba*. I will argue in Chapter 4 that this variation is a parameter of BNF. Some languages allow PPs and CPs to appear in post-NEG$_2$ position, others allow only CPs, and still others allow only *because*-clauses. In Hausa, the rightmost negative can appear before certain adverbs, and heavy complement clauses.

---

[5] Note that the leftmost negative morpheme *bà* fuses with the third person singular morpheme *ya*, yielding *bài*, as in (21)a. This fusion also occurs with the first person, *bà + ni = bàn*. I assume this is a phonological process, and do not offer a particular analysis here. However, this process is generally suggestive of the close syntactic relationship between the leftmost negative marker and the weak subject pronoun in Hausa.

As I mentioned above, there are several other negation strategies available in Hausa, depending on the TMA of the verbal complex. In the negative continuous, for example, a single, pre-verbal negative morpheme *baa* is employed. Consider (22).

(22) **bā** tă sōyà kăzā
      NEG she fry chicken
      'She is not frying chicken.' (Newman 2000:360)

As we see in (22), a single negative morpheme *baa* can stand alone in certain, somewhat restricted environments as the sole marker of sentential negation. According to Newman (1971), the high-tone, long vowel *baa* is historically related to the leftmost negative *bà(a)*, as one can deduce given its phonetic shape. It is thus highly plausible that the negative continuous marker *baa* in (22) has identical featural composition to *bà(a)*, i.e. both have an interpretable negative feature. Tellingly, the final negative morpheme *ba* can never stand alone in this sense. There are no alternative negation strategies with only final *ba*, suggesting, as I argue below in §3.3, that *ba* carries no interpretable negative feature, and that there is a close parallel between the final negative morphemes in the three languages we have seen thus far in the dissertation. If final *ba* contained an interpretable NEG feature, we might expect it to occur as the sole marker of negation in Hausa. This is never attested.

Continuing the discussion of Hausa, I now look at embedded.

3.1.2.2   Hausa Negation in the Context of Embedded Clauses

Next, consider the syntax of negation in Hausa, in the context of embedded clauses. When the matrix clause is negative, and the embedded or relative clause is affirmative, the final *ba* can occur in sentence-final position. Indeed, this is the unmarked position in the dialect described by Newman (2000). Consider (23) below.

(23) a. **bàn** ji dāɗi dà kukà shā giyă **ba**.   HAUSA
NEG-I feel good COMP you-pl drink beer NEG
'I am not happy that you drank beer.' (Newman 2000:359)

b. **bà**i kàmātà tankò yà biyā hàr̃ājī **ba**.
NEG-it appropriate Tanko he pay taxes NEG
'It's not appropriate that Tanko pay taxes.' (ibid.)

c. **bà**n san kō wã ya yi hakà **ba**
NEG-I know even who he do thus NEG
'I don't know who did that.' (ibid.)

In (23)a, we observe that final *ba* follows an affirmative embedded clause. In (23)b, we see that the position of the negative morphemes follows an identical pattern in expletive-like constructions in Hausa. Finally, the negative matrix clause followed by an embedded question in (23)c shows the same behavior. Recall that there is a general heaviness restriction on embedded clauses followed by *ba*. If the clause is too heavy, it is preferable to place *ba* directly following the matrix clause, as in (20) above. This contrasts with Bukusu, in which the final particle *ta* must obligatorily follow the embedded or relative clause. Interestingly, there is again some dialect variation to be found in the position of *ba* vis-à-vis relative and embedded clauses. Newman (2000) describes Western Hausa dialects in which *ba* normally precedes the embedded clause. Consider (24).

(24) **bà**n sanì **ba** kō wã ya yi hakà.   WESTERN HAUSA DIALECTS
NEG-I know NEG even who he do thus
'I don't know who did that.' (ibid.)

Compare (24) to (23)c above. In dialects of Western Hausa, the unmarked position for the rightmost negative marker *ba* is directly following the matrix verb, while the dialect described by Newman (2000) has the unmarked structure as in (23)c. The position of the rightmost negative *ba* remains constant in the context of embedded WH-questions, as in (25).

(25) **bài** gayā minì kō nawà zân biyā **ba**. HAUSA
NEG-he tell 1SG-DAT even how-much fut-I pay NEG
'He didn't tell me how much I should pay.' (ibid.)

As in Afrikaans, we observe that embedded negative relatives have the two negative morphemes bracketing the relative clause, as in (26)a (cf. Chapter Two, example 10). If only the relative clause is negative, the leftmost negative *bà* appears before the weak subject pronoun of the embedded clause, as in (26)b.

(26) a. kōwànè kuřtù dà **bài** ji ùmařnī **ba** zâi shǐga ukù.
any recruit COMP NEG-he hear orders NEG FUT-he enter jam
'Any recruit who doesn't take orders is going to be in a jam.' (Newman 2000:359)

b. inã nēman yāròn dà **bài** cikà fôm **ba**.
I look boy COMP NEG-he fill-out form NEG
'I am looking for the boy who didn't fill out the form.' (ibid.)

When both the matrix clause and the embedded/relative clause are negative, a single, rightmost negative particle *ba* is employed. Consider the sentences in (27). Note that using two contiguous final *ba* morphemes results in ungrammaticality, as in (27)b. These are similar haplology facts to those observed in both Afrikaans (Chapter Two, example 12c) and Bukusu (example (11)b) above.

(27) a. **bàn** ga yāròn dà **bài** tàimàki lādi **ba**
NEG-I see boy COMP NEG-he help Ladi NEG
'I don't see the boy who didn't help Ladi.' (Newman 2000:359)

b. ***bàn** ga yāròn dà [**bài** tàimàki lādi **ba**] **ba**]
NEG-I see boy COMP NEG-he help Ladi NEG NEG (ibid.)

Given what we have observed in Afrikaans, Bukusu, and Hausa, we might be tempted to claim that haplology in the context of identical final negative morphemes in BNF languages is a universal phenomenon. However, Newman (2000) points out the fascinating fact that in Tera, which is a distant relative of Hausa in the Chadic family, two contiguous negative morphemes are perfectly acceptable. He provides the following example, given in (28).

(28) nà gwa njib nəke nà vi nə dam ɓa ɓa   TERA
      he.NEG find man who-is he.NEG enter to out NEG NEG
      'He didn't find the man who didn't come out.' (Newman 2000:359)

Unlike Hausa, the Chadic language Tera allows for two contiguous final negative morphemes. Assuming that Tera can be correctly classified as a BNF language (i.e. if it shows other properties similar to known BNF languages), the data in (28) illustrate that haplology of final NEG is parameterized across these languages.

The Hausa data given in Newman (2000) provides some further insight into the nature of haplology of final NEG. While sequences of two final *ba* morphemes are illicit, a sequence of final *ba* immediately followed by initial *bà* is perfectly well-formed. Consider the data in (29).

(29) a. yāròn dà **bài** tàimàiki Lādi **ba bà** zâi sămi lādā **ba**   HAUSA
         boy COMP NEG-he help Ladi NEG NEG FUT-he get reward NEG
         'The boy who didn't help Ladi will not get a reward.' (Newman 2000:360)

    b. b'idan **bà** kù kasà kûnnē **ba bà** zā ku ji lābāři **ba**
        if NEG you pay attention NEG NEG FUT you hear news NEG
        'If you (pl.) don't pay attention, you won't hear the news.' (ibid.)

The data in (29) serve to illustrate two important facts. First, we see that there is a higher position available for final *ba* in the context of relative clauses, in (29)a. Second, it is clear that haplology affects only identical morphemes. Under my account, the final *ba* associated with the matrix clause and that associated with the embedded, relative, or complement clause occupy the identical position in each clause, *viz.* the head of NegP$_2$. This fact is made surface-evident by the identical phonetic shape of the morphemes. It is crucially not the case that any two contiguous negative morphemes violate the double-NEG filter, as is shown by both sentences in (29). The data in (29) are easily produced in Hausa, owing to the availability of weak subject pronouns which occur without the presence of an overt subject, thus making the leftmost negative *bà* initial in the clause. The analogous sentence to (29)a in Afrikaans would have an overt subject pronoun intervening between the final NEG and the initial NEG of the main clause. Similar examples do exist in Afrikaans, as illustrated in (30).[6]

(30) ...omdat mense wat **nie** werk **nie nie** kan oorlewe **nie.** AFRIKAANS
 ...because people that *nie$_1$* work *nie$_2$ nie$_1$* can survive *nie$_2$*
 '...because people that don't work can't survive.'

The data in (30) reveal that haplology in Afrikaans functions in a similar manner to haplology in Hausa. Only in cases of contiguous morphemes *nie$_2$* does deletion occur. The double-NEG filter does not operate on any two contiguous negative morphemes, even when as in Afrikaans, the two morphemes are homophonous, as are *nie$_1$* and *nie$_2$*. In a syntactic explanation, we could claim that the filter is sensitive to clause boundaries. However, a morphological filter, certainly the simpler explanation, would compute only whether the two morphemes are identical in position and function.[7]

Finally, consider the data in (31), which illustrate that haplology does not operate merely based on a given sequence of phonemes occurring twice in sentence-final position. The final negative morpheme *ba* has the same phonetic shape as the question particle *bâ*. Crucially, the question particle has falling tone, while the

---

[6] Thanks to an anonymous referee from the Triggers proceedings review committee for providing this example.
[7] Note that sentences such as (30) are potentially damaging to Molnárfi's (2002) copy theory for *nie$_2$*. Under his account, *nie$_1$* and *nie$_2$* are identical, the latter being a copy of the former. Therefore, a morphological filter should not be able to distinguish between *nie$_1$* and *nie$_2$* in sentences like (30), and one should be deleted.

negative has high tone, and, furthermore, the two perform very distinct and important syntactic functions.

(31) shī nḕ dīrēbàn dà **bài** zō **ba** bâ
      he STAB driver COMP NEG-he come NEG QUES
      'Is he (not) the driver that didn't come?' (ibid.)

In the next section, I discuss fronting of the leftmost negative in Hausa.

3.1.2.3   Clause-initial *bàa* in Hausa

Recall the following paradigm given in chapter two, from Afrikaans.

(32) a. Hy het **nie** gekom **nie**.   AFRIKAANS
         he has nie_1 come nie_2
         'He didn't come/hasn't come.' (Donaldson 1993)

      b. **Nie** hy het gekom **nie**.
         nie_1 he has come nie_2
         '**He** is not coming.' (Molnárfi 2002)

      c. ***Nie** het hy gekom **nie**.
         nie_1 has he come nie_2 (ibid.)

In Afrikaans, the leftmost negative morpheme nie_1 can appear at the front of the clause, as in (32)b, giving a focus interpretation to the subject. Recall that in Hausa, the leftmost negative morpheme can appear in initial position even when it is not focused, owing to the weak subject pronouns. Consider (33).

(33) a. Taa tàfi Kanò.   b. **Bà** tà tàfi Kanò **ba**.   HAUSA
         she go Kano   NEG she go Kano NEG
         'She went to Kano.'   'She didn't go to Kano.' (Hill 1976:62)

In the affirmative (33)a, the weak subject pronoun is in clause-initial position, while in (33)b, the negative *bà* precedes the weak subject pronoun. Note the difference in vowel length between the subject pronoun in (33)a and (33)b. Now consider the following paradigm from Hill (1976).

(34) a. **Bà** kà tàfi Kanò **ba**.
NEG you go Kano NEG
'You didn't go to Kano'   (Hill 1976:65)

b. **Bàa** kaa tàfi Kanò **ba** nèe.
NEG you go Kano NEG is
'It's not that you went to Kano.' (ibid.)

c. **Bàa** bà kà tàfi Kanò **ba**.
NEG NEG you go Kano NEG
'It's not that you didn't go to Kano.' (ibid.:67)

The example in (34)a shows simple sentential negation in Hausa, with the two negative morphemes bracketing the clause. In (34)b, we see the vowel on the initial negative *bà* has lengthened, as has the vowel of the subject pronoun. The negation in (34)b takes wide scope, negating the truth value of the entire clause – i.e., yielding an 'it-is-not-the-case-that x' reading. Note that the rightmost negative particle *ba* is present, as well as the particle *nèe*, which Hill glosses as 'is' but which is analyzed as a focus particle by Newman (2000). Finally, in (34)c, we see that the truth value of a negative clause can also be negated. Note again the presence of a single rightmost *ba* morpheme, and the absence of the focus particle *nèe*, which in any case is qualified as an optional part of sentences such as (34)b and (34)c by both Hill (1976) and Newman (2000). (34)c provides another example of haplology of a second final negative *ba*. We might expect two final *ba* morphemes, one associated with the *bàa* in focus position, the second with the standard negator *bà*. However, through what Newman (2000:359) terms "a process of morphological haplology," and Hill (1976:72) terms "surface coalescence," only a single instance of final *ba* appears. With only weak subject pronouns, we cannot identify whether (34)b represents movement of the negator *bà* to a higher (focus) position, or whether this is simply a different form of the negator, with a long vowel, which yields the wide scope reading. The data in (35) confirm that movement is involved.

(35)   a. rashìn nāmà **bà** zâi kashè mùtûm **ba**.
       lack   meat NEG FUT kill person NEG
       'Lack of meat will not kill a person.' (Newman 2000:363)

   b. **bǎ** rashìn nāmà zâi kashè mùtûm **ba**.
      NEG lack   meat FUT kill person NEG
      'It is not (the case) that lack of meat will kill a person.' (ibid.)

In (35)a, we see that the negative morpheme *bà* occurs following the overt NP subject. To yield the wide scope reading as in (34)b above, the negator *bà* either moves to the front of the sentence, or is generated in a higher NegP position, as discussed in Chapter 2, §2.4.3.2 above. Note that the position of the rightmost negative marker *ba* remains constant. Also note the absence of the focus marker *nèe* from Newman's (2000) data, indicating that it is merely optional in such cases – a point which he makes explicitly elsewhere (cf. Newman 2000:545). I shall return to a discussion of these data in §3.3 below.

Finally, I wish to briefly consider the case of *because*-clauses in §3.1.2.4.

3.1.2.4 Hausa Negation in *Because*-Clauses

Thus far we have observed that the rightmost negative marker in Hausa, *ba*, follows objects, prepositional phrases, CP complements, and various other post-verbal constituents. Although not a radically-final negative particle like Bukusu *ta*, Hausa *ba* is unmarked in final position, except in cases in which the post-verbal constituent is particularly heavy. Even a heavy complement followed by *ba*, however, is merely degraded, and by no means ungrammatical, as we have seen above.

However, there is one context in which *ba* categorically appears in non-final position in Hausa: in the presence of a *because*-clause complement which falls outside the scope of negation. Consider an example in (36).

(36)　**bà** zā mù　kārā masà àbinci　　**ba**　sabŏdà shī malālācī nĕ
　　　NEG FUT we bring 3SG-DAT food　NEG　because he slacker STAB
　　　'We will not bring him more food, because he is a slacker.'　(Newman 2000)

The sentence in (36) shows the familiar pattern of *because*-clause behavior in BNF languages. The *because*-clause falls outside the scope of negation – i.e. it means 'we will not bring him food' and ***not*** 'we will bring him food, not because he is a slacker.' Note the particle *nèe* at the end of the sentence, which I have glossed as *stabilizer* following Newman's (2000) use of the term. As I mentioned above, this particle is also analyzed as a type of focus marker. As in other BNF languages, the rightmost negative marker *ba* in Hausa can also follow *because*-clauses, in which case negation takes scope over the entire clause. Consider the pair of sentences in (37).

(37)　a.　**bàn**　bā　shì aikìn **ba**, dōmin　nā san　hali-nsà.
　　　　　NEG-I give him job NEG because I　know character-his
　　　　　'I didn't give him the job, because I know his character.'　(Jaggar 2001:453)

　　　b.　**bàn**　bā　shì aikìn dōmin　nā san　hali-nsà **ba**.
　　　　　NEG-I give him job NEG because I　know character-his
　　　　　'I gave him the job not because I know his character.'　(ibid., *my gloss*)

As in Bukusu and Afrikaans, the relative position of the rightmost negative morpheme *ba* plays a crucial role in disambiguating *because*-clauses in Hausa. I will return to these data below in §3.3. Next, consider the third language in our small survey, Nweh.

3.1.3　Nweh

Nweh is a Grassfield Bantu language spoken in Cameroon by approximately 85,000 people, and traditionally divided into nine dialectal varieties (Nkemnji 1995:3-4). Like Bukusu, Nweh has a rich system of noun classes. Nkemnji (1995) establishes the number of noun classes in Nweh as eight. The data in this section come exclusively from Nkemnji's (1995) dissertation on Nweh, and in particular his chapter five, which is entirely devoted to the syntax of negation in Nweh. Nkemnji (1995) presents his own well-argued analysis for Nweh negation, which I will discuss in some detail in §3.3. I cannot hope to touch on all of the data presented by Nkemnji. Therefore, I shall restrict myself to examples relevant to the topic at hand, namely, bipartite negation with final NEG. I will argue in §3.3 that Nweh can be captured under the unified BNF analysis proposed in this thesis. In addition, I argue that several aspects of negation in Nweh, which seem at first to be at variance with the BNF data encountered thus far, are in fact crucial data in fitting together the pieces of the puzzle and presenting a unified, empirically-motivated analysis. To begin, consider negation in matrix clauses.

3.1.3.1   Nweh Negation in Matrix Clauses

The unmarked negation strategy in Nweh follows the by-now familiar pattern of BNF, with some interesting variations on the theme we have encountered thus far. Consider the data in (38). The leftmost negative morpheme in Nweh is *te*, and the rightmost morpheme is *bɔ́*. As illustrated in (38)b and (38)c, absence of either the leftmost or the rightmost negative marker results in ungrammaticality.

(38) a. Njikèm à kè **te** pfɛ́t akèndɔ̀ŋ əjúa **bɔ́**.   NWEH
         N. AGR P-2 NEG eat plantains yesterday NEG
         'Njikem did not eat plantains yesterday.' (Nkemnji 1995:115)

   b. * Njikèm à kè **te** pfɛ́t akèndɔ̀ŋ əjúa.
         N. AGR P-2 NEG eat plantains yesterday (ibid.)

   c. * Njikèm à kè   pfɛ́t akèndɔ̀ŋ əjúa **bɔ́**.
         N. AGR P-2 eat plantains yesterday NEG   (ibid.)

As illustrated in (38)a, the position of the leftmost negative marker *te* in Nweh is somewhat different from that seen in Hausa and Bukusu above. Indeed, as described in detail in Nkemnji 1995:Chapter 5), *te* has a highly fixed position within the verb phrase. It appears before the future tense marker, immediately after the past tense marker, and following the agreement marker. Consider the paradigm in (39).

(39) a. Njikèm à **te** asē pfɛ́la akèndɔ̀ŋ **bɔ́**.   **NWEH**
N. AGR NEG ASP eat-fv plantains NEG
'Njikem is not eating plaintains.' (Nkemnji 1995:114)

b. Njikèm à kɛ̄ **te** pfɛ́t akèndɔ̀ŋ **bɔ́**.
N. AGR P-2 NEG eat plantains NEG
'Njikem did not eat plantains (yesterday).' (ibid.)

c. Njikèm à **te** ló pfɛ́t akèndɔ̀ŋ **bɔ́**.
N. AGR NEG F-2 eat plantains NEG
'Njikem is not eating plaintains (tomorrow).' (ibid.)

The leftmost negative morpheme *te* always follows the subject agreement marker in Nweh. Contrast this with Hausa and Bukusu, in which the leftmost negative maker (in matrix clauses in Bukusu, everywhere in Hausa) obligatorily precedes the subject agreement marker. As illustrated in (39)b, *te* precedes aspectual markers, yet follows the past tense marker, glossed by Nkemnji (1995) as P-2, owing to the complex system of Nweh tense marking, which distinguishes three past tenses and three future tenses (Nkemnji 1995:11). In (39)c, we observe that *te* precedes the future marker (F2) *ló*.

The rightmost negative marker *bɔ́* follows direct objects, as shown in (39), and also prepositional phrases and adverbs, as illustrated in (40).

(40) a. Njikèm à kɛ̄ **te**-fiá nkāp anbó Atem əjúa **bɔ́**.
N. AGR P-2 NEG give money to A yesterday NEG
'Njikem did not give money to Atem yesterday.' (Nkemnji 1995:112)

b. Njikèm à **te** ló fiá nkāp anbó Atem ačɔ̀ʔɔ́ **bɔ́**.
N. AGR NEG F-2 give money to A. tomorrow NEG
'Njikem will not give money to Atem tomorrow.' (ibid.)

As described by Nkemnji (1995:112), Nweh is a strictly head-initial language in terms of constituent order. The verb precedes its complements in almost every environment in Nweh. Interestingly, there are variants of negative sentences in which this strict head-initial character of Nweh does not hold. The basic pattern involves the main verb appearing in sentence-final position in certain negative sentences. Consider the data in (41).

(41) a. Njikèm à kè **te**-fiá nkāp anbó Atem əjúa **bɔ́**.
   N.   AGR P-2 NEG give money to A yesterday NEG
   'Njikem did not give money to Atem yesterday.' (Nkemnji 1995:112)

   b. Njikèm à kè *te* nkāp anbó Atem əjúa *fiá*.
   N. AGR P-2 NEG money to A. yesterday give
   'Njikem did not give money to Atem yesterday.' (ibid.)

   c. *Njikèm à kè *te* nkāp anbó Atem əjúa *bɔ́ fiá* .
   N. AGR P-2 NEG money to A. yesterday NEG give
   'Njikem did not give money to Atem yesterday.' (ibid:.113)

In (41)a, repeated from above, we see what Nkemnji (1995) describes as the unmarked negation strategy in Nweh: two morphemes, *te* and *bɔ́*, bracketing the VP and its complements. However, a very surprising piece of data is revealed in (41)b, in which the verb *fiá* 'give' appears in final position, *contra* the standard Nweh word order. As we see in (41)c, the verb and the rightmost negative marker *bɔ́* cannot co-occur, strongly suggesting, as Nkemnji (1995) claims, that they are in complementary distribution. In the next section, I consider negation in embedded clauses.

3.1.3.2 Nweh Negation in the Context of Embedded Clauses

The discussion in Nkemnji (1995:Chapter 5) centers largely around the fascinating alternation between bipartite negation with final *bɔ́*, and verb-final negation with only the leftmost marker *te*. When a matrix clause is negative, and its embedded complement clause is affirmative, the final *bɔ́* occurs following the embedded clause, as in (42)a below. There is no suggestion of any other possible order in Nkemnji (1995) – an expected result given the very strict clausal ordering of the leftmost negative morpheme *te*. It appear as if the position of *bɔ́* is similarly restricted to the end of the sentence. This suggestes a strong parallel between negation in Bukusu and Nweh, a point to which I return in §3.3. As in root clauses, the verb-final negation strategy is also available in the context of embedded clauses, as in (42)b.

(42) a. mùù n-kɛʔ **te** júʔ lé Njikem a kɘ̀ fiá nkap anbó Atem ɘjúa **bɔ́**.
　　　 I AGR-P-1 NEG hear that Njikem AGR P-2 give money to Atem yesterday NEG
　　　 'I did not hear that Njikem gave money to Atem yesterday.' (Nkemnji 1995:117)

　　 b. mùù n-kɛʔ **te** lé Njikem a kɘ̀ fiá nkap anbó Atem ɘjúa **júʔ**.
　　　 I AGR-P-1 NEG that Njikem AGR P-2 give money to Atem yesterday hear
　　　 'I did not hear that Njikem gave money to Atem yesterday' (ibid.)

In (42)a we see what Nkemnji (1995) describes as the unmarked negation strategy in Nweh. The leftmost negative *te* appears to the left of the main verb, while the rightmost negative marker *bɔ́* appears in clause-final position. The verb-final strategy is also available. Note that the verb which occurs in final position in (42)b is the matrix verb.

There is one context in which the rightmost negative marker *bɔ́* can categorically appear in non-final position, which I consider in the next section.

3.1.3.3   Nweh Negation in *Because*-Clauses

In this final subsection of §3.1, I consider *because*-clauses in Nweh. They present the familiar alternation we observed in Bukusu and Afrikaans. When the *because*-clause falls outside the scope of negation, the rightmost negative marker *bɔ́* appears to the left of the *because*-clause; otherwise *bɔ́* appears in sentence-final position. Consider (43).

(43) a. Njikèm à kɛ̀ʔ **tè** leb Atem **bɔ́** anuzàā júɩ́ a kɛ̀ʔ ase ŋgwàā.
　　　 Njikem AGR P-1 **NEG** beat Atem **NEG** because he AGR P-1 ASP be-sick
　　　 'Njikem did not beat Atem, because he was sick.' (Nkemnji 1995:145)

b. Njikèm à kèʔ **tè** leb Atem anuzàā júī a kèʔ ase ŋgwàā **bɔ́**.
   Njikem AGR P-1 **NEG** beat Atem because he AGR P-1 ASP be-sick **NEG**
   'Njikem beat Atem, not because he was sick.' (ibid.)

As we see in (43), *because*-clauses in Nweh are disambiguated based on the position of the rightmost negative marker – a central property of BNF languages, as I argue in §3.2 below. In Nweh, we have seen that there is a verb-final alternative to BNF which is available in some contexts. This option is also available in the case of *because*-clauses, but, interestingly, only when the *because*-clause falls outside the scope of negation. Consider the data in (44).

(44) a. Njikèm à kèʔ **tè** Atem **leb** anuzàā júī a kèʔ ase ŋgwàā.
         Njikem AGR P-1 **NEG** Atem beat because he AGR P-1 ASP be-sick
         'Njikem did not beat Atem, because he was sick.' (ibid.)

      b. *Njikèm à kèʔ **tè** Atem anuzàā júī a kèʔ ase ŋgwàa **leb**.
         Njikem AGR P-1 **NEG** Atem because he AGR P-1 ASP be-sick beat (ibid.)

The sentence in (44)a has identical truth conditions to the sentence in (43)a. The *because*-clause falls outside the scope of negation. However, there is no verb-final corollary to the sentence in (43)b. This is surprising given the acceptability of sentences such as (42)b above, repeated here in (45).

(45) mùū n-kɛʔ **te** lé Njikem a kɜ̀ fiá nkap anbó Atem ɜjúa **júʔ**.
      I AGR-P-1 NEG that Njikem AGR P-2 give money to Atem yesterday hear
      'I did not hear that Njikem gave money to Atem yesterday' (ibid.)

Compare (45) to (44)b. The two sentences appear on the surface to have very similar structures. Yet the verb-final negation strategy is unavailable in *because*-clauses that fall within the scope of negation. I propose an analysis of these facts in §3.3 below.

3.1.4 Dagara

Finally, I present data on negation in Dagara in this section. Dagara, a Gur langauge of Burkina Faso, is spoken by roughly 1 million people (1.5 million including northern dialects).[8] Dagara is characterized by a relatively complex tense/mood/aspect (TMA) system, and the use of mood particles located between the subject and predicate, suffixed to the verb, or placed in sentence-final position. The data presented here come entirely from Delplanque (1990). To begin, consider Dagara negation in matrix clauses.

3.1.4.1 Dagara Negation in Matrix Clauses

Negation in Dagara, in three of four TMAs, is characterized by a bipartite structure. The leftmost negative marker, realized as *bέ*, *tá*, or *kɜ* depending on the TMA associated with the verb, occurs between the subject and the verb, while the rightmost negative, *έ*, occurs in "absolute final position of the utterance, and this no matter what the number or the length of the arguments following the predicate" (Delplanque 1990:52).[9] Consider three examples in (46).

(46) a. ʔɜ **bέ** mɨ́ yɨ́ έ   DAGARA
      he NEG HAB go-out NEG
      'He doesn't (usually) go out.' (Delplanque 1990:51)

   b. ʔɜ **bέ** kɜ́ kámáànd έ
      he NEG give corn NEG
      'He didn't give corn.' (ibid.:52)

   c. ʔɜ **kɜ** da-n ʔa-kɨ́ ʔabió έ
      he NEG-FUT buy millet tomorrow
      'He will not buy millet tomorrow." (ibid.:53)

   d. ʔɜ **bέ** kɜ́ ʔa pɔ́g kámáànd ʔadɨán έ
      he NEG give the woman corn today NEG
      'He didn't give corn to his wife today.' (ibid.)

---

[8] 1998 statistics from www.ethnologue.com
[9] "A la négation, la marque /*bé*/ est complétée par une particule /*é*/ qui se place [...] **à la finale absolue de l'énoncé, et ce quel que soit le nombre ou la longueur des arguments suivant le prédicat**" (Delplanque 1990:52, my emphasis)

In (46)a-b and (46)d, we see a simple intransitive, negated with the two morphemes *bɛ́* and *ɛ́*. The rightmost negative in Dagara occurs in radically-final position in matrix clauses, whether following a direct object, as in (46)b, or a heavier double-object and temporal adverb, as in (46)c. While the form of the final negative marker is invariable, we observe an alternation between the leftmost negative marker, which can also be spelled-out as *kɜ*, as in (46)c. One explanation for this, suggested by Delplanque (1990), is that the negative particle *bɛ́* is the default marker of sentential negation in Dagara, while *kɜ* (and *tá*, as we shall see below in (49)) are complex particles that contain both a negative component and a TMA component. I will not explore these facts further here, as it appears, given the limited amount of data available, that the three negative markers occur in complementary distribution and occupy the same structural position in the phrase.

As I mentioned above, there is one TMA, the aorist, in which only the leftmost negative appears. Consider the examples in (47).

(47) a. ʔa saánd dɨ-Ø **bɛ́** tig-Ø
 the foreigner eat-AOR NEG full-AOR
 'The foreigner didn't eat until he was full." (Delplanque 1990:54)

b. náàb **bɛ́** puodé baa yaán
 cow NEG greet pond thanks
 'The cow doesn't thank the pond.' (ibid.)

In both (47)a and (47)b, we see examples of the leftmost negative marker *bɛ́* appearing in the absence of the rightmost negative *ɛ́*, suggesting that the leftmost negative is the locus of sentential negation in Dagara. Now consider negation in relative and embedded clauses.

3.1.4.2 Dagara Negation in the Context of Relative and Embedded Clauses

Delplanque (1990) presents a limited amount of data concerning negation in the context of relative clauses in Dagara. One interesting piece of data concerns negation in an embedded relative and in the matrix clause. Consider (48).

(48) ʔa pɔ́g na **bɛ́** tɛ́d daán a **bɛ́** pagd libié yágá **ɛ́**
the woman REL NEG have beer REL NEG earn money a lot NEG
'The woman who doesn't have beer does not earn a lot of money.' (ibid.:55)

In (48) we see two occurrences of the leftmost negative marker *bé*, and a single, sentence-final *é*. Given the absence of aorist mood marking on the verbs, we might expect to find a second marker *é* associated with the embedded relative. However, following Delplanque's (1990) comments, it appears that the final particle *é* cannot appear in any higher positions in the context of relative clauses. Nor do we observe a doubling of the final *é*. Now consider the sentence in (49).

(49) ʔa naa yel-na ʔɛ́ bɛ **tá** ʔɔŋné kɜɔn **ɛ́**
the chief says-AFF that they NEG-OPT[10] draw water NEG
'The chief said that they should not draw water.' (ibid.:56)

In (49) we see the optative negator, *tá*, appearing after the subject and before the verb of the embedded clause. This illustrates that the position of the leftmost negator determines the upper scope of negation in Dagara, as we would expect. Note also that the final negative *é* appears in its canonical position.

Finally, consider the behavior of *because*-clauses in Dagara.

3.1.4.3 Dagara Negation in *Because*-Clauses

Thus far, we have observed that the final negative particle *é* in Dagara occurs in strictly sentence-final position, in both matrix and embedded clauses, and regardless of the relative size or heaviness of the post-verbal complements/adjuncts it follows. As

---

[10] OPT here designates the optative mood, for which *tá* is the leftmost negative particle.

we might expect at this point, however, there is an important exception to the rule, observed in the context of *because*-clauses. Consider the paradigm in (50).

(50) a. bɛ kɜ-n ʔa-kí fɜ na soŋ bɛ a ʔiaŋ
 they give-AFF the-millet you REL help them REL CAUSAL[11]
 'They gave you millet because you helped them.' (Delplanque 1990:57)

b. bɛ **bé** kɜ fɜ kí **έ** fɜ na belɨ bɛ a ʔiaŋ
 they NEG give you millet NEG you REL trick them REL CAUSAL
 'They didn't give you millet, because you tricked them.' (ibid.:58)

c. bɛ **bé** kɜ fɜ kí fɜ na soŋ bɛ a ʔiaŋ **έ**
 they NEG give you millet you REL help them REL CAUSAL NEG
 'They gave you millet not because you helped them.'[12] (ibid.:58)

The data in (50) illustrate the now-familiar role played by the rightmost negative particle *έ* in Dagara *because*-clauses. Note that the position of the leftmost negative marker *bé* does not vary; in both (50)b and (50)c, it appears immediately to the left of the matrix verb. This highlights the important function of the rightmost negative *έ*, which seems to mark the end of negative scope in both (50)b and (50)c.[13]

This concludes the presentation of negation data from Bukusu, Hausa, Nweh, and Dagara. In the next section, I offer a summary of the empirical conclusions regarding negation that we may draw from these four languages. I argue that all four, as well as Afrikaans, can receive a unified analysis, and that all utilize a fundamentally similar negation strategy which I term *bipartite negation with final NEG*, or BNF. As have seen, in addition to their common properties, BNF languages exhibit a good deal

---

[11] Delplanque (1990) glosses this morpheme as "cause" and refers to a relation of "causalité" in these examples. However, if this is some type of functional head, it is very possible that it is involved in *because*-clause displacement in Dagara. I discuss this possibility in §3.3.
[12] Glossed by Delplanque (1990:58) as "Ce n'est pas parce que tu les as aidés qu'ils t'ont donné du mil."
[13] In relation to the sentences in (50)b and (50)c, Delplanque (1990:58) states that "à la négation, la particule finale /έ/ a pour effet de délimiter la portée de l'assertion, car dans les séquences de propositions, sa place est distinctive."

of language-specific variation in their negation strategies. I propose an account of various language-specific variations in Chapter 4. First, I discuss the small cluster of properties shared by BNF languages in §3.2.

3.2 Shared Properties of BNF Languages

This section offers a summary of the empirical observations from chapter two and §3.1, and an analysis of some of the shared properties of the negation strategy under discussion. Thus far, we have seen four languages that, on the surface, appear to share a somewhat similar negation strategy. The strategy involves the use of two separate morphemes to mark sentential negation. To distinguish this strategy from other bipartite strategies, for example French or Moroccan Arabic, I have dubbed it *bipartite negation with final NEG*, or BNF. On a purely descriptive, pre-theoretic level, I propose that BNF languages can be generally characterized by four factors: i) position of the negative markers in the clause; ii) functions of the negative markers; iii) morphology of the negative markers; and, iv) morpho-syntactic processes (i.e. haplology) affecting the negative markers. As I will argue below, these surface-observable characteristics of BNF correspond to deeper morpho-syntactic properties, such as featural composition and categorial status of the negative morphemes, phrase structure in negative clauses, and displacement phenomena. Before moving into a theoretical discussion, however, I wish to review what we know thus far.

All BNF languages use two negative morphemes in most sentential negation environments. The leftmost negative morpheme, which I refer to as NEG_1, is always positioned before the verb, with the important exception of Afrikaans matrix clauses, where verb-second phenomenon cause the verb to appear to the left of the leftmost NEG. The position of NEG_1 is highly restricted. In Nweh, NEG_1 must appear following agreement markers, and between past and future tense markers, crucially always before the main verb. In Hausa and Bukusu, NEG_1 is found preceding all

TMA and agreement markers, directly following full NP subjects. NEG_1 can stand alone as the sole marker of negation, in certain restricted environments, in Afrikaans, Hausa, and Nweh. Finally, NEG_1 does not undergo deletion (haplology) in any BNF language.

The rightmost negative morpheme, NEG_2, normally follow direct and indirect objects, adverbs, and prepositional phrases. In addition, a NEG_2 morpheme associated with a matrix clause can follow non-negative embedded or relative clauses in all of the languages examined. Like NEG_1, the position of NEG_2 is highly restricted. In Bukusu, Nweh, and Dagara, the only position in which NEG_2 can occur, with the important exception of *because*-clauses, is sentence-finally. In both Hausa and Afrikaans, there is more flexibility vis-à-vis the position of NEG_2. In Afrikaans, for example, we saw that prepositional phrases can appear either before or after NEG_2, while in certain dialects of Hausa, even direct objects can occur after NEG_2. In addition, the heaviness of the post-verbal complement or adjunct has a bearing on the acceptability of sentence-final NEG_2 in both Hausa and Afrikaans. Heavier adjuncts and complements prefer to appear after NEG_2, although they can occur before NEG_2 as well. The unmarked position for NEG_2 in both Afrikaans, and the Hausa dialect described by Newman (2000), is sentence-final.

In *Table 2*, I summarize the shared properties of the languages we have examined in Chapters 2 and 3. I list each language in relation to each property, and mark whether the property is directly *confirmed* by the data (✓), *suggested* by the data or by a particular author (?), or remains *unconfirmed* in the data presently available (??). A brief survey of the table reveals that the five languages in question conform to the proposed BNF properties to a surprising degree, given the fact that none are at all closely related typologically. Of the nine proposed properties, only two languages show "unconfirmed" status in a single property, and in only three cases do the data suggest rather than confirm that a particular language conforms to a particular property, placing overall conformity to the proposed properties at roughly 89 percent.

Table 2. Properties of BNF Languages
✓ = confirmed   ? = suggested   ?? = unconfirmed

Property ↓ Language →	Afrikaans	Bukusu	Hausa	Nweh	Dagara
Obligatory bipartite negation strategy	✓	✓	✓	✓	✓
NEG_1 precedes verb	✓	✓	✓	✓	✓
NEG_1 follows DOs, IOs, PPs, Adverbs, and CP complements	✓	✓	✓	✓	✓
Position of NEGs highly restricted	✓	✓	✓	✓	✓
NEG_2 disambiguates *Because*-clauses	✓	✓	✓	✓	✓
Haplology of NEG_2	✓	✓	✓	??	?
2 NEGs are morphologically distinct	?	✓	✓	✓	✓
Neither NEG can move to the left periphery	✓	✓	✓	✓	✓

Table 2 summarizes the shared properties of negation BNF languages. All BNF languages observed up to this point must obligatorily spell out both NEG heads in most contexts. In the next chapter and Chapter 6, we will see examples of BNF languages where spell-out of one head is optional. NEG_1 always precedes the verb, while NEG_2 can follow any XP, including complement clauses, adverbs, and PPs. The position of both NEG markers is highly restricted, strongly suggesting that both are functional categories. All BNF languages in Table 2 disambiguate *because*-clauses via the position of NEG_2, and all have contexts in which NEG_2 undergoes morphological haplology. Finally, NEG_1 and NEG_2 are morphologically distinct in all BNF languages except Afrikaans. In Chapter 6, we will see other examples of creoles and contact languages in which NEG_1 and NEG_2 are homophonous. I argue that this is simply due to the fact that, in the case of Afrikaans, the morpheme *nie* was the most readily available phonological material known to the early speakers of Cape Dutch, and it was therefore used to fill the new functional category $NegP_2$. The fact that all other BNF languages have distinct morphemes for NEG_1 and NEG_2, but that other properties of BNF remain the same across these languages, merely serves to confirm the intuition that nie_1 and nie_2 in Afrikaans are indeed quite different morphemes, with different sets of formal features, as I argue in Chapter 2.

In the next chapter, I discuss several points of variation across BNF languages. These include the position of NEG_1, verb movement to NEG_2^o, relative clause negation, and post-NEG_2 stranding. Also, I return at the end of the next chapter to an analysis of West Flemish, showing that the BNF approach put forth here can also accommodate this language.

CHAPTER FOUR

PARAMETERS OF BNF

In Chapter Three I presented cross-linguistic data on the BNF negation strategy. I argued that BNF is a particular negation strategy made available under UG, and furthermore, that a unified analysis can capture the properties of this strategy across a number of languages. However, there is variation within BNF, as we have seen in the previous chapters. In this chapter, I argue that, in addition to the core properties put forth in Chapter Three, BNF has a number of parameters. I refine and develop my analysis of BNF in a number of ways to take these parameters into account.

I begin the chapter, in §4.1, with a brief typological overview of BNF languages. I then discuss four parameters of BNF. First, in §4.2, I review the data showing that the position of NEG_1 in the clause varies across BNF languages. I propose that this variation is due to the presence of uninterpretable features associated with NEG1 that match features on higher functional heads, triggering head movement of NEG_1 to T^o or Agr^o – the hierarchical ordering of T with respect to the expanded NegP is identical across BNF. Second, in §4.3, I discuss relative clause negation in Bukusu. I argue that, due to the selectional property of [+wh] and [+neg] CPs in Bukusu, NEG_1 is spelled out as a different morpheme, with slightly different syntactic properties, in relative clauses. Third, in §4.4, I present data on verb movement to NEG_2 in Nweh. I argue that this movement is essentially a repair strategy to allow NEG_2 to have an phonetic realization – a general requirement across BNF, as we have seen above. Fourth, in §4.5, I discuss scrambling around NEG_2 (stranding) in BNF. I propose that BNF languages that allow scrambling have dedicated positions to which scrambled constituents and phrases move. Furthermore, I show that there is a correlation between scrambling phenomena such as object shift, and scrambling around NEG_2. For example, direct objects do not scramble around NEG_2, and they are also less likely to scramble to a higher position in Afrikaans (as compared to Dutch). Also, there appears to be a close connection between post-verbal constituents in Dutch and post-nie_2 constituents in Afrikaans, accounting for the restriction on pre-NEG_2 direct objects in Afrikaans. I also show that there are robust scope effects triggered by the relative position of NEG_2 in Afrikaans: elements to the right of NEG_2 fall outside the scope of negation, as revealed by NPI data. Finally, in §4.6, I propose an analysis for West Flemish along the lines of the BNF analysis developed thus far. I conclude the chapter in §4.7.

4.1 Typological Overview of BNF Languages

The BNF languages seen in the previous chapters exhibit a large number of typological similarities, in addition to the similarities in their negation strategies. In the broadest terms, all BNF languages identified at this stage have surface SVO order, with the exception of Afrikaans, which has SVO order in matrix clauses (verb-second) and SOV order in embedded clauses. Verb-second Germanic languages have traditionally been analyzed as underlyingly SOV. However, following the specific analyses of Koster (1994), Zwart (1997) and Haegeman (2002), I assume that Afrikaans is underlyingly SVO, and that SOV order in embedded clauses is a derived order. BNF languages are head-initial: determiners, prepositions, and other particles precede the noun. Verbal tense and aspect markers precede the main verb in most cases, although Bukusu has post-verbal applicative markers, Dagara has post-verbal aorist marking, and case marking in Hausa follows the noun. Both Hausa and Bukusu have subject agreement markers (called 'weak' subject pronouns in the Hausa literature) that directly precede the verb and follow the NEG_1 particle. Such large-scale typological similarities across BNF languages are not surprising given the analysis of negation put forth in this dissertation. I propose that the same structures and movement operations can account for the syntax of negation across all BNF languages. Since the syntax of negation is a central property of human language, we would expect languages with identical negation strategies to behave in similar ways in other areas. Indeed, this is what we observe across BNF languages. Still, as I intimate in Chapters Three and Five, there are a number of significant differences within BNF; differences that I argue below are in fact parameters within the BNF system. I will look in some detail at four such parameters in the next four subsections, beginning with the position of NEG_1 in §4.2.

4.2 The Position of NEG_1 in BNF

The position of NEG_1 varies somewhat across BNF languages. In Hausa, for example, NEG_1 always precedes both tense and subject agreement, and directly follows overt subjects. In Nweh, on the other hand, NEG_1 follows both agreement and tense, although it precedes certain other aspect markers. In this section, I argue that this variation is due to head movement of NEG, which in turn results from the selectional properties of TP across languages. Thus, rather than posit a structural parameter across BNF languages – e.g. some BNF languages exhibit the order NegP > AgrP > TP, while others show AgrP > TP > NegP – I argue that the order TP > NegP is universal (Laka 1994, Chomsky 1995) and that the pre-SA position of NEG_1 results from of head movement. This ordering follows from Laka's (1994:3) *Tense C-command Condition*, which states that tense must c-command all propositional operators (i.e. all functional heads that operate on the clause) at the level of S-structure, i.e. at Spell-Out.

As we have seen, NEG_1 in Hausa always occurs directly following the overt subject, and preceding both subject agreement (weak subject pronoun) and any tense markers. Consider the data in (1).

(1) a. **bà** mù kāmà ɓàrāwòn **ba**   HAUSA
NEG₁ we catch thief NEG
'We didn't catch the thief.' (Newman 2000:358)

b. Bintà **bà** tà ga Hàawaa **ba**.

Binta NEG₁ she see Haawaa NEG
'Binta didn't see Haawaa.' (Hill 1976:63)

c. rashǐn nāmà **bà** zâ-i kashè mùtûm **ba**.
lack meat NEG₁ FUT-3sg kill person NEG
'Lack of meat will not kill a person.' (Newman 2000:363)

d. **bà** zā sù shā giyã **ba**.
NEG₁ FUT they drink beer NEG
'They are not going to drink beer.' (ibid.)

In Hausa, the NEG₁ particle *bà* precedes both subject agreement, (1)a-b, and tense, (1)c-d. Note the ordering of tense with respect to subject agreement. When a sentence contains an overt tense marker, it precedes subject agreement. This suggests multiple head movement of NEG, which first forms a complex head with T°, then with Agr°. The derivation of is represented in (2)b.

(2) a. **bà** zā sù shā giyã **ba**.
NEG₁ FUT they drink beer NEG
'They are not going to drink beer.' (ibid.)

b.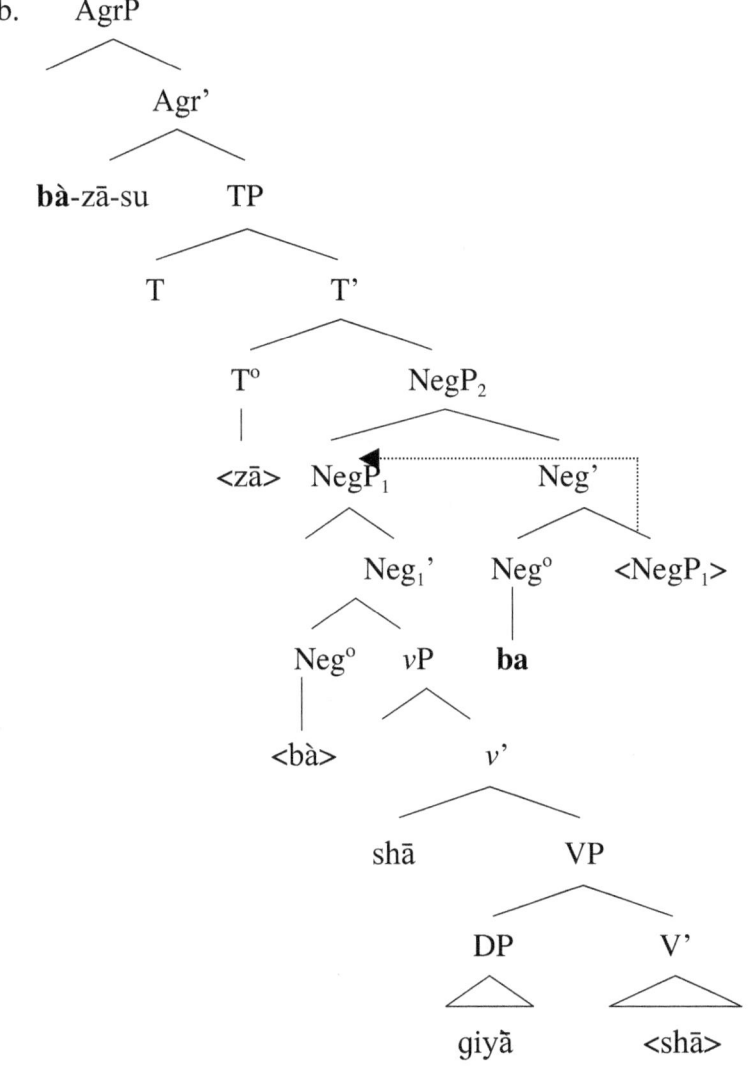

I propose that head movement of NEG_1 accounts for the observed word order in Hausa. As shown in the derivation in (2)b, the negative particle *bà* moves first to T°, where it adjoins with the tense morpheme. This complex head then moves to Agr°, yielding the surface order.

Similar data exist in Bukusu. Consider examples (3)a-b.

(3)   a. Peter **se**-a-liča-ng-a-xo   mu McDonald's **ta**.   **BUKUSU**
        Peter NEG_1-SA-TNS-eat-SA-ever at McDonald's NEG
        'Peter never eats at McDonald's.'

b. Peter **se**-a-la-kula sitabu **ta**.
   Peter NEG1-SA-TNS-buy book NEG
   'Peter will not buy a book.'

However, the order of the Tense and Agreement morphemes in Bukusu is reversed, with subject agreement preceding tense. If we are to follow a roll-up style derivation of head movement, such as that proposed for Hausa, this implies one of the following: i) T selects Agr in Bukusu; ii) Agr selects T, and NEG_1 moves directly to Agr; or, iii) Agr dominates T, and NEG_1 moves to T and then excorporates and moves to Agr. We can easily exclude option (i), since the ordering in non-negative clauses is also $Agr^o > T^o$, and there is no motivation for the agreement morpheme moving to T^o. Both option (ii) and option (iii) violate principles of head movement: (ii) violates the HMC, while (iii) violates the general ban on for excorporation (cf. Haegeman 1995). I argued above in Chapter Two that negative heads are not subject to the HMC as blockers in Afrikaans, thus it seems that option (ii) is perhaps the most viable, and allows us to maintain identical hierarchical relations across BNF languages. Also, as we shall see in a moment, Bukusu relative clauses present further data supporting the order AgrP > TP > NegP.

Nweh presents a different ordering of NEG_1 relative to agreement, tense and aspect morphemes. Consider the following examples in (4)a-c.

(4) a. Atem à kèʔ **te** túa akendɔŋ npfét **bɔ́**. **NWEH**
       Atem Agr P-1 roast plantains eat
       'Atem roasted plantains and ate (them). (ibid.:142)

   b. Njikem à **te** ló lée **bɔ́**.
      Njikem AGR NEG_1 F-2 sleep-fv NEG
      'Njikem was not sleeping yesterday.' (ibid.)

   c. Njikèm à **te** asē pféla akèndɔŋ **bɔ́**.
      N.   AGR NEG_1 ASP eat-fv plantains NEG
      'Njikem is not eating plaintains.' (Nkemnji 1995:114)

As we observe in (4)a-c, subject agreement in Nweh always precedes negation, as do the past-tense markers (of which there are three), including the past-1 tense marker kὲʔ (Cf. Nkemnji 1995). There are also tense/aspect markers that follow negation, including the present continuous marker *asē* in (4)c and the future-2 marker *ló* in (4)b. Following Nkemnji (1995), I assume that these latter morphemes are aspect heads and reside in an AspP dominated by NegP – or the expanded NegP, in my analysis. Unlike Hausa and Bukusu, NEG_1 in Nweh does not undergo head movement to $T°$ and $Agr°$ in Nweh, but remains *in situ*. Thus head movement of NEG_1 to T/Agr is parameterized in BNF, but the underlying ordering of Agr > T > NegP can be maintained across BNF.

In the next section, I will consider negation in relative clauses in Bukusu.

4.3 Relative Clause Negation in BNF

Negation of relative and embedded clauses follows a predictable pattern across BNF languages. As in matrix clauses, NEG_1 precedes the verb in the embedded/relative clause, while NEG_2 is in phrase-final position. As I discussed in Chapter Five, there are examples of 'partial' or developing BNF languages, such as Palenquero and Vernacular Brazilian Portuguese, which can spell out a single particle (either NEG_1 or NEG2) in sentential negation. In Palenquero, a phrase-final negative particle following a relative or embedded clause can be associated either with matrix negation or with relative/embedded clause negation, resulting in some interesting ambiguities. These ambiguities do not arise in VBP, nor in any other BNF language.

Consider a few examples of negation in the context of embedded questions and relative clauses across BNF, beginning with Afrikaans in (5)a-c.

(5)   a. Piet weet **nie** wie John by die winkel gesien het **nie**.
        Peter knows NEG_1 who John at the store seen has NEG_2
        'Peter doesn't know who John saw at the store.'

b. Piet weet wie John **nie** by die winkel gesien het **nie**.
   Peter knows NEG$_1$ who John at the store see has NEG$_2$
   Peter knows who John didn't see at the store.'

c. Piet weet **nie** wie John **nie** by die winkel gesien het **nie**.
   Peter knows NEG$_1$ who John NIE$_1$ at the store see has NEG$_2$
   'Peter doesn't know who John didn't see at the store.'

Examples (5)a-c illustrate negation in the context of embedded question in Afrikaans. When the matrix clause is negative, NEG$_2$ can appear either before the embedded clause (the scrambled order) or in sentence-final position. When the embedded clause is negative, the two negative morphemes bracket the entire clause, just as they do in embedded clauses. Other BNF languages follow the same pattern: relative clause negation is entirely analogous to other cases of sentential negation. Consider the examples in (6).

(6) a. **bàn** san kō wã ya yi hakà **ba**.   HAUSA
       NEG1-I know even who he do thus NEG
       'I don't know who did that.' (ibid.)

    b. inã nēman yārǒn dà **bà**-i cikà fôm **ba**.
       I search boy COMP NEG1-he fill-out form NEG
       'I am looking for the boy who didn't fill out the form.' (ibid.)

Negation in Hausa employs two negative particles which normally bracket the entire clause when the matrix clause is negative, as in (6)a. The same particles are used in relative clause negation, as in (6)b. Note that, in both examples (6)a-b, NEG$_1$ adjoins with the weak subject pronoun (which can also be analyzed as a subject agreement marker). I assume this adjunction is due to head movement of NEG$_1$ (*bà*) to Agr^o (see §4.2 above).

Now consider the following data from Bukusu. We have seen in Chapter Three that NEG$_1$ in Bukusu matrix and embedded clauses occupies a position identical to NEG₁ in Hausa. It follows overt subjects, but precedes the subject agreement marker. Consider the examples in (7).

(7) a. Peter **se**-a-la-kula sitabu **ta**.   **BUKUSU**
    Peter NEG1-SA-TNS-buy book NEG2
    'Peter will not buy a book.'

   b. **Se**-a-la-kula sitabu **ta**.
    NEG1-SA-TNS-buy book NEG2
    'He/she will not buy a book.'

   c. * Peter a-**se**-la-kula sitabu **ta**.
    Peter SA-NEG1-TNS-buy book NEG2

   d. * a-**se**-la-kula sitabu **ta**.
    NEG1-SA-TNS-buy book NEG2

The only available position for NEG₁ *se* in Bukusu is directly preceding the subject agreement marker in matrix clauses. This generalization also holds for embedded clauses. Consider (8).

(8) Peter **se**-a-bolele John ali Sally **se**-a-mala ekasi **ta**.   **BUKUSU**
    Peter NEG1-SA-tell John COMP Sally NEG1-SA-finish work NEG
    'Peter did not tell John that Sally did not finish her work.'

Embedded clauses in Bukusu are also negated with the particle *se*, which appears in pre-SA position. Now consider the following sentences, in which a relative clause is negated.

(9) a. Peter **se**-a-manyile omuundu niye John a-a-bona xu-soko **ta**.   **BUKUSU**
    Peter NEG1-SA-know person REL John SA-TNS-see P-market NEG2
    'Peter doesn't know the person who John saw at the market.'

   b. Peter a-manyile omuundu niye John a-**xa**-bona xu-soko **ta**.
    Peter SA-know person REL J. SA-NEG-see P-market NEG
    'Peter knows the person who John didn't see at the market.'

   c. Peter **se**-a-manyile omuundu niye John a-**xa**-bona xu-soko **ta**.
    Peter NEG-SA-know person REL John SA-NEG-see P-market NEG2
    'Peter doesn't know the person who John didn't see at the market.'

Unlike matrix and embedded clauses, both subject and object relative clauses, in (9), employ the particle *xa*, in conjunction with the phrase-final negative *ta*. In addition to its distinct morphological form, *xa* appears following the subject agreement marker, giving it a distinct distribution from *se*. Negative variants of this type are attested in other Bantu languages. Consider for example data from Kurundi in (10).

(10)   a. Yohani **nti**-a-á-somye ivyo bitabo.   **KIRUNDI**
          John NEG-3s-PST-read:PERF those books
          'John didn't read those books.' (Ndayiragije 1999:419)

        b. Ivyo bitabo **nti**-bi-á-som-u-ye na Yohani
          those books NEG-3p-PST-read-PASS-PERF by John
          'Those books were not read by John.' (ibid.)

        c. Ibitabo$_i$ [$_{CP}$ Op$_i$ [$_{TP}$ Yohani a-**ta**-á-somye t$_i$]]
          books   John   3s-NEG-PST-read-PERF
          'Books that John didn't read.' (ibid.)

        d. *Ibitabo$_i$ [$_{CP}$ Op$_i$ [$_{TP}$ Yohani **nti**-a-á-somye t$_i$]]
          books   John   NEG-3s-PST-read:PERF (ibid.)

In Kirundi, we observe an alternation in negative particles. Both declarative and passive matrix clauses, as in (10)a-b, employ the negative particle *nti*. As in Bukusu, *nti* in Kirundi precedes subject agreement markers. In Kirundi embedded clauses we find the particle *ta*, as in (10)c. Indeed, Ndayiragije (1999:419) states that *ta* is found in embedded clauses and "in all clauses (either matrix or embedded) involving *wh*-movement to initial [Spec,CP]." Kirundi also has OVS constructions, in which the object is located in [Spec,TP], according to Ndayiragije (1999). OVS constructions pattern with declarative and passive in using *nti*, not *ta*. Consider (11).

(11)   a. Ibitabo **nti**-bi-á-somye Yohani
          books NEG-3p-PST-read:PERF John
          'John (not Peter) didn't read the books.' (ibid.)

       b. * Ibitabo bi-**ta**-á-somye Yohani
           books 3p-NEG-PST-read:PERF John (ibid.)

Ndayiragije (1999) argues for an A-movement analysis of the OVS construction in Kirundi, based on the data in (10)-(11), as well as data from object *pro*-drop, raising, weak crossover effects, adjunct distribution, and case-marking facts. Object fronting of the Kirundi type is illicit in Bukusu, so we are unable to compare Kirundi directly with Bukusu along these same lines. Also, Kirundi has no overt NEG_2 particle, and there is little indication of BNF-style negation. However, we observe that both Kirundi and Bukusu show an alternation in the position and morphological form of NEG_1 in certain clause types.

Although the Kirundi negation data suggest a structural parallel between declarative, passive, and OVS constructions on the one hand, and *wh*-movement constructions on the other – a parallel strongly supported by other data – it is not clear from the discussion in Ndayiragije (1999) precisely why certain clause types license *nti*, while others license *ta*. What mechanisms are at work here? For example, while it appears logical that *books* in (11)a is in [Spec,TP], standard assumptions also require that *Yohani* 'John' be in [Spec,TP] in both (10)a and (10)c. This suggests that there is no structural difference between the TP domain in (10)a and the TP domain (10)c. Therefore, no structural difference, such as an intervening head blocking head movement, can explain the difference between (10)a and (10)c.

In Kirundi, the NEG_1 morpheme *ta* is licensed by a [+wh] CP. *Ta* undergoes head movement to T°, suggesting that the tense head and NEG_1 enter into an Agree relation, licensing movement to eliminate some uninterpretable feature. In the absence of a [+wh] CP, NEG_1 is spelled out at *nti*, and moves to Agr°, suggesting that Agr° and NEG_1 enter into a similar relation. Note that the two NEG_1 particles have different morphological forms. I argue that both are heads of NegP, but that each has a distinct set of uninterpretable features. While *ta* matches features with T° and moves to tense, *nti* matches features with Agr° and moves to Agr. Assuming that NEG_1 heads are not subject to the HMC (see Chapter Two and §4.2 above), this straight-forwardly explains both the positional and morphological differences between the two particles. In Kirundi, *ta* is licensed by a [+wh] CP. In Bukusu, the distribution of *xa* is restricted to relative clauses, *wh*-questions, and negative imperative and negative subjunctive constructions. First, consider the data from *Wh*-questions in (12)-(13).

(12) a. Naanu o-wa-bon-a John xu-sooko? BUKUSU
     who Agr-SA/tns-see-fv John at-market
     'Who saw John at the market?'

   b. Naanu oo-**xa**-bon-a John **ta**?
     who Agr-neg-see-fv John neg
     'Who didn't see John at the market?'

   c. * Naanu **se**-oo-bon-a John **ta**?
     who neg-Agr- see -fv John neg

(13) a. John a-a-bon-a naanu xu-sooko?
     John SA-pst-see-fv who P-market
     'Who did John see at the market?

   b. Naanu niye John a-**xa**-bon-a xu-sooko **ta**?
     who REL John SA-NEG$_1$-see-Fv P-market NEG$_2$

   c. *John **se**-a-bon-a naanu xu-sooko **ta**?
     John NEG$_1$-SA-see-Fv who P-market NEG$_2$

   d. *John a-**xa**-bon-a naanu xu-sooko **ta**?
     John SA-NEG$_2$-see-Fv who P-market NEG$_2$

In negative *Wh*-questions we find the negative particle *xa* rather than *se*. The cleft construction in (13)b could be due to the blocking effects of negation. These data strongly suggest that the particle *xa* is associated with the presence of a [+wh] CP. Next, consider the data in (14)-(15).

(14) a. βa-**xa**-kona   **ta**!   BUKUSU
       SA-NEG1-sleep NEG2
       'Let them not sleep!'

b. *βa-**se**-kona **ta**.
      SA-NEG1-sleep NEG2

   c. **Se**-βa-kona **ta**.
      NEG1-SA-sleep NEG2
      * 'Let them not sleep.'
      √ 'They don't sleep.'

(15) a. βa-**xa**-kona **ta**?
        SA-NEG1-sleep NEG2
        'Should they not sleep?'

   b. *βa-**se**-kona **ta**?
      SA-NEG1-sleep NEG2

   c. **Se**-βa-kona **ta**?
      NEG1-SA-sleep NEG2
      * 'Should they not sleep?'
      √ 'Don't they sleep.'

The NEG$_1$ particle *xa* occurs in relative clauses, and also in negative imperatives, (14)a and negative subjunctives, (15)a. In Kirundi, the negator *ta* is licensed by a [+wh] CP. Similarly, I propose that in Bukusu, *xa* is licensed by certain CPs – a [+wh] CP in the case of relative clauses and imperatives, and a [+neg] CP in the case of negative subjunctives. This proposal finds cross-linguistic support in Spanish, where sentences headed by a [+neg] complementizer must be in the subjunctive mood (Laka 1994:140). Thus we can posit the following structures for (14)a and (14)c above, repeated below in (16)a-b.

(16) a. βa-**xa**-kona **ta**!   **BUKUSU**
        SA-NEG$_1$-sleep NEG$_2$
        'Let them not sleep!'

b.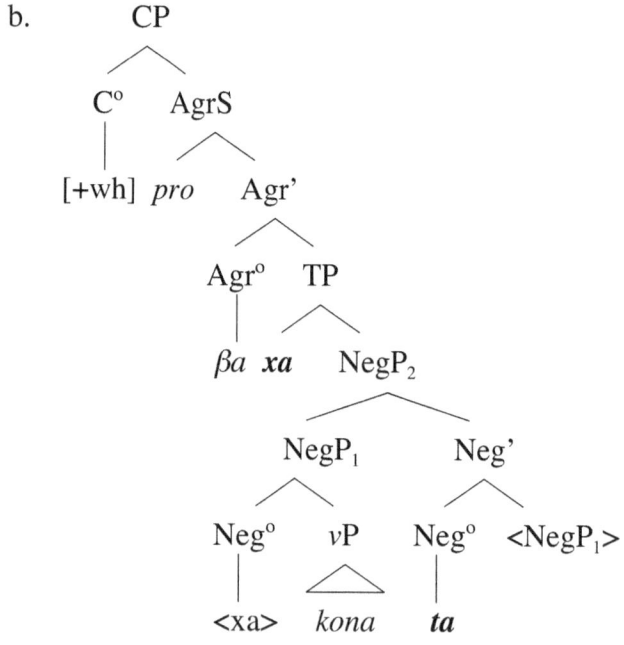

I assume that imperatives such as (16)a contain a CP in Bukusu, as they do in English. It is possible that the subject agreement moves to C°, although there is no empirical evidence to support or refute this possibility. To explain the distribution of the negative morphemes across these clause types, I propose that the head of CP in imperatives is [+wh], in the sense of Laka (1994) – that is, in Bukusu, it licenses the presence of the negative *xa*, rather than *se*, exactly as in Wh-questions and relative clauses. The particle *xa* moves to tense, although this movement is string-vacuous in example (16), since there is no overt tense particle. Note that imperatives with a modal auxiliary are NPI-licensers in English, suggesting, if we are to draw a parallel with Kirundi, the presence of a [+wh] C°, which serves as an NPI licenser. Consider the English data in (17), which suggest a similar interaction between questions and imperatives with let.[1]

(17)   a. Can anyone stand against me?
        b. ? Let anyone stand against me (and he will meet his doom)!
        c. *Anyone stood against me.

---

[1] Wayne Harbert (personal communication) points out the similarity between imperatives with *let* and if...then clauses, especially in mathematical language, e.g. 'Let x be a whole number...'

In simple declaratives, the negative particle *se* must obligatorily move to Agr°. If C° is present in these clauses, it is [-neg], and licenses the presence of the 'default' negative *se*. Consider the example and the derivation in (18)a-b.

(18)   a. **Se-βa-kona ta**.
           NEG1-SA-sleep NEG2
           √ 'They don't sleep.'

   b.
```
                    AgrS
                   /    \
                Agr°    TP
                 |     /  \
               se-βa       NegP₂
                          /     \
                       Spec      Neg'
                        |       /    \
                      NegP    Neg°   <NegP₁>
                     /   \     |
                        Neg'   ta
                       /   \
                    Neg°    vP
                     |      △
                    <se>   kona
```

Example (18)b is ungrammatical, since *se* has not moved far enough, leaving some feature unchecked. The derivation of (18)a is given in (18)c, where *se* has adjoined via head movement with Agr°. Not surprisingly, (18)a can only mean 'they do not sleep', the imperative reading being reserved for the structure with a [+wh] CP, which in turn licenses the presence of *xa* rather than *se*. Bukusu is the only BNF language in our dataset that exhibits this contrast, although, as I have shown, the variation between *se* and *xa* is easily captured within the theory of negation put forth here.

Movement of NEG$_1$ to either T° or Agr° is not the only head movement phenomenon in BNF. There are also examples of verb movement to NEG$_1$ found in Nweh. I consider these data in the next section.

4.4   Verb Movement in BNF

As we saw briefly in Chapter 3, Nweh shows an alternation between a phrase-final negative particle, which I argue to be an instantiation of NEG$_2$ in the BNF system, and the verb, which can also appear in final position in certain contexts. The verb in final position and the NEG$_2$ particle occur in complementary distribution. Consider (19)a-c.

(19)   a.   Njikèm à kè **te-**fiá nkāp anbó Atem əjúa **bɔ́**.   NWEH
           N.   AGR P-2 NEG$_1$ give money to A yesterday NEG
           'Njikem did not give money to Atem yesterday.'   (Nkemnji 1995:112)

       b.   Njikèm à kè *te* nkāp anbó Atem əjúa *fiá*.
           N. AGR P-2 NEG$_1$ money to A. yesterday give
           'Njikem did not give money to Atem yesterday.' (ibid.)

       c.   *Njikèm à kè *te* nkāp anbó Atem əjúa *bɔ́ fiá* .
           N. AGR P-2 NEG$_1$ money to A. yesterday NEG give
           'Njikem did not give money to Atem yesterday.' (ibid:.113)

The NEG$_2$ particle *bɔ́* appears in phrase-final position in Nweh. However, the main verb can also appear in this position, (19)b. The two cannot co-occur, as the ungrammaticality of (19)c shows, suggesting they occupy the same position. Nkemnji (1995) argues that the data in (19)b result from verb movement to Neg° (i.e. NEG2). I essentially adopt Nkemnji's (1995) analysis here, with some modifications related to the implementation of a BNF analysis. I propose that verb movement to NEG$_2$ is a parameter of BNF, illustrating the general requirement across BNF languages that NEG$_2$ have an overt realization. In Nweh, NEG$_2$ may be spelled out either as *bɔ́*, or as the verb. I assume that this is determined at the numeration. If the numeration contains *bɔ́*, the verb remains *in situ*, since there is phonetic material to fill NEG$_2$°. If the numeration does not contain *bɔ́*, then the verb must move to NEG$_2$° before Spell-Out. Below, I argue that adopting a BNF analysis can account for some issues that remain unresolved in the spec-head analysis presented by Nkemnji (1995). First, consider (20)a and (20)b below.

(20) a. Njikèm à kè *te* nkāp anbó Atem əjúa *fiá*.
N. AGR P-2 NEG$_1$ money to A. yesterday give
'Njikem did not give money to Atem yesterday.' (ibid.)

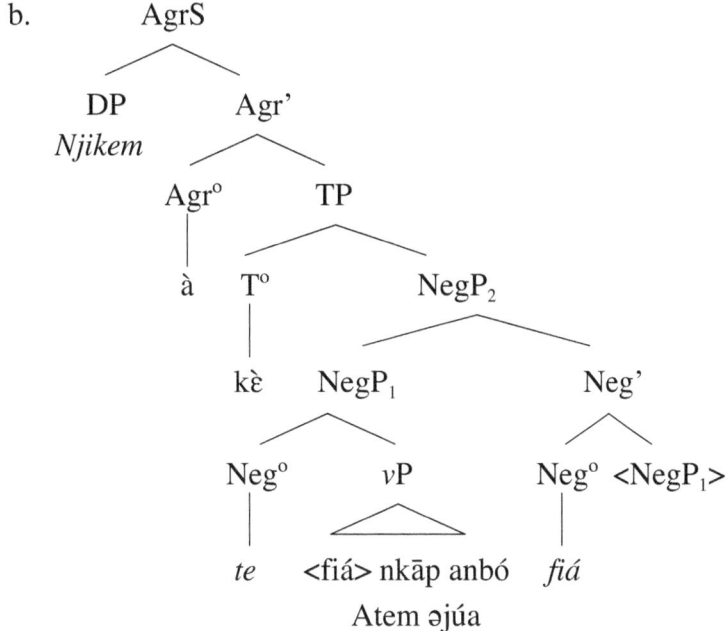

Following Nkemnji (1995), I assume that the phrase-final position of the verb in negative contexts results from verb movement to a negative head position. However, *contra* Nkemnji (1995), I propose that the position in question is the head of NegP$_2$. NEG$_2$° attracts the verb. Subsequently, the NegP-remnant moves to Spec,NegP$_2$. As above, the negative head *te* does not block head movement of the verb, further confirming the status of negative heads as inactive in any (possible) HMC computation.

Verb movement to NEG₂ is not unrestricted in Nweh. Consider the data in (21).

(21)   a. Njikèm à *te* ló *fiá* nkāp anbó Atem ač̀ɔʔɔ́ *b́ɔ*.
         Njikem AGR NEG₁ F-2 give money to Atem tomorrow NEG
         'Njikem will not give money to Atem tomorrow.' (Nkemnji 1995:113)

    b. * Njikèm à *te* ló nkāp anbó Atem ač̀ɔʔɔ́ *fiá*.
         Njikem AGR NEG₁ F-2 money to A. tomorrow give
         'Njikem will not give money to Atem tomorrow.' (ibid.)

In the presence of the future aspect particle *ló*, the verb cannot move to NEG2°. The aspectual head *ló* blocks verb movement. Consider the derivation of (21)b in (22).

(22)

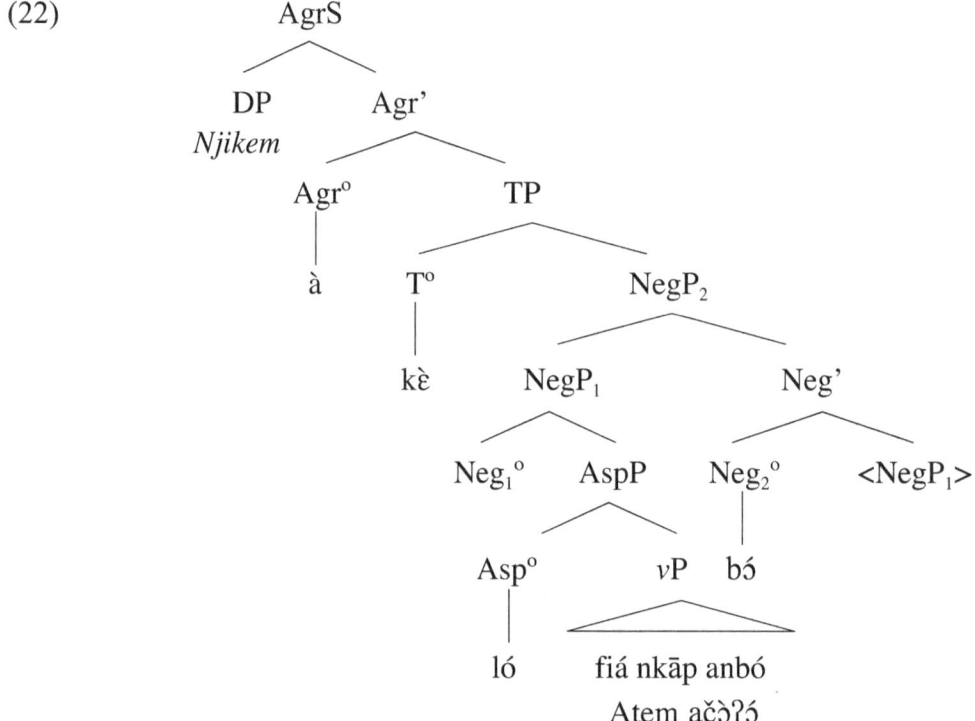

In (22) the verb must remain *in situ*, and is pied-piped along with everything contained in NegP₁ to Spec,NegP₂. Head movement of the verb is locally blocked by the aspectual head *ló*. Verb movement is also blocked in the case of serial verb constructions (SVCs). Consider the data in (23)a-d.[2]

(23) a. Atem à kèʔ ntúa akendɔŋ npfét.
   Atem Agr P-1 roast plantains eat
   'Atem roasted plantains and ate (them).' (Nkemnji 1995:141)

   b. Atem à kèʔ **te** túa akendɔŋ npfét **bɔ́**.
   Atem Agr P-1 roast plantains eat
   'Atem roasted plantains and ate (them). (ibid.:142)

   c. * Atem à kèʔ te túa akendɔŋ (n)pfét
   Atem Agr P-1 roast plantains eat (ibid.:142)

   d. * Atem à kèʔ te pfét akendɔŋ (n)túa
   Atem Agr P-1 roast plantains roast (ibid.:142)

Nweh has object-oriented SVCs, such as (23)a, which can be negated as in (23)b. Assuming a standard analysis of SVCs in which each verb heads its own VP (Collins 1997), movement of the lower verb is naturally blocked by the higher verb, ruling out (23)c (Nkemnji 1995). However, movement of the higher verb is also ungrammatical, as shown in (23)d, suggesting a freezing effect in SVCs: a verb cannot be moved from inside an SVC.

Nkemnji (1995) characterizes verb movement to Neg° (NEG_2) as the marked option in Nweh. In the context of simple intransitives, however, the overt NEG_2 head *bɔ́* is illicit. Consider the data in (24).

(24) a. Njikem à kè **te** lé.   **NWEH**
   Njikem AGR P-2 NEG_1 sleep
   'Njikem did not sleep (yesterday)' (Nkemnji 1995:132)

---

[2] Similar data exist for verbal focus constructions, which involve a doubling of the verb. These may only be negated in Nweh using both negative morphemes. The verb-final negation strategy is not available. Nkemnji (1995) proposes a unified analysis of these facts, which can straight-forwardly be adapted to the analysis proposed herein. I do not discuss the focus facts for lack of space, but I refer the reader to the excellent discussion in Nkemnji (1995:138-142)

b. *Njikem à kɛ̀ **te** lé **bɔ́**.
   Njikem AGR P-2 NEG$_1$ sleep NEG

c. Njikem à kɛ́ **te** lé əjúa **bɔ́**.
   Njikem AGR P-2 NEG$_1$ sleep-fv yesterday NEG
   'Njikem was not sleeping yesterday.' (Nkemnji 1995:133)

d. Njikem à kɛ́ **te** əjúa lée.
   Njikem AGR P-2 NEG$_1$ yesterday sleep-fv
   'Njikem was not sleeping yesterday.' (ibid.)

In simple intransitives, the verb must appear in final position, as in (24)a. As Nkemnji (1995:132) points out, there are (at least) two possible analyses for the contrast in (24)a-b. Either the verb has moved to NEG$_2$, or the verb has remained *in situ* and *bɔ́* is blocked from surfacing for some other reason. Given the fact that NEG$_2$ must have an overt instantiation in all other contexts in Nweh, I argue for the former scenario: the verb has moved to NEG$_2$° in (24)a, though this movement is string-vacuous. As support for such an analysis, consider (24)c-d. When the *v*P contains more material than a simple intransitive verb, both negative variants are allowed. In fact, these data are highly reminiscent of intransitive data in Afrikaans. Recall the data from Chapter Two, repeated below in (25).

(25) a. Ek weet **nie** (*nie).   **AFRIKAANS**
         I know *nie$_1$* *nie$_2$*
         'I don't know.' (Donaldson 2000:68)

     b. Hy sal **nie** kom **nie**.
         he shall *nie$_1$* come *nie$_2$*
         'He won't come.' (ibid.)

     c. Ek kyk **nie** televisie **nie**.
         I watch *nie$_1$* television *nie$_2$*
         'I don't watch television.' (ibid.)

Nie$_1$ and *nie$_2$* cannot be surface contiguous in Afrikaans, owing to the Double-NEG filter (see Chapter Two, Robbers 1997). *Nie$_2$* is deleted in simple intransitives in

Afrikaans, as in (25)a, unless there is some intervening material, for example, as in (25)b, where the auxiliary moves to second position and the main verb intervenes between *nie₁* and *nie₂*, blocking morphological haplology. It appears that there is also a Double-NEG filter at work in Nweh. The filter in Nweh is sensitive to intervening structure. There must be more than a simple verb separating NEG_1 and NEG_2 in Nweh. Compare example (24)c in Nweh and (25)c in Afrikaans above. *Modulo* verb-second in Afrikaans, these sentences are structurally very similar. In (25)c the direct object intervenes between *nie₁* and *nie₂*, while in (24)c the adverb intervenes, adding the required structure and preventing haplology. In other words, the verb moves to $NEG_2°$ in Nweh obligatorily in the absence of an overt NEG_2 morpheme. The NEG_2 morpheme is deleted when *v*P contains only a simple verb, and there are no intervening aspect heads. Further support for this analysis comes from the following data on the interaction between aspect heads and verb movement. Consider (26)a-d.

(26) a. Njikem à kè **te** ase ndéē **bɔ́**.
       Njikem AGR P-2 NEG_1 ASP sleep-fv NEG
       'Njikem was not sleeping yesterday.' (Nkemnji 1995:133)

   b. * Njikem à kè **te** ase ndéē.
       Njikem AGR P-2 NEG_1 ASP sleep-fv
       'Njikem was not sleeping yesterday.' (ibid.)

   c. Njikem à **te** ló lée **bɔ́**.
       Njikem AGR NEG_1 F-2 sleep-fv NEG
       'Njikem was not sleeping yesterday.' (ibid.)

   d. * Njikem à **te** ló lée.
       Njikem AGR NEG_1 F-2 sleep-fv
       'Njikem was not sleeping yesterday.' (ibid.)

In (26)a *v*P contains only a verb, thus we might predict NEG_2 deletion. In the case of (26)b, the numeration does not contain *bɔ́*. However, verb movement is blocked by the aspect head. The derivation crashes since $NEG2°$ must have an overt phonetic form. Nkemnji (1995:133) proposes no concrete answer for the admittedly perplexing facts on NEG2-deletion in Nweh.

Across BNF languages, $NEG_2°$ must be spelled out as a separate morpheme, either obligatorily (Afrikaans, Hausa, Bukusu, Nweh, Dagara, Santome) or optionally (Palenquero, VBP). NEG_2 is sometimes homophonous with NEG_1 (Afrikaans, Palenquero, VBP), and sometimes takes a different phonetic shape (Bukusu, Hausa, Nweh, Santome, Dagara). Nweh presents a further option: verb movement to $NEG_2°$. Verb movement to $NEG_2°$ in Nweh can thus be viewed as a repair strategy when a numeration does not contain the NEG_2 head *bɔ́*.

4.5 Post-NEG$_2$ Stranding in BNF

As we observed in Chapter Two and Chapter Three, some BNF languages allow constituents and phrases to be stranded to the right of NEG_2. These include CPs and PPs in Afrikaans, CPs and some adverbs in Hausa, and, as we will see in Chapter Six, PPs and CPs in the Spanish-based creole language Palenquero. Other BNF languages are much more restrictive in this area, and require NEG_2 to appear in phrase-final position. I argue in this section that post-NEG_2 stranding is the result of XP-movement to a position internal to the expanded NegP, followed by remnant movement of $NegP_1$ to Spec,$NegP_2$. Only the languages that allow post-NEG_2 stranding have such a position. Thus, stranding appears to be another parameter within BNF.

Post-NEG_2 stranding is restricted to certain constituents and phrases in at least some BNF languages. In Afrikaans, DPs can never appear in post-NEG_2 position. I argue that this is directly related to the fact that DPs cannot appear in post-verbal position in Afrikaans or Dutch. Interestingly, some dialects of Hausa *do* allow DPs in post-NEG_2 position. I provide an analysis of post-NEG_2 DPs in Hausa below. Then, in Chapter Seven, I argue that the BNF system can be extended to French. To begin, consider again the case of Afrikaans.

4.5.1 Afrikaans

As we saw briefly in Chapter Two, the categories that can be stranded to the right of NEG$_2$ in Afrikaans are CP and PP. Recall the data, repeated in (27)a-d.

(27)   a.   Sy het **niks**   gesê op die vergadering **nie**.   **AFRIKAANS**
            she has nothing said at the meeing   *nie$_2$*
            'She said nothing at the meeting.' (Oosthuizen 1998)

       b.   Sy het **niks**   gesê **nie** op die vergadering.
            she has nothing said *nie$_2$* at the meeing
            'She said nothing at the meeting.' (ibid.)

       c.   Ek het **nie** geweet dat hy sou   kom **nie.**
            I AUX *nie$_1$* know   that he would come *nie$_2$*
            'I didn't know that he would be coming.' (Donaldson 1993)

       d.   Ek het **nie** geweet **nie** dat hy sou   kom.
            I AUX *nie$_1$* know   *nie$_2$* that he would come
            'I didn't know that he would be coming.' (ibid.)

DP complements, on the other hand, can never appear to the right of NEG$_2$ in Afrikaans. Consider the following data.

(28)   a. Hy het **nie**   die boek gekoop **nie**.   **AFRIKAANS**
          he has NEG$_1$ the book bought NEG$_2$

       b. *Hy het **nie** gekoop **nie** die boek.
          he has NEG$_1$ bought NEG$_2$ the book

Many speakers of Afrikaans accept both PPs, as in (27)b, and CPs, as in (27)d, in post-NEG$_2$ position. As I mentioned in Chapter Two, not all speakers of Afrikaans allow such stranding. For example, one native-speaker consultant with whom I worked completely rejected the sentences in (27)b and (27)d in favor of their NEG$_2$-final counterparts in (27)a and (27)c. For those speakers who do find such stranding grammatical, it is far from clear whether there are any information structure related effects induced by scrambling, (i.e. focus or anti-focus, changes in presupposition, etc). Neither Oosthuizen (1998) nor Donaldson (1993) mention any such effects for the pairs in (27)a-b and (27)c-d. Rather, they both suggest that stranding is a purely syntactic option with no discourse-related properties. My native-speaker consultants who accepted such sentences generally agreed with this assessment. In certain cases, the stranded PP was perceived as a kind of "afterthought" to the main utterance, such as in (27)b for example. However, the anti-focus effect was, impressionistically, accompanied by a significant pause following NEG_2, and also a distinct intonation pattern on the PP when compared to the unmarked intonation. Thus the effect may be at least partially phonologically induced. Although post-NEG_2 stranding may not be related to information structure, there is a much clearer correlation between post-verbal constituents and post-NEG_2 constituents, which I explore in the next section.

4.5.1.1   Post-posed *Nie₂* & Post-verbal Constituents: Afrikaans & Dutch

It is a well-known fact that certain constituents in Dutch can only appear to the left of the main verb, while others can only appear to the right. Consider the data in (29)a-b.

(29)   a. Hij heeft [$_{DP}$ dat] gezegd (*dat)   **DUTCH**
           he has   that   said
           "He has said that."

        b. Hij heeft (*dat hij komt) gezegd [$_{CP}$ dat hij komt]
           he has   that he comes said   that he comes
           "He has said that he comes."   (Koster 1994)

Dutch DPs cannot occur in post-verbal position. If we adopt the proposal that Dutch is underlyingly SVO (Zwart 1997, Haegeman 2002), then we must assume that the DP in (29)a has undergone movement to some position to the left of *v*P. I assume that this is an object agreement position such as AgrO (Koster 1994). Movement of a DP to AgrO allows case to be assigned to the DP in Dutch. CPs, on the other hand, do not require case marking, and thus do not (and indeed cannot) move to the left of the verb, as in (29)b.

Definite DPs in Dutch show some variation in their distribution. Consider the data in (30)a-b.

(30) a. omdat Paul zondag *de was* gaat doen.
because Paul Sunday the wash goes do

b. omdat Paul *de was* zondag gaat doen.
because Paul the wash Sunday goes do
"because Paul is going to do the laundry on Sunday" (Koster 1994)

According to Koster (1994), the DP in (30)a receives a predicate incorporation reading, while the scrambled DP in (30)b receives a strong reading. In his analysis, Koster proposes that the strong reading is available when DP moves to AgrO, while the predicate incorporation reading is available when DP moves to Spec,PredP, where PredP is a projection intermediate between AgrO and VP (*v*P in Minimalist terminology). The proposed phrase structure is given in (31).

(31)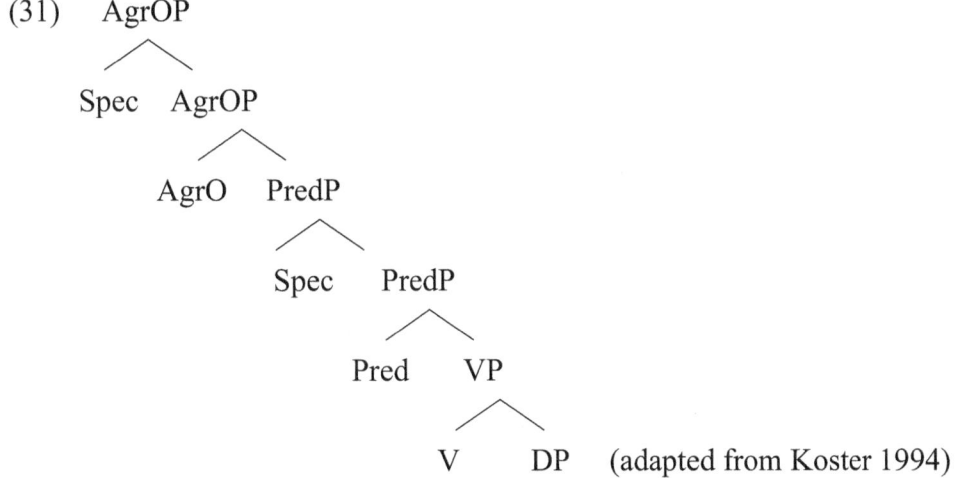

(adapted from Koster 1994)

The articulated left-of-*v*P structure proposed in (31) accounts for the different readings available for Dutch DPs. Definite DPs receive a strong reading when they move to AgrO, and a predicate incorporation reading when they move to PredP.

Indefinite DPs like *a man* are normally not able to scramble to AgrO, but instead receive their case marking (and their non-generic non-specific reading) by moving to PredP.

PPs, unlike DPs, can appear in either post-verbal or pre-verbal position, as illustrated below in (32). In certain cases there may be some information structure effects associated with post-verbal PPs in Dutch. However, according to Koster (1994), these effects are not reliably produced, and may also have to do with intonational factors – for example, phrase-final stress on a post-verbal constituent such as *in de tuin* in (32)d.

(32) a. ... dat Jan *aan zijn vader* dacht.   **DUTCH**
        that John of his father thought
        "...that John thought of his father..."

    b. ... dat Jan dacht *aan zijn vader*.
        that John thought of his father
        "...that John thought of his father..."

    c. Ik geloof dat de katten *in de tuin* spelen.
        I believe that the cats in the yard play
        "I believe that the cats play in the yard."

    d. Ik geloof dat de katten spelen *in de tuin*.
        I believe that the cats play in the yard
        "I believe that the cats play, namely in the yard." (Koster 1994)

Interestingly, post-verbal PPs are not allowed in certain cases, for example with locative PP complements and idiomatic expressions. Consider the data in (33).

(33) a. ...dat hij *naar huis* ging.   **DUTCH**
        that he to house went
        "...that he went home..."

    b. *dat hij ging *naar huis*.

    c. ...dat hij *aan de weg* timmerde.
        that he on the road carpentered
        "...that he was fond of the limelight"

d. *...dat hij timmerde *aan de weg*.

e. ...dat hij *er op* rekende.
   that he there on counted
   "...that he counted on it..."

f. *...dat hij rekende *er op*   (Koster 1994)

According to Koster (1994), the data in (33)a-f reflect the fact that *weak* PPs (those without independent argument status) must obligatorily move to Spec,PredP. *Strong* PPs such as those in (32) (those with independent argument status) can remain *in situ* in post-verbal position, or they can scramble to PredP – just as strong DPs can either scramble to AgrO or move to PredP. In certain cases, these two positions trigger two different readings, as in (32)c-d. Interestingly, Afrikaans appears to show similar restrictions on post-nie_2 PPs. Consider the data in (34).

(34) a. Ek weet dat hulle **oor die huis** praat.   AFRIKAANS
        I know that they about the house talk
        'I know that they talk about the house'

   b. Ek weet dat hulle **nie oor die huis** praat **nie**.
      I know that they *nie₁* about the house speak *nie₂*
      'I know that they don't talk about the house.'

   c. ?Ek weet dat hulle **nie** praat **nie oor die huis**.
      I know that they *nie₁* speak *nie₂* about the house
      'I know that they don't talk about the house.'

   d. Ek weet dat hulle **in die huis** is.
      I know that they in the house are
      'I know that they are in the house."

   e. Ek weet dat hulle **nie in die huis** is **nie**.
      I know that they *nie₁* in the house are *nie₂*
      'I know that they aren't in the house.'

   f. *Ek weet dat hulle **nie** is **nie in die huis**.
      I know that they *nie₁* are *nie₂* in the house

Compare (34)a-c to (34)d-f. The PP in (34)a-c, *oor die huis*, is an adjunct. The unmarked position of PP adjuncts in Afrikaans is shown in (34)b. However, placing the adjunct in post-*nie₂* position results in only a slight degradation. Now consider (34)d-f. I assume that the locative PP *in die huis* is a *v*P complement and, as in Dutch (33)b,d, must move to Spec,PredP and cannot be stranded in post-*nie₂* position, i.e. post-verbal position. Consider the structure in (35)b.

(35) a. ?Ek weet dat hulle **nie** praat **nie oor die huis**.
I know that they *nie₁* speak *nie₂* about the house
'I know that they don't talk about the house.'

b.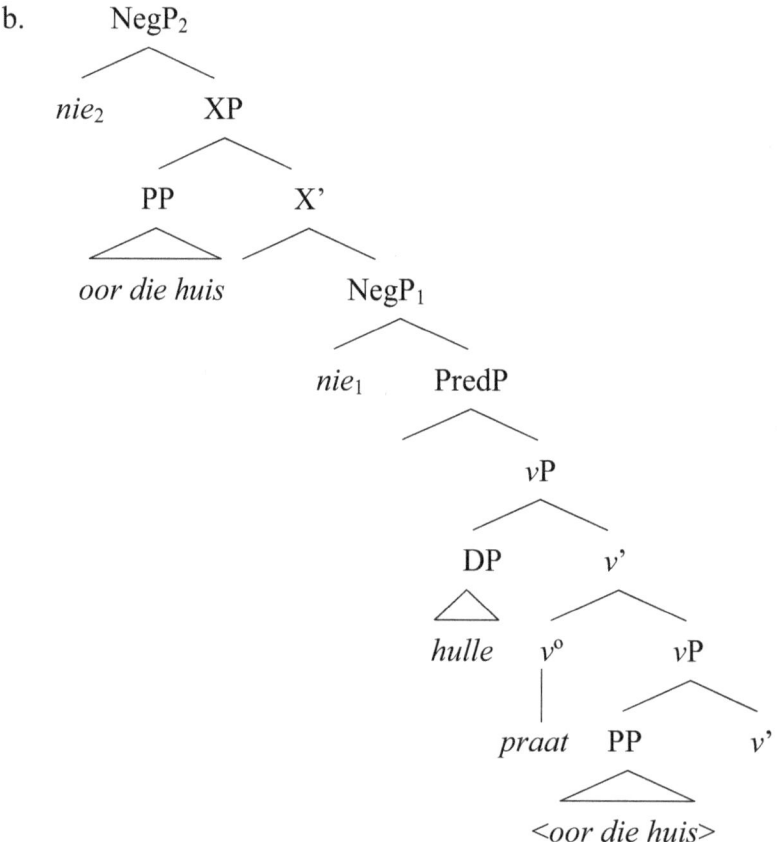

The PP-adjunct *oor die huis* has independent argument status. It is a *strong* PP in the sense of Koster (1994), and need not stay in [Spec,PredP]. As a result, it can move to [Spec,XP], where it will be stranded in post-*nie₂* position following NegP₁ movement to [Spec,NegP$_2$], as I illustrate in (35)b. Now consider the case of a locative PP-complement.

(36) a. Ek weet dat hulle **nie in die huis** is **nie**.   **AFRIKAANS**
     I know that they *nie$_1$* in the house are *nie$_2$*
     'I know that they aren't in the house.'

b. *Ek weet dat hulle **nie** is **nie in die huis**.
   I know that they *nie$_1$* are *nie$_2$* in the house

c.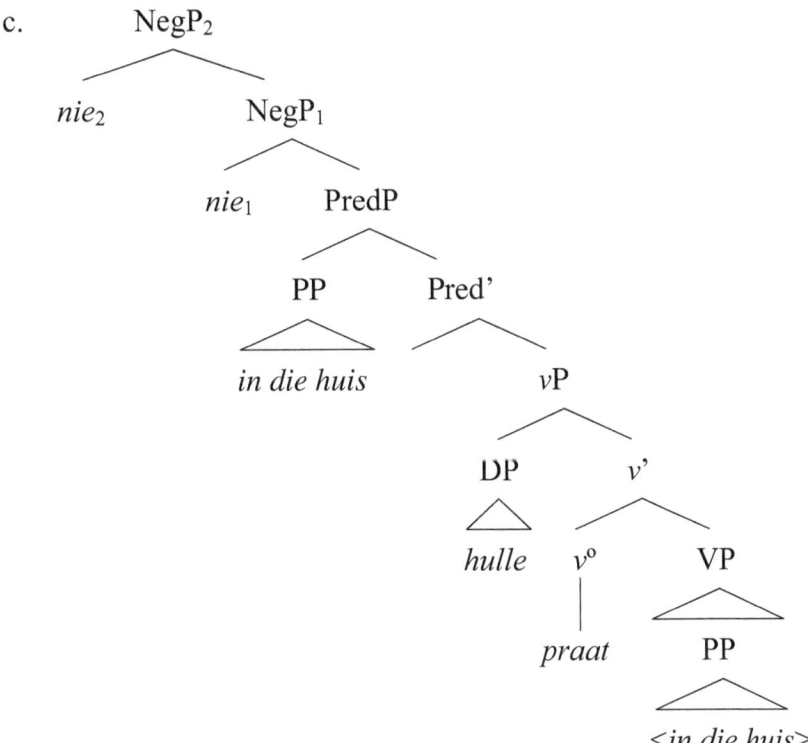

The locative PP-complement *in die huis* must move to [Spec,PredP], because it is a *weak* PP in the sense of Koster (1994). I propose that the PP in (36)a undergoes freezing once it moves to [Spec,PredP], preventing it from further scrambling to [Spec,XP]. This accounts for the ungrammaticality of (36)b.

As we observed in (29)a above, DPs in Dutch cannot appear in post-verbal position. Furthermore, we saw in (28)a-b above that DPs in Afrikaans cannot appear in post-*nie$_2$* position. PPs in Dutch can appear post-verbally, and they can appear post-

nie₂ in Afrikaans. There is a very close correlation between the distribution of post-*nie₂* constituents in Dutch and post-verbal constituents in Afrikaans. Consider the data in *Table 3*.

*Table 3. Post-verbal constituents in Dutch and Post-*nie₂* constituents in Afrikaans.*

DISTRIBUTION OF POST-VERBAL CONSTITUENTS IN DUTCH	DISTRIBUTION OF POST-NIE₂ CONSTITUENTS IN AFRIKAANS
(37) a. **DP V** dat hij *het boek* las that he the book read b. **PP V** dat hij *aan zijn moeder* dacht that he of his mother thought c. **AP V** dat hij *ziek* was that he sick was d. ***CP V** *dat hij *dat zij kwam* dacht that he that she came thought (38) a. ***V DP** *dat hij las *het boek* b. **V PP** dat hij dacht *aan zijn moeder* c. ***V AP** *dat hij was *ziek* d. **V CP** dat hij dacht *dat zij kwam*	(39) a. **DP *nie₂*** dat hy nie *die werk* gedoen het nie that he nie₁ the work do has nie₂ b. **PP *nie₂*** dat hy nie *in dié kamer* gerook het nie that he nie₁ in that room smoke has nie₂ c. **AP *nie₂*** dat hy nie *siek* is nie that he nie₁ sick is nie₂ d. **CP *nie₂*** Ek het nie geweet *dat hy sou kom* nie I have nie₁ know that he would come nie₂ (40) a. ****nie₂* DP** dat hy nie gedoen het nie *die werk* b. ***nie₂* PP** dat hy nie gerook het nie *in dié kamer* c. ****nie₂* AP** dat hy nie is nie *siek* d. ***nie₂* CP** Ek het nie geweet nie *dat hy sou kom*

As we see in *Table 3*, when a constituent can appear in post-verbal position in Dutch, then it can also appear in post-*nie₂* position in Afrikaans. Similarly, if a constituent is illicit in post-verbal position in Dutch, then it is also illicit in post-*nie₂* position in Afrikaans. Consider the case of DPs, comparing (37)a and (39)a with (38)a and (40)a. In Dutch, following Koster (1994), DPs must move to either [Spec,PredP] or [Spec,AgrO] to receive case.[3] They cannot remain *in situ*, and thus

---

[3] For ease of presentation, I do not consider further movement to AgrO. I assume that, if an object agreement position exists in Afrikaans, it is projected directly above PredP, and thus such movement would be string-vacuous for the purposes of the analysis at hand.

cannot appear in post-verbal position. In Afrikaans, I assume that DPs must undergo a similar movement to [Spec,PredP]. As in the case of PPs above, I posit that this movement entails freezing: no further movement of the DP is possible. Consider the structure below in (41)b.

(41)   a.   ...dat hy **nie** *die werk* gedoen het **nie**.   AFRIKAANS
              that he nie$_1$ the work do   has nie$_2$
            '...that he hasn't done the work.'

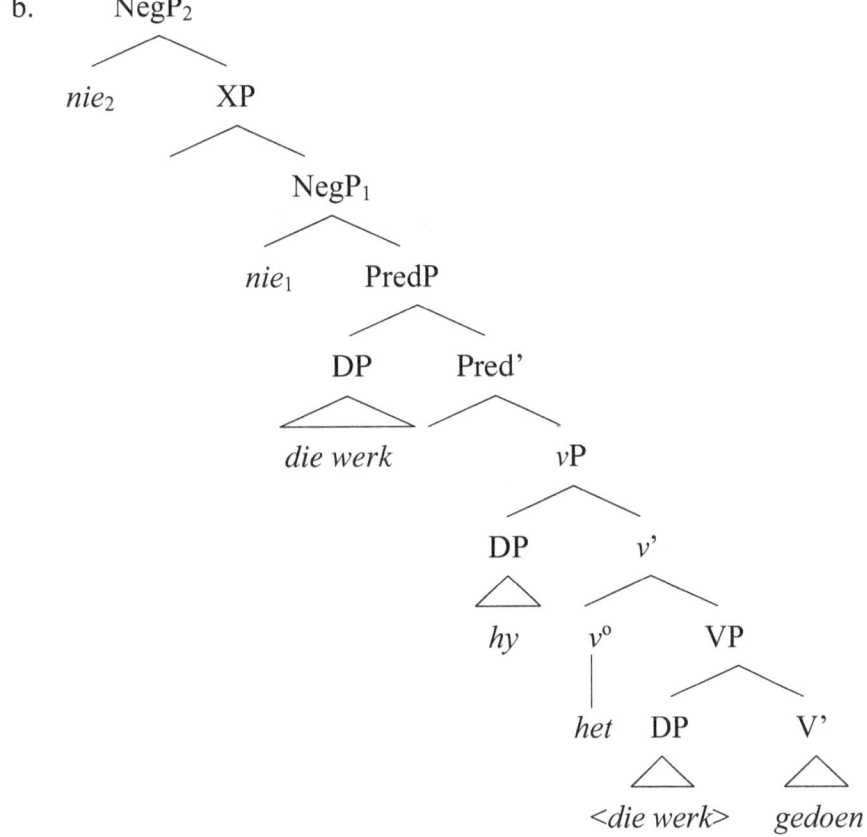

In the structure above, the DP object *die werk* has moved to [Spec,PredP], following Koster's (1994) analysis of DP-movement and case assignment in Dutch. I argue that the DP is frozen in this position, and is not able to move to [Spec,XP]. NegP$_1$ then moves to [Spec,NegP$_2$], pied-piping PredP and effectively preventing any subsequent movement of the DP to [Spec,XP]. Thus we see that a similar movement operation, DP to [Spec,PredP], accounts for the absence of post-verbal DPs in Dutch and post-*nie₂* DPs in Afrikaans. All DPs, as well as some PPs, undergo freezing once they move to [Spec,PredP], and cannot move further into [Spec,XP].

In the next section, I discuss the semantic effects of post-NEG₂ stranding of PPs in Afrikaans.

4.5.1.2 Scope Effects of Post-NEG₂ Stranding

As I mentioned above, post-NEG₂ stranding of a PP or CP in Afrikaans, for many speakers, gives an 'afterthought' interpretation to the PP or CP. Consider examples (42)a-c.

(42)   a. Sy het **niks** *op die vergadering* gesê **nie**.   **AFRIKAANS**
          she has nothing at the meeing   said *nie₂*
          'She said nothing at the meeting.'

        b. Sy het **niks** gesê *op die vergadering* **nie**.
          she has nothing said at the meeing   *nie₂*
          'She said nothing at the meeting.' (Oosthuizen 1998)

        c. Sy het **niks** gesê **nie** *op die vergadering*.
          she has nothing said *nie₂* at the meeing
          'She said nothing at the meeting.' (ibid.)

All of the examples in (42)a-c are grammatical. They are listed in order of preference, based on the judgments of a native Afrikaans consultant. Example (42)a is preferred, while (42)b is also perfectly acceptable. Example (42)c is grammatical, but the prepositional phrase *op die vergadering* 'at the meeting' receives a parenthetical or 'afterthought' interpretation. We have also seen that stranding certain constituents following *nie₂* leads to a change in negative scope. This is the case with *because*-clauses. Recall the data from Chapter 2, repeated below.

(43)   a. Piet het **nie** vertrek **nie**, omdat dit gereën het.
          Peter has *nie₁* left *nie₂* because it raining has
          'Peter didn't leave, because it was raining.'

b. Piet het **nie** vertrek omdat dit gereën het **nie**, (maar het vetrek omdat ...)
   Peter has *nie*₁ left because it raining has *nie*₂ (but has left because)
   'Peter left not because it was raining, (but because ...)'

When a *because*-clause is stranded to the right of *nie*₂, as in (43)a, it falls outside of the scope of negation. When the *because*-clause is to the left of *nie*₂, as in (43)b, then it falls within the scope of negation. This same effect is not possible to discern in examples such as (42)c. Although the 'afterthought' interpretation is triggered by post-NEG₂ stranding, there is no evidence of a difference in negative scope in (42)a-c. Now consider the data in (44), similar to that in (42)a-c above.

(44) a. Sy het niks *vir haar suster* gesê **nie**.
        she has nothing to her sister said *nie*₂
        'She said nothing to her sister.'

   b. Sy het niks gesê *vir haar suster* **nie**.
      she has nothing said to her sister *nie*₂
      'She said nothing to her sister.'

   c. ?Sy het niks gesê **nie** *vir haar suster*.
      she has nothing said *nie*₂ to her sister
      'She said nothing to her sister.'

A native speaker judged (44)a-b to be roughly equivalent in terms of grammaticality, with a slight preference for (44)a. The PP in (44)c recieved the standard 'afterthought' interpretation, and the example was judged to be slightly degraded by the same consultant. Finally, consider the following examples, in which the DP *haar suster* 'her sister' has been replaced by the negative polarity item (NPI) *enige iemand* 'anybody'.

(45) a. Sy het niks vir enige iemand gesê **nie**.
        she has nothing to any someone said *nie*₂
        'She said nothing to anybody.'

b. Sy het niks gesê vir enige iemand **nie**.
   she has nothing said to any someone *nie₂*
   'She said nothing to anybody.'

c. * Sy het niks gesê **nie** vir enige iemand.
   she has nothing said *nie₂* to any someone

Unsurprisingly, given the grammaticality of (44)a-b, (45)a-b are grammatical. However, there is a sharp contrast in grammaticality between (44)c and (45)c. While (44)c is only slightly degraded, (45)c is ungrammatical. This is a surprising fact, considering that prepositional phrases are normally allowed in post-NEG₂ position in Afrikaans. However, Afrikaans, like English, requires NPIs to be in the scope of negation. Recall from the *because*-clause data that elements stranded to the right of *nie₂* fall outside the scope of negation. Therefore, we can easily explain the contrast between (45)c and (44)c if we assume that phrases and constituents stranded to the right of *nie₂* fall outside the scope of negation. In this sense, *nie₂* functions as a type of scope-delimiter, effectively marking the rightward edge of negative scope.

A similar effect is attested in West Flemish, where PP complements containing nominal DPs can follow the verb, as in Dutch. However, PPs containing N-words such as *niemand* 'no one' cannot be postposed. Consider the following paradigm.

(46) a. ...da ze ketent **van euren coiffeur** was. **WEST FLEMISH**
         that she contented of her hairdresser was
         '...that she was pleased with her hairdresser.'

   b. ...da ze **van euren coiffeur** ketent was

   c. ...da ze ketent was **van euren coiffeur**

(47) a. ...da ze ketent **van niemand en**-was.
         that she contented of no one *en* was
         '...that she was happy with no one.'

   b. ...da ze **van niemand** ketent **en**-was.

   c. *da ze ketent **en**-was **van niemand**.   (Haegeman 1995b:117-118)

PPs containing an N-word such as *niemand* in West Flemish cannot be stranded following the negative particle *en*, while PPs containing a DP can easily appear in post-verbal position, as we see in (46). I argue that the N-word in West Flemish must move to a position within the scope of negation, presumably to trigger a concord reading, as opposed to a double-negative reading. This suggests a strong structural correlation between Afrikaans and West Flemish – in both languages, items that must appear within the scope of negation move to a position to the left of the righmost negative clausal head. I develop a BNF analysis of West Flemish in §4.6 below.

In the next section, I look at post-NEG_2 stranding in Hausa.

4.5.2 Hausa

Hausa allows stranding of CPs to the right of NEG_2. Heavy CPs are more likely to occur to the right of NEG_2. Compare (48)a with (48)b.

(48) a. **bài** yi kirā gà mutānē **ba** dà sù zō dandàlī.   **HAUSA**
    NEG-he make call toward people NEG COMP they come town-square
    'He did not call upon the people to come to the town square.' (Newman 2000:359)

   b. ? **bài** yi kirā gà mutānē dà sù zō dandàlī **ba**
    NEG-he make call towards people COMP they come town-square NEG
    'He did not call upon the people to come to the town square.' (ibid.)

Newman (2000) describes (48)b as being somewhat degraded, but not entirely ungrammatical. Hausa differs from Afrikaans in this respect, since heavy or light CPs (and PPs) can appear before or after NEG_2 with equal ease. Consider the Afrikaans sentences in (49)a-d.

AFRIKAANS
(49) a. Ons het **nooit** die mense geken wat in hierdie huis gebly het **nie**.
    we AUX never the people know who in this house live AUX nie_2
    'We never knew the people who lived in this house.' (Donaldson 1993)

b. Ons het **nooit** die mense geken **nie** wat in hierdie huis gebly het.
we AUX never the people know *nie$_2$* who in this house live AUX
'We never knew the people who lived in this house.' (ibid.)

c. Hoekom word daar **nie meer** ingegaan op die direkte invloed van
how come is there no more delve into the direct influence of

die bruin Afrikaanssprekendes **nie**?
the colored Afrikaans-speakers *nie$_2$*

'How come one isn't delving any more into the influence of coloured speakers of Afrikaans?' (ibid.)

d. Hoekom word daar **nie meer** ingegaan **nie** op die direkte invloed
how come is there no more delve *nie$_2$* into the direct influence

van die bruin Afrikaanssprekendes?
of the colored Afrikaans-speakers

As we observed above, heaviness plays a role in post-NEG$_2$ stranding in Hausa, though again there are no information structure effects mentioned in the two main grammars of Hausa, Newman (2000) and Jagger (2001). Under the analysis adopted here, the CP-stranding data receive a natural explanation. It appears that in Hausa, heavy pied-piping is generally dispreferred. When NEG$_2$ is in final position, NegP$_1$ has moved to Spec,NegP$_2$, pied-piping everything contained in it. When NegP$_1$ contains a heavy CP, it is quite simply too heavy to move in one piece, as indicated by the degraded status of (48)b above. Rather, as I suggest above in Chapter Two, the CP first moves to an intermediate position inside the expanded NegP. The remnant-NegP$_1$ is then free to move to Spec,NegP$_2$. I illustrate a partial derivation in (50)b below.

(50) a. **bài** yi kirā gà mutānē **ba** dà sù zō dandàlī. **HAUSA**
NEG-he make call towards people NEG COMP they come town-square
'He did not call upon the people to come to the town square.' (Newman 2000:359)

b.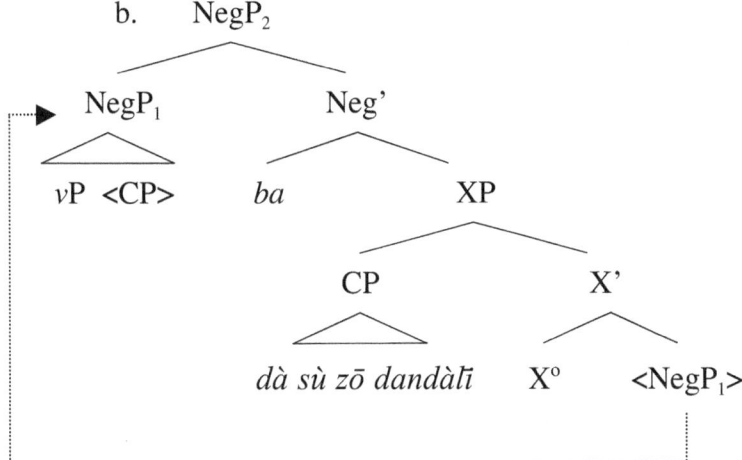

In (50)b, NegP₁ has been partially evacuated prior to moving to Spec,NegP₂. Hausa and Afrikaans are similar in allowing certain constituents and phrases to move out of NegP₁. In Hausa, the movement is linked to heaviness, while in Afrikaans the movement is simply a variation in the (unmarked) NEG₂-final structure.

Hausa also allows certain sentential adverbs to appear in post-NEG₂ position. Consider the data in (51)a-d.

(51) a. mālàm **bà** zâi gyārà tàkàr̃dun-mù gŏbe **ba**
teacher NEG FUT mark papers-our tomorrow NEG
'The teacher will not mark our papers tomorrow.' (Jaggar 2001:453)

b. mālàm **bà** zâi gyārà tàkàr̃dun-mù **ba** gŏbe
teacher NEG FUT mark papers-our NEG tomorrow
'The teacher will not mark our papers tomorrow.' (ibid.)

c. **bà** mù fàhìnci muhimman-čìn-sà sōsai **ba**
NEG we understand importance-of-it completely NEG
'We didn't understand its importance completely' (ibid.)

d. **bà** mù fàhìnci muhimman-čìn-sà **ba** sōsai
NEG we understand importance-of-it NEG completely
'We didn't understand its importance completely' (ibid.)

According to Jagger (2001:453-4), there are no discourse-related effects of adverb stranding in negative sentences. Rather, it appears that the movement is a purely syntactic option made available (in certain BNF languages) under UG. The most natural assumption about adverb-stranding is to say that it is also XP-movement, most probably to the same position as used in CP-stranding; that is, an intermediate position inside the expanded NegP.

Finally, we should note that some dialects of Hausa allow direct objects to appear following NEG_2. Compare (52)a, from standard Hausa, to (52)b, which Newman (2000) describes as a Northern Hausa dialect.

(52) a. **bà** mù kāmà ɓàrāwòn **ba**　　　　　　　　　　**HAUSA**
　　　　NEG we catch thief　NEG
　　　　'We didn't catch the thief.'　(Newman 2000:358)

　　　b. **bà** mù kāmà **ba**　ɓàrāwòn　　　　　　　**NORTHERN HAUSA**
　　　　NEG we catch NEG　thief
　　　　'We didn't catch the thief.'　(Newman 2000:358)

　　　c. Nous **n'**avons **pas** arrêté le voleur.　　　　　　**FRENCH**
　　　　we　*ne* have　NEG stopped the thief
　　　　'We didn't stop (apprehend) the thief.'

While standard Hausa does not allow direct objects to follow NEG_2, as in (52)a, Northern Hausa dialects as in (52)b permit this structure. I note in passing the surface similarities between Northern Hausa and French – a point to which I shall return in Chapter Seven.

Returning to Hausa, let us assume that the two Hausa dialects, which Newman (2000) describes as closely related, vary in their negation strategies in the following way: Northern Hausa allows *v*P-movement to a NegP-internal XP, while standard Hausa does not. This allows us to maintain the basic BNF architecture, while neatly explaining the difference between the two dialects. Furthermore, it builds on the notion that various constituents and phrases can move out of $NegP_1$ prior to $NegP_1$ movement to Spec,$NegP_2$. Depending on what is permitted to move, we can derive

Afrikaans (PPs and CPs), Hausa (CPs and adverbs), Northern Hausa (*v*P), and perhaps even French (*v*P). Consider the derivation of the Northern Hausa sentence in (53).

(53) a. **bà** mù kāmà **ba** ɓàrāwòn   **NORTHERN HAUSA**
     NEG we catch NEG thief
     'We didn't catch the thief.' (Newman 2000:358)

b.

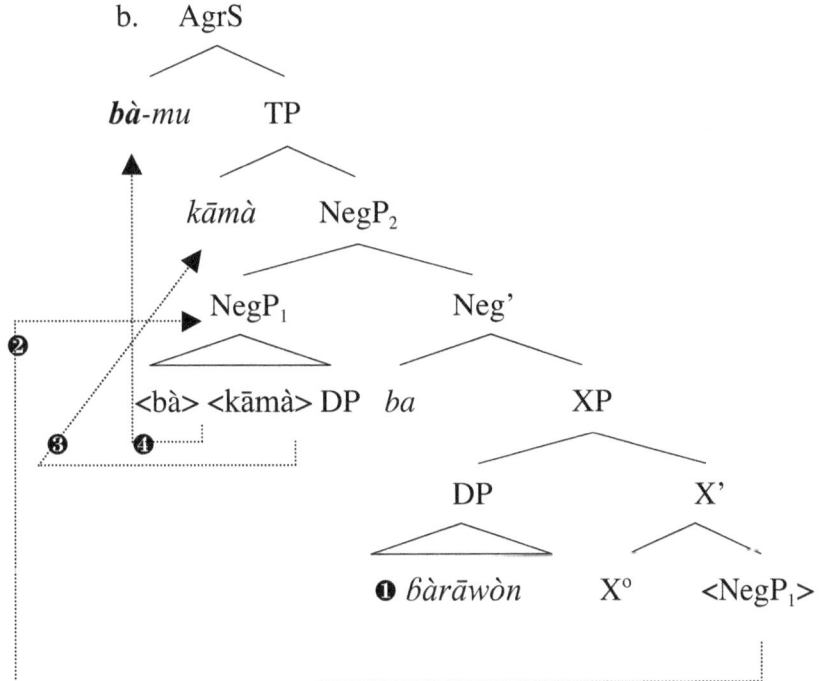

The derivation in (53) shows how we can straight forwardly account for the position of the direct object DP in northern dialects of Hausa. Unlike Standard Hausa, Norther Hausa allows DPs to follow NEG$_2$. I argue that this is dialect is simply a less restrictive variant of BNF. In addition to PPs and CPs, Northern Hausa allows DPs to move to [Spec,XP], effectively stranding them to the right of NEG$_2$. Once the DP has moved (❶), then NegP$_1$ moves to [Spec,NegP$_2$] (❷)

I assume that NEG$_1$ undergoes head movement to Agr° in Hausa, accounting for its position preceding the agreement marker. Furthermore, I assume that the Hausa verb moves to T°, again as in §4.2, skipping over the NEG$_1$ head, which does not block head movement in BNF. The *v*P in Northern Hausa moves to Spec,XP. Note that it is also possible that, in Northern Hausa, XP is in fact an object agreement phrase AgrO which attracts the object. Assuming the verb can still move to T, such an analysis would also account for the Northern Hausa word order facts (Cf. Haegeman 2002 on West Flemish, where she proposes an AgrO projection dominated by PolP that selects NegP). I do not generally assume the existence of AgrO in this dissertation, nor is there any evidence in Hausa (for example, an object agreement marker similar to the subject agreement marker) to substantiate such an analysis. Following vP-movement to Spec,XP, the NegP$_1$-remnant can move to Spec,NegP$_2$.

In Hausa, the normally phrase-final particle *ne* and its feminine form *ce* also allow certain phrases to be stranded behind them. In the next section, I discuss these facts, arguing that XP-movement is a more widely employed strategy in Hausa.

4.5.2.1 Post-Stabilizer stranding in Hausa

I have argued that there is a dedicated position in some BNF languages, including Afrikaans and Hausa, to which phrases and constituents such as those in above can scramble. Unlike Afrikaans, Hausa does not generally allow scrambling above negation, and has a somewhat more restricted word order. However, we observe a striking parallel between post-NEG$_2$ stranding, and stranding to the right of the stabilizer (STAB) particle *nē/cē*. I propose that post-STAB stranding provides independent evidence for XP-movement followed by remnant movement resulting in stranding. As we shall observe, the same types of constituents and phrases can appear after STAB and NEG$_2$. Furthermore, heaviness plays a role in both post-STAB and post-NEG$_2$ stranding.

The stabilizer functions as an equational or identificational particle, a focus marker, and what Newman (2000:545) terms a "clause-level reinforcement marker." Consider examples of each of these main functions in examples (54)a-e.

(54) a. tēbùr̃i **nē**.   **HAUSA**
    table STAB
    'It's a table.' (Newman 2000:545)

    b. haladù wàkīlin-mù **nē**.
    Haladu representative-1pl STAB
    'Haladu is our representative.' (ibid.)

    c. hàɗizà **cē** na gani bã kànde ba.
    Hadiza STAB 1sg see NEG$_1$ Kande NEG$_2$
    'It was *Hadiza* I saw not Kande.' (Newman 2000:546)

    d. audù **nē** mālàmī.
    Audu STAB teacher
    'It is *Audu* who is a teacher.' (ibid.)

    e. kằkànnin kằkànninsù sun zō **nẽ** dàgà arẽwa.
    ancestor ancestor-3pl 3pl come STAB from north
    'Their ancestors came from the north.' (ibid.)

The STAB particle is found in copular environments such as (54)a-b, focus constructions such as (54)c-d, and is also as a clause-level reinforcement marker, as in (54)e. In this last role, the position of the STAB can vary with respect to certain constituents and phrases. Newman (2000:546) states that, in these cases, "the STAB sometimes occurs at the very end of the sentence, and sometimes at the end of the core sentence but before adverbial adjuncts or complements." The unmarked position for STAB is phrase-final. However, adverbs can be stranded to the right of STAB. Consider the following data.

(55) a. mãtí dà shēhù yârā nàgàr̃tàttū **nẽ**.
    Mati and Shehu children well-fed STAB
    'Mati and Shehu are well-fed children.'

    b. mãtí dà shēhù yârā **nẽ** nàgàr̃tàttū.
    Mati and Shehu children STAB well-fed
    'Mati and Shehu are well-fed children.'

c. kĕkên sābō fil **nĕ**.
bicycle new very STAB
'The bicycle is brand new.'

d. kĕkên sābō **nĕ** fil.
bicycle new STAB very
'The bicycle is brand new.' (Newman 2000:168)

Adverbs are not the only elements that can occur after STAB. CPs can also appear in post-STAB position, exactly as they appear in post-NEG$_2$ position in example (48)a above. This is due to a heaviness effect, according to Newman (2000:168). Compare the following examples of post-STAB stranding in (56)a-b to the post-NEG$_2$ stranding data from (48)a-b above, repeated as (56)c-d.

(56) a. audù shī mùtûm **nē** dà kĕ sôn à kulā dà shī. HAUSA
Audu 3sg person STAB that ASP like PREP care PREP 3sg
'Audu is a person who likes to be looked after.' (Newman 2000:169)

b. ?? audù shī mùtûm dà kĕ sôn à kulā dà shī **nē**.
Audu 3sg person that ASP like PREP care PREP 3sg STAB (ibid.)

c. **bài** yi kirā gà mutānē **ba** dà sù zō dandàlī.
NEG-he make call towards people NEG COMP they come town-square
'He did not call upon the people to come to the town square.' (ibid: 359)

d. ? **bài** yi kirā gà mutānē dà sù zō dandàlī **ba**
NEG-he make call towards people COMP they come town-square NEG
'He did not call upon the people to come to the town square.' (ibid.)

The STAB particle in (56)a-b functions not as a focus marker, but as a clause-level reinforcement marker. There is no difference in meaning between (56)a and (56)b. However, (56)b is seriously degraded compared to (56)a. A heavy CP complement cannot appear in pre-STAB position, but must evacuate prior to what I analyze as remnant *v*P-movement to Spec,StabP. Consider the structure in (57)b.

(57) a. audù shī mùtûm **nē** dà kĕ sôn à kulā dà shī.   HAUSA
Audu 3sg person STAB that ASP like PREP care PREP 3sg
'Audu is a person who likes to be looked after.' (Newman 2000:169)

b.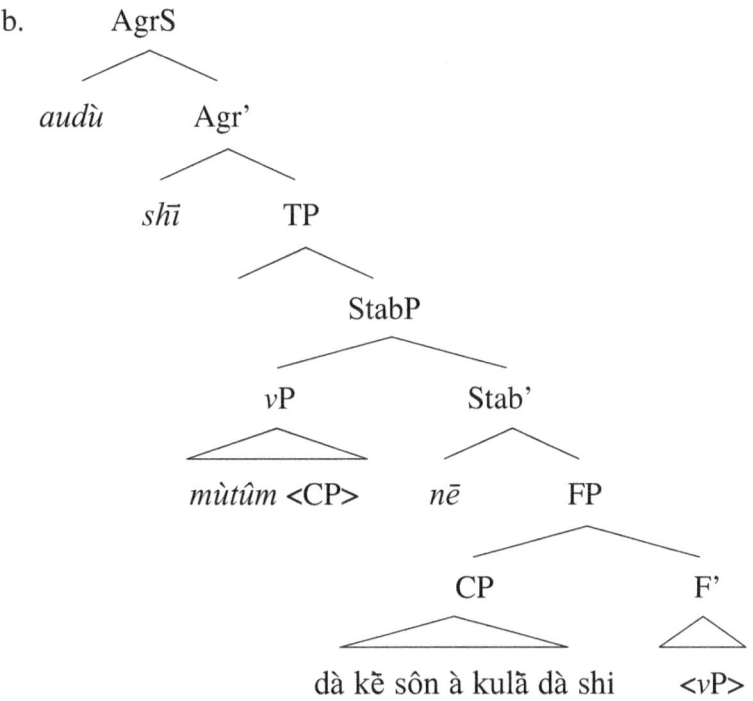

I propose that the stabilizer particle *ne* projects its own phrase StabP in Hausa. TP selects StabP, and StabP selects FP. In examples such as (57)a, the heavy complement clause moves to Spec,FP. The *v*P-remnant then moves to Spec,StabP, much in the same way that NegP$_1$ moves to Spec,NegP$_2$. The CP is thereby stranded to the right of the otherwise final stabilizer particle. Similarly, in cases of negation as in (56)c-d above, heavy CP complements result in marginal sentences when they appear to the left of NEG$_2$, and must evacuate to the intermediate position available in BNF before remnant movement of NegP$_1$ to Spec,NegP$_2$. I propose that a highly similar set of movement operations can account for both post-STAB and post-NEG$_2$ stranding, providing strong evidence for the viability of the proposed analysis of post-NEG$_2$ stranding.

4.6 Negation in West Flemish

In this section, I examine negation in West Flemish (WF) in light of the analysis I have develop for Afrikaans and other BNF languages in Chapters Two and Three. The basic question I will address is whether or not WF falls under the rubric of BNF. As I stated in Chapter Two, much of my analysis draws on notions first developed by Haegeman (1995) for the NEG Criterion. However, I have argued that the Minimalist analysis of the expanded NegP can derive the crucial aspects of the NEG Criterion, while dispensing with those that do not hold for BNF languages, thus allowing us to adequately capture the syntax of negation in BNF without reference to well-formedness constraints on syntactic structure. The NEG Criterion was developed with data from WF. Thus, it is interesting to look at these data with a fresh eye and attempt to accommodate them with the theory proposed here.

Like Afrikaans, WF allows two negative words in simple sentential negation, although one, the particle *en*, is optional. *Contra* Haegeman (1995), I will argue that WF. like Afrikaans and other BNF languages, has two negative clausal functional heads. One of these, *nie*, corresponds to NEG_1. The other, *en*, corresponds to NEG_2. I argue that Afrikaans nie_2 and WF *en* occupy the same structural position, differing in their phonetic form and syntactic feature content. To begin, consider the basic data on negation in WF.

4.6.1 West Flemish Negation: The Data

In this section I present the basic data on sentential negation in West Flemish, with special attention to the similarities and differences to negation in Afrikaans. West Flemish has by and large the same word order as Afrikaans and Dutch. Surface order is SVO in matrix clauses and SOV in embedded clauses. As in Afrikaans and Dutch, the position of PP adjuncts in WF is subject to variation. To begin, consider the data in (58).

(58) a. ... da Valère dienen boek **nie** **en**-kent. WEST FLEMISH
that Valère that book *nie* *en*-knows
'...that Valère doesn't know that book.' (Haegeman 2002)

b. ...da Valère gisteren **nie** tegen zen voader geklaapt eet.
that V. yesterday *nie* against his father talked has
'...that Valère did not talk to his father yesterday.'

Like Afrikaans, WF has a negative morpheme *nie* that occurs between the subject and the verb. Haegeman (1995) describes the distribution of WF *nie* as follows:

> *Nie* has a fixed position in the middle field, the domain between the subject and the verb: unlike negative time adverbs like *nooit* ('never'), for instance, *nie* cannot occur in the sentence-initial position of root clauses and it cannot precede NP arguments. (Haegeman 1995:117)

WF *nie* can stand alone as the sole marker of negation. Unlike Afrikaans, WF *nie* does not occur with an obligatory second negative particle like nie_2. However, WF has an optional negative particle *en* that is left-adjacent to the finite verb. Consider the following data.

(59) a. ... da Valère die boeken **nie** an zen voader getoogd (**en**)-oat. WF
that V. those books *nie* to his father showed *en*-had
'...that V. had not shown those books to his father.'

b. ... da Valère ier **niemand** (**en**)-kent.
that V. here no one *en*-knows
'... that V. doesn't know anyone here.'

c. ... da Valère ier **niemand nie** (**en**)-kent.
'... that V. doesn't know anyone here.'

In (59)a, we see a case of simple sentential negation in WF with the optional particle *en* left-adjacent to the verb. In (59)b we see that *en* can appear along with an N-word (*niemand*). (59)c shows that *nie* can also appear in sentential negation with an N-word and *en*. (59)b and (59)c have the same meaning, illustrating that *nie*, along with *en*, is optional. In recent work, Haegeman (2002) develops a new analysis of negation in WF based in part on the fact that *en* can add emphasis, at least in certain cases, to negative sentences:

> The precise semantic characterization of the contribution of *en* awaits further study. The best I can say at the moment is that it resembles the emphatic use of *do* in positive sentences in English: 'I don't think it will rain, but if it DOES rain, don't forget to close the windows.' (Haegeman 2002:181)

Like Afrikaans *nie$_2$*, WF *en* cannot be the sole marker of sentential negation. Rather, the presence of *en* is licensed by the presence of sentential negation (i.e. the presence of N-word(s), *nie*, or both). Consider the data in (60).

(60) *... da Valère die boeken an zen voader getoogd **en**-oat.   **WF**
        that V   the books to his father showed *en*-had.

Compare (60) to (59)a. (60) is ill-formed without the overt presence of *nie*, which apparently carries the negative force (the interpretable negative feature) in WF simple sentential negation.

Unlike Afrikaans *nie$_2$*, WF *en* occurs to the left of the verb in matrix clauses as well. Consider the data in (63).

(61)   a.   Valère **en**-eet **niemand** gevroagd.
              V.   *en* has nobody asked
              'V. did not ask anyone.'

      b.   **Niemand en**-eet Valère gevroagd.
              nobody *en* has V. asked.
              'Valère asked nobody.'

In (61)a, the particle *en* occurs to the left of the finite verb *eet* 'has'. The difference between (61)a and (61)b is focus; the N-word is fronted in (61)b, but (61)a and (61)b have identical truth conditions. Corresponding Afrikaans sentences would place *nie$_2$* at the end of the sentence.

Finally, like Afrikaans, PPs can follow [*en* V], as in (62).

(62)　... da Valère **nooit en**-klaaptige [over den voetbal]　　　　**WF**
　　　　that V.　never en talked about the football
　　　'... that V. never talked about football.'

As in Afrikaans, the position of PP adjuncts is variable in WF. This includes PP adjuncts in negative sentences, which can occur to the right or the left of [*en* V].

In the following sub-sections, I will argue that the BNF analysis presented above can be adapted to capture WF. This will allow us to unify WF under the rubric of BNF. In fact, we will see that certain areas of variation between WF and Afrikaans can be reduced to parameters within BNF – for example, as we saw in the case of Bukusu and Nweh, the position of NEG_1 appears to be parameterized. I will argue that the position and selectional properties of NEG_2 (spelled out as *en*) are parameterized. To begin, I consider the more recent work of Haegeman (2002).

4.6.2　Haegeman (2002)

In recent work, Haegeman (2002) has adapted her earlier work on the NEG Criterion to bring it in line with Kayne's (1994) LCA and the general theory of word order in Dutch put forth in Koster (1994) and Zwart (1997). As we will see, Haegeman's (2002) approach to WF is quite similar to the as that presented for BNF languages here. She proposes an "extended NegP", which is selected by a polarity projection PolP housing *en*. The proposal is highly reminiscent of Oosthuizen's (1998) proposal for Afrikaans, except that for Haegeman PolP is in the domain of IP.

Recall from above that the verb is in final position in WF embedded clauses, and that the negative particle *en* is left-adjacent to the verb, as in (63), repeated from above.

(63)　a. ... da Valère dienen boek **nie**　**en**-kent.　　　　**WF**
　　　　　 that Valère that book　　*nie*　*en*-knows
　　　　　'...that Valère doesn't know that book.' (Haegeman 2002)

Haegeman (2002) proposes the following structure for negative clauses in WF.

(64)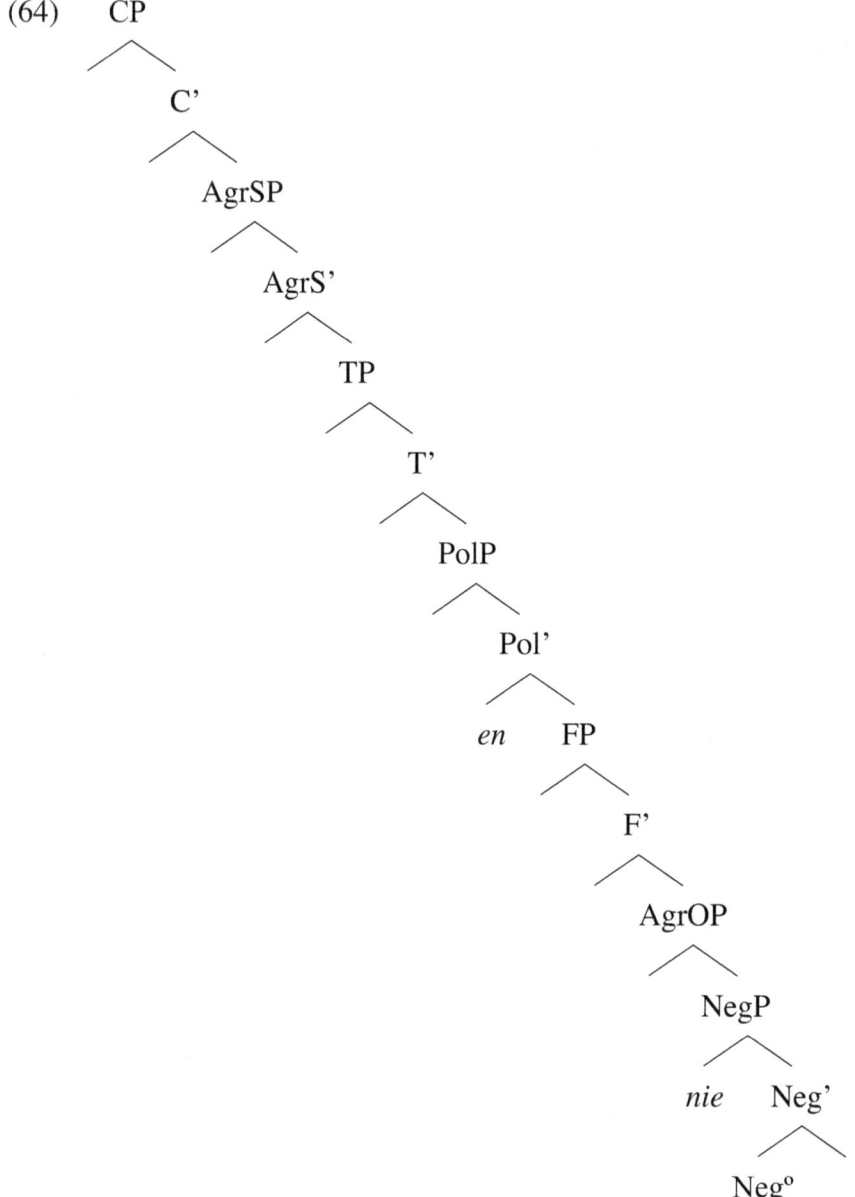

In (64), AgrOP serves as the landing site for objects (cf. Koster 1994), while FP serves as a landing site for the verb in infinitival contexts. As Haegeman states, "the sentence-final position of the verb is achieved by remnant movement of the complement of F, i.e. an extended projection of V, which (minimally) includes the trace of V and AgrOP, NegP and VP" to Spec,TP (Haegeman 2002:175). Below, I give a complete derivation based on Haegeman (2002).

(65) a. ... da Valère dienen boek **nie** **en**-kent.   **WF**
      that Valère that   book *nie* *en*-knows
      '...that Valère doesn't know that book.' (Haegeman 2002)

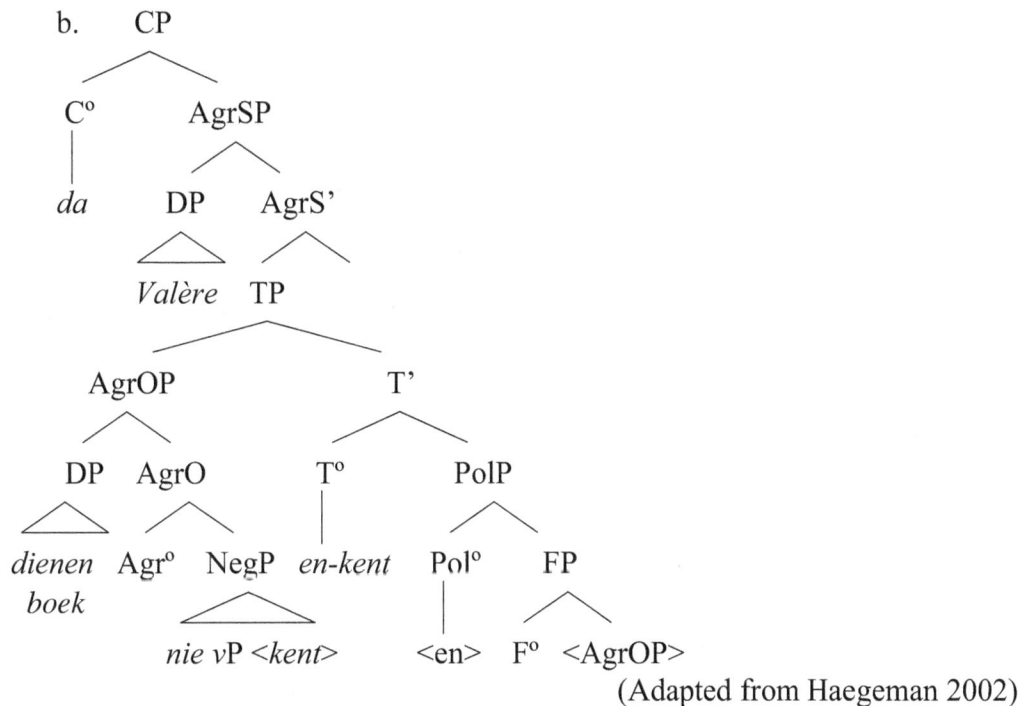

(Adapted from Haegeman 2002)

The structure in (65)b represents Haegeman's (2002) proposal for finite negative embedded clauses in WF. The object has moved to Spec,AgrO (Cf. Koster 1994), and the verb has undergone head movement to T° (presumably passing through F°). T° then targets the "complement of F" for movement to Spec,TP, effectively stranding the verb and the polarity head *en* in phrase-final position. The polarity head then adjoins to the verb via clitic movement, yielding the observed surface order.

Clearly, this account of negation in WF has much in common with the account of BNF that I have developed thus far. There is an "extended" NegP that includes higher functional projections, one of which is the landing site for the non-finite verb

(F°). Surface order is derived through XP- and remnant movement. In Haegeman's (2002) analysis these XPs are part of the Tense-Agreement complex (TP and AgrP). In the BNF analysis, they are part of the expanded NegP complex (NegP$_1$ and NegP$_2$). Haegeman (2002) invokes feature movement to allow for the proper checking relations, while the BNF analysis developed here relies on uninterpretable features, *Agree*, and *OCC*.

As we have seen in Chapters 2-3, and in this chapter, the BNF analysis has broad cross-linguistic applicability. Although Haegeman's (2002) analysis nicely captures the data in West Flemish, it is unclear whether it could be successfully applied to Afrikaans or the other BNF languages described above. However, the BNF analysis can easily be adapted to accommodate the WF data. To begin, I will argue that both negative particles *nie* and *en* in WF are functional categories, and head NegP$_1$ and NegP$_2$ respectively.

4.6.3 Categorial status of N-words, *nie* and *en* in West Flemish

Following Haegeman (1995, 2002), I assume that the particle *en* is a clausal functional category. However, I will argue *contra* Haegeman (1995, 2002) that WF *nie* is also a clausal functional category, and that WF *en* does not head a polarity phrase but a NegP.

Haegeman (1995:117-119) claims that *nie* in West Flemish is a lexical category. She argues against applying the head analysis of Bavarian *nicht* in Bayer (1990) to *nie* in WF. In Bayer's (1990) analysis, the head *nicht* and the verb incorporate to form a complex head [$_{v°}$ Neg+V]. Haegeman shows, through various syntactic arguments, that this type of complex head with *nie* incorporated into the verb is not possible in West Flemish:

> I assume that *nie* is a maximal projection and that it is the WF equivalent of French *pas* and that it occupies [Spec, NegP]. [...] Since we have to admit that WF *nie* is a maximal projection external to VP in at least some cases, I propose that in all its occurrences *nie* is a maximal projection (p.117-119).

It is clear that *nie* in WF does not incorporate with V to form a complex head. However, it is possible to analyze *nie* in WF along the lines of nie_1 in Afrikaans, as the head of $NegP_1$. Adopting this analysis, we can immediately explain the fixed position of WF *nie* noted by Haegeman (1995): N-words are lexical categories and can undergo A- and A-bar movement; WF *nie* is a head, and cannot undergo these types of movement.

There are other felicitous results of the head analysis for WF *nie*. Consider the data in (66).

(66) a. ... da Valère **niemand nie** kent. WF
that V. no one *nie* knows
'...that V. doesn't know anybody.'

b. ... da Valère **nie niemand** kent.
'...that V. doesn't know nobody.' (Haegeman & Zanuttini 1991:234)

Haegeman and Zanuttini (1991) argue that (66)a is a case of NC, since both *nie* and *niemand* are N-words with their own negative force in their analysis. (66)b has a double negative reading because *niemand* has not scrambled out of VP to take sentential scope along with *nie*. Thus Haegeman and Zanuttini (1991:235) propose that, "one condition for negative constituents to enter into an NC [Negative Concord] relation is that their scope domains be identical." This condition apparently exists alongside the NEG Criterion as another well-formedness condition on negative sentences – here allowing NC to obtain. Under a head analysis of WF *nie*, the data in (66) result directly from the NEG Criterion. In (66)a, the N-word *niemand* is in a spec-head relation with the head *nie*. In (66)b, a Spec-head relation does not obtain, resulting in a double negative reading (see Watanabe 2004 for a highly detailed discussion of negative concord facts in WF and many other languages, and a well-developed Minimalist account of negative-factorization in NC languages).

I now argue that WF *en* is not a polarity head, but the head of NegP$_2$. Haegeman (2002) puts forth the following facts about WF *en*:

(67)   i.   *en* is optional
        ii.   *en* is emphatic
        iii.   *en* is used only in tensed clauses

For Haegeman (2002), the facts about *en* in (67)i-ii are evidence for the existence of a polarity phrase. The difference between Dutch and WF negation, according to Haegeman (2002), reduces to the availability of the PolP projection: WF has it; Dutch does not. I give three arguments against the PolP analysis. First, I propose that the emphatic nature of *en* is directly related to its optionality, based on cross-linguistic data. Second, I argue that *en* has no positive counter-part, for example the equivalent of *do*-support in English. Third, I propose that *en* occurring only in tensed clauses is a parameter of BNF.

First, I argue that the behavior of *en* is very much in line with the behavior of NEG particles in certain creoles and CLs, such as Palenquero and Vernacular Brazilian Portuguese (see Chapter 6). Both Palenquero and VBP employ two negative particles in simple sentential negation. However, as in WF, one of the particles is normally optional. When both particles are present, there is a tendency for speakers to perceive a slight emphasis on the negation that they do not perceive when only one particle is present. This emphasis is not a manifestation of polarity. Rather, it results from the spell-out of an optional NEG particle. The languages in question, Palenquero and VBP, exhibit many of the properties of BNF. Yet they do not have obligatory spell-out of both NEG particles. Neither does WF. When both are spelled out, there is a natural tendency to perceive a slight emphasis, as in WF. This does not occur in "standard" BNF since both particles are obligatory.

Second, if *en* were a polarity item, licensed in negative contexts, we might expect to find some positive polarity item occurring in positive emphatic contexts. Indeed, Haegeman (2002) likens the behavior of *en* to emphatic *do* in English in sentences such as the following:

(68)   I don't think it will rain, but if it DOES rain, don't forget to close the windows.

A more convincing argument for PolP in WF could be drawn if some positive polarity item, perhaps along the lines of English *so*, and its correlate in Basque, argued by Laka (1990:118) to head ΣP in certain contexts, as in (69).

(69)   *Speaker A*: You did not go to the store.
       Speaker B: I did **so** go to the store.

To the best of my knowledge, and based on the discussion in Haegeman (2002), there is no such correlate of *en* in WF. Yet we could argue that the positive correlate of *en* is simply null in WF. However, there are other arguments against the PolP analysis.

Third, *en* can only occur in tensed clauses. This fact seems utterly unrelated to polarity. Are tensed clauses the only clauses that can receive negative emphasis, or undergo polarity shifts? As I show in the next section, a more satisfactory answer for the distribution of *en* can be provided if we analyze *en* as the head of NegP$_2$, and further assume that it has tense features that must be eliminated, much as NEG$_1$ *se* in Bukusu must move to Tense. I argue that this is simply a parameter of BNF manifested on either NEG$_1$ or NEG$_2$.

4.6.4 BNF Analysis of WF Negation

Recall my basic analysis of negation in BNF. Both NEG_1 and NEG_2 are functional categories, and head the projections $NegP_1$ and $NegP_2$, respectively. $NegP_2$ dominates $NegP_1$. In Afrikaans, N-word(s) move to [Spec,$NegP_1$] to eliminate the OCC feature on NEG_1. NEG_2 enters into an *Agree* relation with NEG_1, and $NegP_1$ is pied-piped to [Spec,$NegP_2$] to eliminate the OCC feature on NEG_2.

In what follows, I argue that WF *nie* is the equivalent of Afrikaans nie_1, and WF *en* is the equivalent of Afrikaans nie_2. WF *nie* heads $NegP_1$, and *en* heads $NegP_2$. I give a rough-and-ready representation of a BNF approach to WF in (70).

(70)
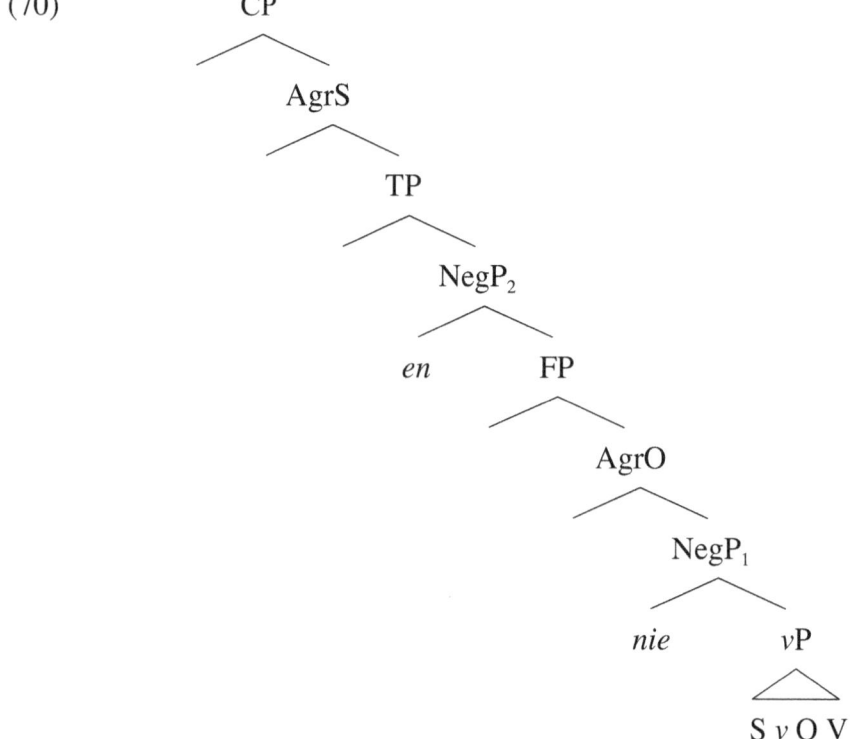

The structure in (70) is virtually identical to that proposed by Haegeman (2002) for WF. I have simply substituted $NegP_2$ for PolP. I assume that, as in other BNF languages, there are intermediate functional projections inside the expanded NegP. In WF, these may include FP, which Haegeman (2002) proposes as the landing site for infinitival verbs, and AgrOP, for case checking of objects. Although I do not assume the existence of AgrOP in the case of Afrikaans, I incorporate as much of Haegeman's (2002) analysis here as possible, since it has wider positive implications for the derivation of word order in West Flemish outside the particular context of negation. Note that there may also be intermediate XP and YP projections to serve as landing sites for stranded post-verbal PPs and *because*-clauses respectively. I do not discuss these projections here.

Now consider the derivation of the same WF negative sentence shown in the discussion of Haegeman's (2002) analysis, repeated below in (71).

(71) a. ... da Valère dienen boek **nie** **en**-kent.   **WF**
        that Valère that book *nie* *en*-knows
        '...that Valère doesn't know that book.' (Haegeman 2002)

b.

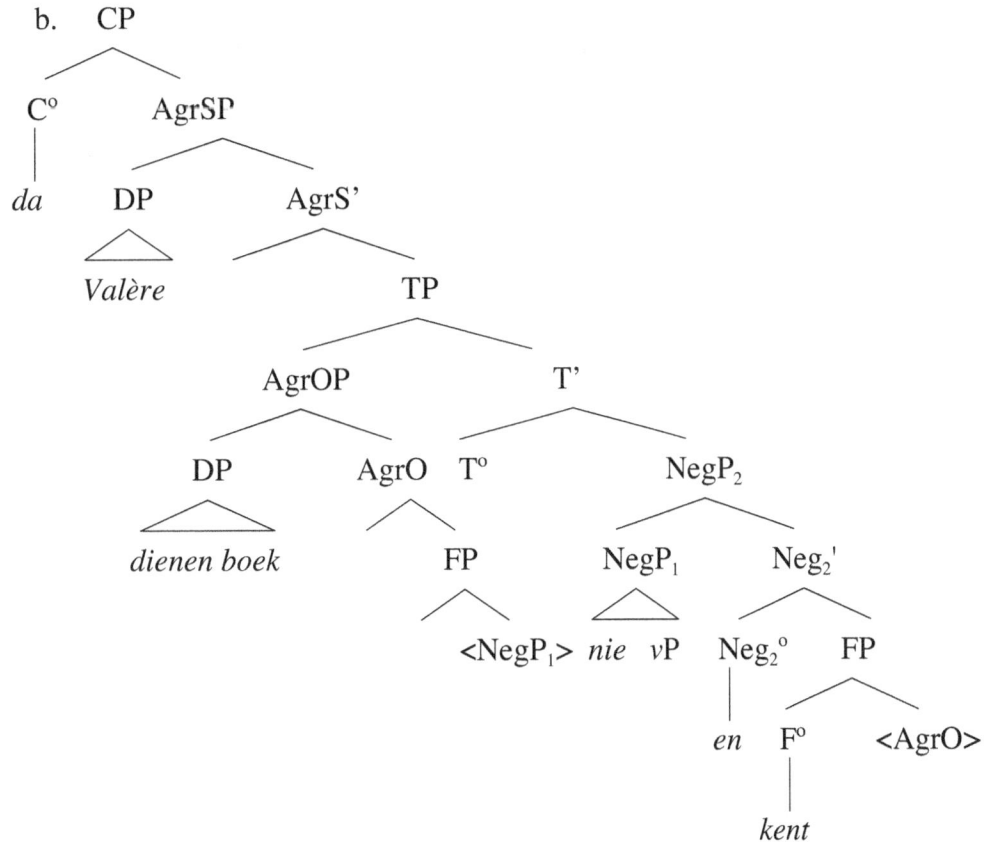

In (71)b I propose a BNF analysis of embedded-clause negation in WF. As in all BNF languages, there are two negative functional categories in WF, NegP$_1$ and NegP$_2$. NegP$_1$ houses the particle *nie* in WF, which possesses an interpretable negative feature [+neg], while NegP$_2$ houses *en*, which possesses an uninterpretable feature [uNeg]. Prior to NegP$_1$ movement to Spec,NegP$_2$, the *v*P is partially evacuated – the DP object moves to Spec,AgrO and the DP subject moves to Spec,AgrS to check their φ-features and receive case. Also, I argue that the verb moves to F°. This position is reserved for non-finite verbs in Haegeman (2002). However, I stipulate that it is the landing site for finite verbs in embedded clauses.[4] After verb movement, NegP$_1$ moves to Spec,NegP$_2$, at which point the derivation converges. The particle *en* remains *in situ* to the left of the verb – the only true structural difference between WF and Afrikaans negation.

Recall that WF *en* also has a slightly different distribution from Afrikaans *nie*$_2$. While *nie*$_2$ can appear in infinitival clauses, WF *en* cannot. Consider the following data.

(72) a. Marie goa preberen van dienen boek nie (***en**)-te (***en**)-vergeten. **WF**
Marie goes try of that book not (*en)-to (*en)-forget
'Marie will try not to forget that book.' (Haegeman 2002)

b. Dit is moeilik om **nie** te hoor **nie**. **AFRIKAANS**
it is difficult *om nie*$_1$ to hear *nie*$_2$
'It is difficult to not hear.'

c. Sy sal dit moet **nie** betaal **nie**.
she will it must *nie*$_1$ pay *nie*$_2$
'She will have to not pay it.'

---

[4] Another possibility, suggested to me by Chris Collins (personal communication), would involve verb movement to T°, *en* cliticization on the verb, and finally NegP$_2$ remnant movement to some higher position. I opt for the analysis in (71)b, in keeping with the spirit of Haegeman (2002).

WF *en* is illicit in infinitival clauses, while Afrikaans *nie₂* is obligatory. Haegeman (1995, 2002) suggests a close relationship between Tense and *en*, arguing that *en* cliticizes to the verb in T°. Under my analysis, the verb does not move to T° but to F°, an intermediate projection inside the expanded NegP. I propose that there is in fact a close relationship between the verb and *en* in West Flemish, but that this relationship is manifested, in the case of finite clauses, through the selectional properties of NegP₂. In particular, I argue that NegP₂ can optionally spell out *en* in finite clauses, and selects FP. In non-finite contexts, NegP₂ does not spell out *en*, and selects AgrOP. The verb is pied-piped with NegP₁ to Spec,NegP₂ in non-finite clauses, as in Afrikaans, resulting in identical word order, with the only difference being the overt spell out of *en*.

4.7 Chapter Summary and Conclusions

In this chapter I have shown that, in addition to the core properties of BNF outlined in Chapter Three, BNF languages also vary in a number of significant ways. Rather than detract from the unified picture of BNF, I argue that these differences add strength to the analysis, since they can easily be captured as parameters within the unified BNF system made available under UG. The parameters include the position of NEG₁, relative clause negation, verb movement, and post-NEG₂ stranding.

In the last section of the chapter, I develop an analysis of negation in West Flemish in line with the general principles of BNF. I show that a BNF analysis can indeed capture the WF data with minimal adjustments to the theory. Moreover, Haegeman (2002), in independent research, has developed an account of negation in WF that is highly similar to my analysis of BNF. I argue against one aspect of her analysis, the adoption of a PolP, but otherwise observe that both analyses lead to very similar results for WF.

The next chapter of the dissertation moves away from a synchronic analysis of the syntax of negation and into a discussion of the historical development of BNF in Afrikaans. I argue, based on the historical data available, that a borrowing played a significant role in the adoption of a second NEG morpheme in Afrikaans. However, borrowing cannot account for the development of the properties of BNF, which I argue are the result of a universal component. This proposal predicts the existence of languages that are in the process of developing BNF. Such languages do exist, and I turn to them in the Chapter Six of the dissertation.

CHAPTER FIVE

THE DEVELOPMENT OF BNF IN AFRIKAANS

Thus far in the dissertation I have considered the syntax of negation from a purely synchronic perspective. In this chapter, I wish to examine the historical development of negation in one of the languages in the dataset: Afrikaans. The discussion will involve both sociolinguistic and syntactic analysis. Then, in Chapter Six, I will look at data from a number of (other) creole and contact languages (CCLs) with strikingly similar patterns of negation to Afrikaans, and discuss to what extent these languages may be in the process of developing full-fledged BNF.

To summarize the dissertation up to this point, I have argued that a single, unified negation strategy exists across a number of relatively unrelated languages. This system, which I have called Bipartite Negation with Final NEG, or BNF, is characterized by the use of two negative particles in simple sentential negation: one particle appears in a pre-verbal position, while the other normally occurs phrase-finally. In addition to this basic structural fact, there are a number of morpho-syntactic properties shared among BNF languages (see Chapter Three), as well as parametric variation among BNF languages (see Chapter Four).

I argue for a unified syntactic analysis of BNF across the languages considered thus far. The position of the negative particles in the clause is obtained via XP-movement and remnant movement of various constituents and phrases to dedicated positions within the expanded NegP. For example, the final position of NEG_2, the second negative particle, is derived through movement of the lower NegP ($NegP_1$) to Spec,$NegP_2$, effectively stranding NEG_2 in final position. Postposed elements such as PPs (in Afrikaans), adverbs (in Hausa), and *because*-clauses (across BNF languages), move out of vP to NegP-internal positions. In this way the vP is partially evacuated prior to remnant-NegP$_1$ movement. I argue that the movement operations in question are purely feature-driven, and thus do not rely on syntactic well-formedness constraints such as the NEG Crieterion.

At this juncture, then, we have thoroughly explored the synchronic syntax of BNF with data from five languages. In this and the following chapter, I move into a discussion of BNF in diachronic perspective. Unfortunately, there is precious little extant historical data for the languages discussed in Chapters Three and Four – Bukusu, Dagara, Hausa and Nweh.[1] As a result, any discussion of the development of BNF in these languages would be highly speculative, at best. Fortunately, this is not the case for Afrikaans, which is a relatively "young" language (the Dutch presence of the Cape was established as early as 1590) with relatively rich historical documentation. There is a large literature devoted to the historical development of Afrikaans, including work specifically focused on the development of negation. An adequate diachronic analysis of the syntax of negation in Afrikaans must take the sociolinguistic facts into account. Therefore, I begin this chapter, in section 5.1, with a general discussion of the history of the Cape colony. In §5.2, I discuss the main theories of Afrikaans genesis, followed in §5.3 by a detailed discussion of the sociolinguistic and syntactic development of bipartite negation in Afrikaans.

In §5.4, I move into a detailed discussion and analysis of the syntactic development of BNF in Afrikaans. I am concerned *en gros* with the following two questions: first, what were the exact mechanisms of the development of BNF in Afrikaans; and, second, to what extent, if any, was the development of BNF in Afrikaans contact-induced? I argue, based on the discussion from §§5.1-5.3, that there is no evidence of BNF, as described above in Chapters 2-4, in any of the purported

---

[1] Newman (2000) has some historical reconstructions for certain Hausa lexical items and grammatical structures, but these are of no direct relevance to the phenomena currently under discussion.

substrates of Afrikaans, nor in any Germanic dialect which may have served as lexifier to Afrikaans. However, I also show that there are several potential sources of transfer of a *final* negative particle, including Khoekhoe and some Dutch dialects. I argue that the growth of BNF in Afrikaans can be captured within a five-stage development model. The model breaks the development of BNF into stages based primarily on the sociolinguistic data that I will outline in a moment. Broadly, the model proposes that a long period of co-habitation between Cape Dutch and Creole Dutch was followed by a period of more intense contact, and a subsequent period of standardization, during which Afrikaans developed all the properties of BNF. I present this model in detail in the final section of the chapter. From a theoretical perspective, I argue that this account is incompatible with a pure relexification analysis of Afrikaans (at least for negation). Borrowing played an important role, but there is also a universal component to the development of the full range of properties of BNF. The universal component exercised pressure in the formation of BNF, as did standardization.

In addition, as I show in the next chapter, there are a number of (other) creole and contact languages that exhibit patterns of negation similar to BNF in Afrikaans. Intriguingly, none of these languages shows a fully developed BNF system with all the known concomitant morpho-syntactic properties – (e.g. obligatory bipartite marking, *because*-clause disambiguation, etc). I argue that these languages reflect partially-developed BNF systems. By examining these languages, we may gain a better understanding of the precise stages in the development of BNF.

To begin, I discuss the population demographics on the Cape during the early years of Dutch colonial expansion in §5.1.

5.1 History of the Cape Colony from 1590

In this section I outline the history of the Cape Colony and the early history of speakers of Cape Dutch. I pay special attention to the place of Khoisan[2] peoples in the Cape colony, and to the status of Cape Dutch in the development of Afrikaans.

5.1.1 Early Years

The first Dutch trading frontier was maintained as early as 1590 at Table Bay, near present-day Cape Town on the South-West coast of South Africa. The Dutch had profitable trade relations with the Cape Khoekhoe from the outset, exchanging tobacco, beads and copper for beef and mutton. Indeed, "trade with Khoekhoe was a major concern for the early Dutch commanders" (Elphick 1989:12).

In 1652 the Dutch East Indies Company (VOC) established a trading post at Table Bay. The colony was small and grew slowly compared to Caribbean or West African colonies, as population data from Elphick (1989) reveals. In 1662, there were 394 Europeans and slaves – "slaves" here referring to men and women forcibly removed from other parts of Africa and Asia and brought to the Cape, and crucially *not* to Khoisan or other indigenous Cape peoples. Fifty-two years later, in 1714 there were only 3,878 Europeans and Slaves: a relatively small 10-fold increase. Compare these data to French colonies in the Caribbean such as Martinique, which saw a 25-fold increase in population over roughly the same period (*The Americas* online demographic data). The Cape Dutch colony was not one of rapid expansion, but of slow, steady growth. The small population of Europeans was surrounded by roughly 50,000 Khoekhoe who lived on the Cape in the 17th century (Elphick 1989). Thus

---

[2] *Khoisan* (or *Khoesan*) is a neologism consisting of the word *khoi* ('man' in several Northern and Central Khoisan languages), and the word *san* ('people' in Southern Khoisan languages). It is a cover term for the entire family of languages, as well as the people who speak them. The Khoekhoe (a.k.a. the Nama) are a specific Khoisan group – of particular interest here due to their presence on the Cape during Dutch colonial times.

there were ample opportunities for social and linguistic contact between the two groups.

5.1.2 Contact with the Khoekhoe

After 1652, trade in the Cape Colony was vigorous, and the Khoekhoe became more and more dependent on the new economy brought by the Dutch. This growing dependence was reflected in ever-closer contact between Khoekhoe servants and their Cape Dutch employers, as pointed out by Elphick (1989).

> By the mid-1690s some Khoikhoi were in permanent employment and lived with their families and livestock on the farmers' land, but in their own huts. In the early eighteenth century, if not before, servants were given space in one of the masters' main buildings." (Elphick 1989:17)

With increased dependence on the Dutch settlers came increased proximity and greater contact between the Cape Dutch and the Khoekhoe. Despite the frequent conflicts and wars fought between the Cape Dutch and the Khoekhoe, historians are quick to point out the willing part that the Khoekhoe played in their affiliation with the Dutch, and their continued status as 'non-slaves' in the Cape Colony. The relationship between the Cape Dutch and the Khoekhoe is described in Elphick (1989) as one of mutual benefit, although obviously the spoils of the colony remained firmly in Dutch hands. Still, it is clear from the quote above that the Khoekhoe maintained a certain degree of independence vis-à-vis their Cape Dutch 'masters'. As we will see below, this independence played a key role in the development of Afrikaans.

5.1.3 From Dutch to Afrikaans

The language spoken by the colonizers on the Cape began to diverge from European (dialects of) Dutch very early on. Writings of Cape Dutch colonists and travelers confirm the existence of non-standard varieties of Dutch spoken by Cape Dutch, slaves, and Khoekhoe. We know, for example, that from the early years of

Dutch colonization (*circa* 1610) there existed a large percentage of speakers of mixed blood, the children of the first Dutch settlers and their slaves or servants (Zimmer 1992). Furthermore, the writings of a Dutch traveler in the early 18th century confirm that these slaves and servants were the primary care givers, raising Dutch children and teaching them, as the same traveler states, "from the outset a very pitiful Dutch" (Thomason and Kaufman 1988:257). There are other commentaries of this nature from early travelers, including the following from 1685, taken from the journal of the Baron H.A. van Rheede, then Commissioner-General of the VOC:

> It is a custom among all our people [Cape Dutch] that when these natives [Khoekhoe] learn the Netherlandish speech and speak it in their way in a very crooked and almost unintelligible manner, our Netherlanders imitate them, indeed yes in such a way that if the children of our Netherlanders also accustom themselves to it, a broken language will be established which it will be impossible to overcome afterwards, still less to introduce the Dutch language among the Hottentots [Khoekhoe], although they are not lacking in ability.. (Cited in Smith 1952:18 and Elphick 1989:208)

Early writings such as these provide anecdotal evidence of changes in the Dutch spoken on the Cape. The "broken language" or "pitiful Dutch" to which these authors refer so disdainfully is none other than the predecessor to Standard Afrikaans – often referred to as Cape Dutch (Roberge 2002, Deumert 2004) or Cape Dutch Pidgin (den Besten 2002). Interestingly, both of the writers cited above make explicit reference to the roll that contact plays in the observed changes. The second quote specifically names the "Hottentots," meaning the Khoekhoe, as prime movers in effecting changes – perceived as negative in the colonial context – on the 'pure' Dutch language.

5.1.4 Varieties of Dutch

The early Dutch settlers of the Cape hailed from various regions within, and outside of, present-day Netherlands. There were speakers of many Dutch dialects, from regions throughout modern-day Netherlands, as well as speakers of more easterly Germanic dialects (Elphick 1989). Thus the Dutch brought to the Cape during the early years of colonization was far from a homogenous language. Indeed, Roberge (2002a) suggests the possibility that a koine or interlanguage existed in urban regions of Holland in the 17th century. If this is the case, then at least some speakers of Dutch arriving at the Cape may have already been speaking a mixed form of Dutch.

Regarding the mix of Dutch dialects on the Cape, Valkhoff (1966:15) states that in 1657 Dutch and German settlers outnumbered West Flemish nearly fifteen to one. In other words, West Flemish speakers were so few in number in the early years that their collective influence on the development of Cape Dutch was most likely quite minimal. As we saw above in Chapter Four, West Flemish employs a bipartite negation strategy that I argue to be structurally similar to BNF in Afrikaans – a strategy that, while considered somewhat archaic at present (Haegeman 1995), was the dominant negation strategy of several southern and western Dutch dialects in the 17th century (Burridge 1993, Ponelis 1993). As I discuss in greater detail below, we could easily posit that West Flemish was the (main) source of influence in the development of BNF in Afrikaans, since 17th century dialects contained, at the very least, somewhat similar structures. However, to prove that a given construction is a contact-induced borrowing, it is not enough to show that it existed in a known contact language (for example, West Flemish dialects of Dutch). Rather, as Thomason and Kaufman (1988) remark, one must show that speakers of this dialect were present in sufficient numbers to effect a change, before one can argue convincingly for language change through contact (cf. also Harris and Campbell 1995, chapter 4). I return to a detailed discussion of the possible role of Dutch dialects in the adoption of a final negative particle (and subsequent development of BNF) in the following sections.

To briefly summarize this section, I have shown that the Khoekhoe and the Dutch had close contact from the beginning of the Dutch invasion of southern Africa. Furthermore, anecdotal writings reveal that contact between the Khoekhoe and the Cape Dutch was viewed as having an adverse effect on Cape Dutch. These writings document the first stages of language change through contact, as seen through the eyes of colonial prejudice.

I now turn from an examination of general historical data to a closer look at the development of Afrikaans and, in particular, the rise of the second negative particle *nie*$_2$ and subsequent development of BNF.

5.2 The genesis of Afrikaans

Throughout the 20th century, and before, there was much controversy surrounding the question of the origin of Afrikaans, both among linguists and linguistically-naive political and social groups. Although it was the language of the Dutch East Indies company and the early years of Dutch colonization, Afrikaans took a back seat to English after the British takeover. Thus, Afrikaans was not purely the language of the colonial oppressor. As is the case today, Afrikaans was spoken by more non-whites than whites. After British takeover, Afrikaans became integral to the "struggle on the part of the Afrikaner people for political self-assertion" (Roberge 1992:31). The status of Afrikaans was anything but prestigious during this period:

> For the greater part of the nineteenth century, the Cape Dutch Vernacular we know today as Afrikaans was considered a peasant dialect – a 'miserable, bastard jargon . . . unworthy of the name of language' and unfit for educated discourse (quoted selection from the *Cape Argus*, 19 September 1857, cited in Roberge 1992:31).

To assert their political power and national identity, not only the Afrikaner people but the Afrikaans language had to be viewed as European, pure, superior, etc. Thus developed what Roberge terms the 'myth of ontogenesis', the central tenet being that

Afrikaans is a pure descendant of Dutch. Much of the early linguistic work on Afrikaans, especially within South Africa, adheres closely to this myth, which is often referred to, in more scientific terms, as the *Stammbaum* ('family tree') model. Understandably, language contact plays virtually no role in this theory. Most differences between Standard Dutch and Afrikaans are viewed as internally-motivated change, or are attributed to the influence of non-standard varieties of Dutch, or to dialect leveling. Consider as an example the following passage from the introduction to W. Kempen's (1962) *Grammar of Afrikaans*:

> This volume proves that Afrikaners have remained infinitely more Dutch than people have realized hitherto. Afrikaans is not different [from Dutch]; it is the same language. (W. Kempen, 1962, cited in Valkhoff 1966:193)

Valkhoff (1966), building on early work by Hessling (1899), suggests that Afrikaans is essentially a relexified Malay-Portuguese creole; a language whose grammar is the result of extensive contact with non-Germanic languages. In a radical departure from scholars who he terms "diachronic purists," Valkhoff states,

> If [Afrikaans and Dutch] are more or less the same language, everything becomes easy: one need not look for special social conditions to explain the rise of Afrikaans, and it is unnecessary to adduce linguistic explanations from outside the field of Dutch and Flemish. If, however, as I would suggest, Afrikaans and Dutch have become **two totally different languages**, one has to account for the birth of the "Daughter language" [...] and for its separate development. In that case, one is compelled to take into consideration the influence, first of foreign languages at the Cape – even those spoken by Non-Whites – and, later on, of English. (Valkhoff 1966:194-195, my emphasis)

Valkhoff's hypotheses have today gained wide-spread acceptance, especially with the rise of creole studies, and the dismantling of the 'simple creole' orthodoxy (DeGraff 2001). Thomason and Kaufman (1988; henceforth T&K) propose that Afrikaans is what they term a 'semi-creole', arguing that Afrikaans resulted from both internally motivated changes *and* contact with Khoisan and Malay-Portuguese:

> Afrikaans is historically a descendant of Dutch [. . .] because it preserves a significant portion of Dutch structures in all its grammatical subsystems. [. . .] But its development into a separate language was in fact heavily conditioned by nonwhites who learned Dutch imperfectly as a second language. (T&K:256)

T&K's observe that, throughout the history of the Cape colony, there existed a "socially stable core" of Cape Dutch speakers who lived alongside slaves and indigenous peoples. They did not intermingle as extensively as other colonial groups, nor were they overwhelmed by the extreme population demographics created by other colonial powers (cf. as in Martinique). At the same time, because Afrikaans shows some non-Dutch features (absence of verb inflection, periphrastic constructions, reduplication, object marking with *vir*, etc.), T&K posit that contact played a crucial role in the genesis of this new language. These arguments have been further developed in the recent work of Roberge (1999, 2002a, 2000b), who proposes a model of linguistic convergence which takes into account several factors in the development of Afrikaans, including i) the variability of the Dutch superstrate; ii) the existence of a jargonized (pidgin) Dutch; iii) the role of innovation in language change; and, iv) the existence of a linguistic continuum in the Cape colony (Roberge 2002a 67-71). The convergence model has the distinct advantage of recognizing the highly complex nature of Cape Dutch society, and views the development of Afrikaans across several generations, as a continuous process of both L2- and L1-acquisition (cf. DeGraff 1999).

The strong creolization hypothesis is most fully developed in the research of Hans den Besten (den Besten 1978, 1985, 1989, 2002). Den Besten and Roberge share many theoretical assumptions regarding language contact and change, and are largely in agreement on the sociolinguistic facts. Den Besten, however, argues that the early Cape Dutch Pidgin is a relexified Khoekhoe; in other words, grammatical categories from Khoekhoe were replaced with Dutch words, forming a new language (cf. Lefebvre 1998 on relexification). Cape Dutch Pidgin, alongside Orange River Afrikaans (and perhaps other co-existing dialects, see den Besten 2002:18-22), served in large part as the superstrate in the later development of Standard Afrikaans, while contact with Khoekhoe continued to influence its development. This continued contact helps to elucidate the rapid emergence in Afrikaans, during the 19th century, of features that were not present in Dutch or the Cape Dutch of the 17th and 18th centuries (den Besten 1989, Roberge 1995), such as bipartite negation. It also explains the existence of non-standard dialects of Afrikaans, especially those spoken by Khoisan peoples, such as Orange River Afrikaans: these dialects are the surviving strands of Cape Dutch Pidgin. (see also Zimmer 1992; Luijks 2000, 2001; Deumert *forthcoming*). Finally, it recognizes the existence of a dialect continuum, continuing to the present day. I summarized the den Besten model in Figure 1 below.

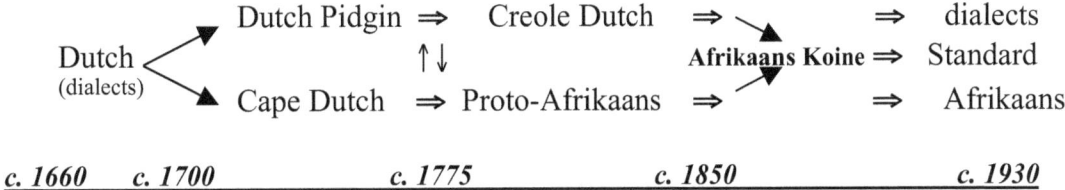

Figure 1. Model of Afrikaans genesis, adapted from den Besten (1989:226)

In this simplified diachronic model, the Dutch dialects spoken on the Cape split into a Dutch Pidgin/Creole (top strata) and an acrolectal Cape Dutch (bottom strata). These two dialects evolved separately, with mutual contact, from c.1680 to c.1800, when the two began to merge (where *merge* refers essentially to a period of very heavy contact resulting in a synthesis of the two dialects in certain areas). As represented in Figure 1, strands of Creole Dutch still exist, such as Orange River Afrikaans. However, there are no extant strands of Cape Dutch as it was spoken in the early 19th century, before convergence with Creole Dutch. As I show below, many of the core non-Dutch features entered into Cape Dutch/proto-Afrikaans over a very brief period, transforming Cape Dutch into modern Afrikaans (den Besten 1989, 2002; Roberge 1995, 2002). Furthermore, I argue below that dialect convergence is directly attributable to contact between Cape Dutch and the primary speakers of Creole Dutch, the Khoekhoe, in the 1790s (Elphick 1989:35).

With this overview of the development of Afrikaans in mind, let us return to the central concern of the chapter, namely, the development of BNF in Afrikaans. In the remaining sections, I will proceed as follows. First, in §5.3, I will review the historical data on the rise of the second negative particle, *nie*$_2$, in Afrikaans. Then in §5.4, I look at several possible structural origins for *nie*$_2$, including Khoekhoe, Dutch dialects, Malay-Portuguese, and internal development. I discuss which of these is most probable. Then, in §5.5, I return to a discussion of relexification in the development of BNF in Afrikaans. I argue that, although final *nie* may have been transferred through contact from another language, the BNF negation strategy arose via the influence of language universals (UG).

5.3 The history of *nie*$_2$ in Afrikaans

In this section I trace the history of *nie*$_2$ in Afrikaans. I make an important distinction here between the adoption of *nie*$_2$ as a second negative particle, and the development of BNF as a sentential negation strategy in Afrikaans. I view the latter as a separate process from the former for two reasons. First, as I will show, there are no languages from either superstrate(s) (e.g. dialects of Dutch) or substrates (e.g. Khoisan) with BNF. This immediately excludes the possibility that BNF was borrowed or transferred. Second, there are cross-linguistic data from other creoles and contact showing intermediate stages of BNF development – in other words, adoption of bipartite negation, with *some* of the accompanying BNF properties. I illustrate these data in chapter 6.

Over the last two hundred years, Afrikaans has adopted a phrase-final negative particle *nie$_2$*, and BNF – the properties of which I detail in chapters 2 and 3. Today, in Standard Afrikaans, *nie$_2$* is obligatory in most sentential negation environments. Grammars and language manuals such as Donaldson (1993, 2000) prescribe the use of *nie$_2$* in all but a few contexts. Native speaker judgments confirm that in cases of standard sentential negation, *nie$_2$* must be present or the sentences are not grammatical.

To trace the development of *nie$_2$* in Afrikaans, scholars rely on texts of early Cape Dutch, including personal diaries, travel writings, administrative logs, and the rare first-hand account of the developing language, such as I illustrate above. Some of these writings have recently been the subject of extensive linguistic analysis (see Luijks 2000, Deumert *forthcoming*). A number of diary fragments provide important evidence on the structure of acrolectal Cape Dutch in the 18th and early 19th centuries – i.e. the Cape Dutch which in den Besten's (1989) model (see Figure 1 above), developed into *proto*-Afrikaans. One of these is the unpublished diary fragment of Johanna Duminy (1797):

> Acrolectal Cape Dutch [...] is preserved in the diary fragment of Johanna Duminy. The Duminy diary is no less important for the hallmark Afrikaans features that it **does not show: the double negation (*nie . . .nie*)** the demonstrative pronoun 'herdie' (*this*), reduplication, [. . .] etc. (Roberge:1995:79,my emphasis)

The Duminy diary, like other writings of the same period (Luijks, 2000), shows a marked absence of *nie$_2$*. Rather than using bipartite negation with N-words/*nie$_1$* and *nie$_2$*, Duminy employed a single pre-verbal negator in her writings (Roberge 1995). The absence of *nie$_2$* in the Duminy diary suggests that the construction was not prevalent in informal written Cape Dutch, and, by extension, in spoken registers. The absence of *nie₂* from writings such as the Duminy diary raise interesting questions for any account claiming a purely Germanic origin for the particle. If *nie₂* entered into Afrikaans from (non-standard) 17th century Dutch dialects, as argued for example by Ponelis (1993), why is it not observed in late 18th century writings in Cape Dutch? What can explain this apparent 150-year gap in the use of *nie₂* in Cape Dutch/proto-Afrikaans?

Valkhoff (1966) argues that the adoption of *nie₂* is the result of contact with Khoekhoe speakers of Creole Dutch, as evidenced by the relatively late development of *nie₂* in Cape Dutch as compared to Creole Dutch:

> I do not think that it is mere chance that in the history of Afrikaans the double negative [i.e. Negative word(s) **and** final *nie*] occurs first, as well as most frequently, in the mouths of the Hottentots [the Khoekhoe]. Valkhoff (1966:131)

Based on a number of textual sources, it appears that Khoekhoe speakers of Creole Dutch were among the first speakers to use *nie₂* in sentential negation. Valkhoff (1966) cites a textual study by G.S. Nienaber (1955) that analyses transcriptions of Cape Dutch and Creole Dutch speech from the period 1826 to 1844. Nienaber (1955) shows that, in the Creole Dutch of Khoekhoe speakers, *nie₂* was found in 50% of all negative sentences, while the Cape Dutch employed *nie₂* in only 16% of negative sentences. Consider *Table 4*.

Table 4. Nie₂ in Cape Dutch and Creole Dutch, 1826-1844 (**from Valkhoff 1966**)

Speakers	Total number of negative sentences	Total with second *nie*	Percent *nie₂* used:
Khoekhoe	107	54	50%
Cape Dutch	45	7	16%

The data in *Table 4* show that nie_2 was far from obligatory in either dialect of Afrikaans in the early to mid-19th century. They also show that Khoekhoe speakers of Creole Dutch used nie_2 much more frequently than Cape Dutch speakers. Consider these data in light of the model of Afrikaans genesis illustrated in *Figure 1*. In the early 19th century, nie_2 was uncommon in Cape Dutch (16% of negative sentences), while it was more common in Khoekhoe Creole Dutch (50% of negative sentences). Sometime in the late 19th century, nie_2 became more prevalent among Cape Dutch speakers as the dialects merged, due to influence from Creole Dutch. As *Table 4* suggests, nie_2 was not obligatory in Creole Dutch of the early 19th century. Interestingly, nie_2 is not obligatory in Khoekhoe dialects of Afrikaans, such as Orange River Afrikaans, at present (Ponelis 1993). As I discuss shortly, nie_2 became obligatory in Afrikaans under pressures of standardization, and, presumably, under pressure from the universal component of BNF.

Ponelis (1993:472) argues, *contra* Valkhoff (1966), that Nienaber "misrepresents the lectal distribution of nie_2 in the early 19th century to the effect that it was more strongly associated with Khoi speakers." Ponelis (1993:476) provides data to counter-exemplify the claims in Valkhoff (1966) and Nienaber (1955). However, even in Ponelis' (1993) counterexamples, the highest percentage of nie_2 recorded before 1850 occurs in the writings of a Khoekhoe speaker of Creole Dutch (Boniface, 1830-1832: 62% nie_2). Fifteen years later, the writings of a Cape Dutch speaker show only half as many occurrences of nie_2 (Meurant, 1844-1847, 31%). And fifteen years later, in 1861, the percentage of nie_2 in Meurant's (Cape Dutch) writings rises to 80% – suggesting, interestingly, a change in his own grammar over time.

By the mid to late 19th century, Afrikaans was undergoing a process of standardization (Elphick 1989, Ponelis 1993, Roberge 1999). As the language of Afrikaner nationalism, Afrikaans gained a higher status in certain speech communities, and was taught for the first time in both primary schools, later, at universities. This period also saw the publication of the first grammars of Afrikaans. By the early 20th century, there was a wealth of linguistic work on the 'purely Dutch' origins of the language (Roberge 1995, 1999).

At the same time, it was evident that Afrikaans had developed certain features absent in Dutch, for example, the use of *nie*$_2$. At some point in the early 20th century, as *nie*$_2$ became an ever-more-present part of negative sentences in Afrikaans, many speakers began to identify with this construction as "pure" Afrikaans (Cf. Deumert 2003). Molnárfi (2002) points out that *nie*$_2$ has long functioned as a shibboleth for Afrikaners, marking their language as distinct from European Dutch. The obligatory use of *nie*$_2$ in Standard Afrikaans also distinguished it from other Afrikaans dialects, which continued to use *nie*$_2$ optionally, while it became obligatory in Standard Afrikaans. The fact that *nie*$_2$ is obligatory in Standard Afrikaans while it remains optional in dialects such as the heavily Khoe-influenced Orange River Afrikaans presents something of a puzzle, however. If Khoe-influenced Afrikaans was the source of *nie*$_2$, we might expect *nie*$_2$ to be obligatory in these dialects as well. Indeed, Ponelis points out precisely this fact, which he views as a problem for theories of Khoe-influenced transfer:

> In the strongly Khoi-influenced northwestern variety of Afrikaans, *nie*$_2$ is facultative, which means that the onus of [...] grammaticisation [...] remains with the other varieties of Afrikaans that have less Khoi influence. (Ponelis 1993:472)

Ponelis (1993) argues that facultative *nie*$_2$ in modern Khoe-influenced dialects of Afrikaans is damaging to a Creole Dutch borrowing hypothesis for *nie*$_2$, since it shows that the Khoe-influenced dialects did not continue on the trajectory to obligatory *nie*$_2$ as did Standard Afrikaans. However, as the historical data suggests, one need simply to separate transfer of *nie₂* from standardization of *nie₂*. We know that *nie₂* was more prevalent among Khoe speakers of Creole Dutch in the early 18th century, i.e. during the transfer period, when *nie₂* began to appear, to a lesser extent, in Cape Dutch. Once adopted in Cape Dutch, *nie₂* continued to gain ground in this dialect, while remaining optional in Creole Dutch, and, thereby, in Orange River Afrikaans today. This simply means that, in diachronic perspective, the Khoe-influenced Creole Dutch never had obligatory *nie₂* – nor is it necessary to claim that it ever did. The fact that *nie₂* was common (50% of negative sentences in one corpus, for example) in Creole Dutch is sufficient to propose that it was borrowed, through contact, into Cape Dutch.

As I have already suggested, *nie₂* became obligatory in Standard Afrikaans under normative and social pressures. In addition, as we will see in Chapter Six, languages that adopt a final negative particle also tend to adopt the properties associated with BNF. Thus it seems prudent to speak also of pressure from the grammar to adopt these morpho-syntactic properties. In terms of social pressures, consider the history of negation in French as a point of comparison (cf. Jespersen 1917). Old French used a single preverbal negator *ne*. From the 16th century onwards, certain post-verbal nominals such as *pas* 'step', *rien* 'thing', and *goutte*, 'drop' became more and more common in the context of negation – first as emphatics, and later as purely grammatical markers of negation – with *pas* eventually becoming the default negator. The grammarians at the *Académie Française* and Port Royal, by the 18th century, were prescribing the use of both *ne* and *pas* in sentential negation (Picoche et al. 1989:291), and the bipartite structure was generally adopted as the 'correct' form in the influential (i.e. socially desirable) Ile de France dialect. However, very early in the grammaticalization of the post-verbal negators appear examples of purely post-verbal *pas*:

(1)   Elles me touchent **pas** tant   que le malheur   qui ...   FRENCH
      3pl me affect   NEG as-much as the unhappiness which ...
      'They do not affect me as much as the unhappiness which ...' (LaFontaine, 17th C.)

Data such as (1), from a letter by the poet LaFontaine, suggest that a period of obligatory *ne ... pas* was most likely very brief. Rather, it seems that normative pressures and prescriptive rules played a large role in public perception of *ne...pas* as the 'correct' form, while in normal speech the post-verbal *pas* very quickly took over. The French facts reveal the power of social and normative pressures, which I argue to have been the prime movers in the adoption of obligatory *nie*$_2$ in Afrikaans. Standard Afrikaans is akin to Standard (prescribed) French in the obligatory use of two negative particles, while dialects (vernaculars) of both French and Afrikaans have continued to use a bipartite strategy only optionally.

The history of negation in Afrikaans differs from that in French in at least two relevant respects. First, in Afrikaans, normative and social pressures have led to the adoption of obligatory *nie*$_2$ by a certain group of speakers, whereas no group of French speakers uses obligatory *ne...pas* – it is purely a prescriptive convention (Ashby 1981). Second, unlike French, Afrikaans has developed the BNF negation strategy, available under UG, which uses a phrase-final negative particle and has a number of related morpho-syntactic properties. In point of fact, the modern Khoe-influenced dialects of Afrikaans, which never underwent standardization, continue to use facultative *nie*$_2$ – as vernacular French employs facultative *ne*. I will argue in Chapter Seven that *nie*$_2$ and French *ne* occupy the same syntactic position. Also, I will show in the next chapter that certain creole and contact varieties of Spanish and Portuguese use a facultative second negative particle.

To summarize the chapter thus far, I have given data on the history of the Cape colony that show close contact between Khoekhoe and Cape Dutch inhabitants during the early years of colonization of the Cape. This contact increased throughout the 18th and 19th centuries, precisely the point at which certain Khoe-influenced features such as *nie*$_2$ emerged in Afrikaans. I have presented the central theories on the genesis of Afrikaans, with special attention to the creolization hypothesis of Valkhoff (1966) and the contact and convergence models of Roberge (1995, 2002) and especially den Besten (1989, 2002). Corpus data show that *nie*$_2$ was absent from 18th century Cape Dutch, but prevalent among Khoe speakers of Afrikaans in the mid-19th century. *Nie*$_2$ gained obligatory status in Standard Afrikaans under normative and social pressures over the last 150 years.

In the next section, I turn to a detailed examination of the possible sources of *nie*$_2$ in syntactic terms.

5.4 Structural origins of *nie*$_2$ in Afrikaans

In the broadest terms there are two possible accounts of the syntactic shift to obligatory *nie*$_2$ in Afrikaans: i) *nie*$_2$ is an internally-motivated change; or ii) *nie*$_2$ is a borrowing. The default assumption in this dissertation is (ii), that *nie*$_2$ is a borrowing. We may exclude the internal change hypothesis on the following grounds, the first of which was illustrated above, and the second two of which are the subject of this section. First, we have observed the relatively rapid emergence and adoption of *nie*$_2$, over a period of (less than) 100 years. This rapid emergence is inconsistent with many internal changes, which can occur over periods of several hundred years (Harris & Campbell 1995; cf. negation in French), but is consistent with general notions of creolization and language change under intense contact conditions. Second, as I will show in a moment, there is a marked absence of data from Middle Dutch dialects showing anything resembling *nie*$_2$. If *nie*$_2$ were an internally-motivated change, we would expect to find historical data suggesting a change in progress, and perhaps another modern dialect of Dutch with a very similar strategy, even if optional. Neither are attested. Third, there are convincing data from Khoekhoe showing a phrase-final negative particle – clearly a possible source of transfer/borrowing. However, as I will show, Khoekhoe does not show other BNF properties, suggesting a two-part development path: adoption of nie_2, followed by adoption of BNF.

I begin with a discussion of the Germanic data in §5.4.1-5.4.3. Then, in §5.4.4, I present the Khoekhoe data. Finally, in §5.4.5, I argue that even Khoekhoe could not have provided the model for the development of BNF in Afrikaans.

5.4.1 Negative tags in Germanic

Sociolinguistic data strongly suggest that nie_2 is not the result of internally motivated change. However, it is worth considering several possibilities from historical syntax, so as to eliminate this possibility definitively. First, consider the argument that a negative tag grammaticalized into a phrase-final negative particle. Germanic in general makes use of negative tags in yes-no questions. Consider the following example from Modern Dutch.

(2)   Hij zei toch dat hij **niet** wilde komen, **niet**?   **MODERN DUTCH**
       He said MOD that he not wanted come,   not
       "He said he didn't want to come, didn't he?"

The negative tag *niet* in Modern Dutch appears in sentence-final position, exactly the position where such tags appear across Germanic and Romance languages in general, and, exactly where we find nie_2 in Afrikaans. The basic argument then says that negative tags such as *niet* were grammaticalized into a final negative marker nie_2 in Afrikaans. However, this is an unlikely source for nie_2 in Afrikaans for several reasons. First, it is clear that a tag has a unique discourse function that is wholly unlike a functional head. This is evidenced in, for example, stress and intonation on tags, which normally distance them from the clause. In contrast to this stress pattern,

Afrikaans speakers fully integrate nie_2 into the intonational pattern of the sentence. Impressionistically, nie_2 receives no stress (Molnárfi 2002).

Secondly, grammaticalized negative tags would have initially been available only in negative yes/no questions, and gradually, by extension, in other sentence types. We would thus expect to find historical evidence of an intermediate stage, contrary to fact. Given the rapid rise of the construction, and the total absence of historical evidence that negative tags were more prevalent in Cape Dutch than in other Dutch dialects, for example, this hypothesis appears highly implausible on syntactic grounds. A more plausible scenario would see *niet* become a marker of yes/no questions, as with the Tibeto-Burman particle *ma* (Harris and Campbell 1995:79). However, this is not evidenced in Afrikaans.

Finally, Afrikaans possesses a negative tag found in yes-no questions, the particle *né*, which is also the equivalent of English *no* in Afrikaans. Consider (3).

(3) Die mielies is nou al ryp, **né**? **AFRIKAANS**
 the corn is now all ripe, no
 'The corn is already ripe, isn't it?' (Donaldson 1993:417)

If nie_2 had grammaticalized from a negative tag, we might expect to find *nie* still in use in this context. Instead, as example (3) illustrates, we see that Afrikaans *né* 'no', fills the role of negative tag.

In the next section, I consider the development of negation in Dutch during the period of Dutch colonial expansion.

5.4.2 Negation in Dutch

The period referred to as Middle Dutch extends from roughly 1100 to 1550, when Modern Dutch began to develop (Burridge 1993). If nie_2 transferred into Afrikaans from a Dutch dialect, then we must examine in detail the negation strategies of Middle and early Modern Dutch, since this corresponds roughly to the period of colonization of the Cape. Furthermore, if *nie*₂ is an internal development in Afrikaans, we might expect to see some early signs of its emergence in Middle Dutch.

Middle Dutch normally employed a bipartite negation scheme similar to that observed in modern West Flemish (see Chapter Four). The historical development of negation in Dutch main clauses closely parallels that of French, as described above. Over a 1000-year period, Dutch has gone from preverbal negation (pre-1100) to a bipartite strategy (1100-1550), and finally to post-verbal or post-auxiliary negation (1550-present) – a paradigmatic example of the Jespersen cycle.

(4)   Jespersen cycle in Dutch

Stage 1: Old Dutch (pre-1100).
Preverbal (clitic) negation: *ne/en* +V
ic **en** was siec.
I NEG was sick
'I wasn't sick.'

Stage 2: Middle Dutch (1100-1550).
Embracing negation: *en* +V+*niet*
ic **en** was **niet** siec.
I NEG was NEG sick
'I wasn't sick.'

Stage 3: Modern Dutch (1550-present).
Postverbal negation: V+*niet*
ic was **niet** siec
I was NEG sick
'I wasn't sick.'   (Hoeksema 1997:140)

Stage 2 from example (4) above is most relevant to the discussion at hand, since the first inhabitants of the burgeoning Cape colony arrived in southern Africa in the early 1500s. Like modern-day West Flemish, Middle Dutch had SOV order in embedded clauses, with negation and the negative clitic *ne* (*en* in West Flemish, as in Old Dutch) preceding the finite verb. Consider the data in (5).

(5) ...dat ics vergheten **niet ne** mach   MIDDLE DUTCH, C. 1350
     that I-it forget   NEG NEG may
     '...that I may not forget it.' (Hoeksema 1997:150)

As a potential model for transfer of a final negative particle, Middle Dutch as represented in (5) fails the test, for the obvious reason that there is no final particle. Indeed, although it may be minimally different in terms of syntactic structure (see Chapter Four), the negation pattern in Middle Dutch shows no rightmost final particle, and shows none of its related properties (see Burridge 1993; Hoeksema 1997; Haegeman 1995, 2002). Even taking the highly charitable view that some dialect of Middle Dutch with bipartite negation did serve as a model for transfer, there is evidence bipartite negation was losing ground at the exact time when it would have been exported to the Cape. Hoeksema (1997:141) points out that, "over a period of centuries, the negative clitic [*ne* or *en*] gradually loses territory [in Middle Dutch], until it finally disappears around the beginning of the 18th century." Thus we observe that Dutch negation and Afrikaans negation appear to be moving in entirely opposite directions from the 17th to the 18th century. Just prior to the point at which Afrikaans (in particular, Creole Dutch) began developing *nie$_2$*, Dutch had all but lost its negative clitic *ne*.

Some dialects of late Middle and early Modern Dutch show a phrase-final negative particle in certain environments. Ponelis (1993), who argues strongly for a Dutch origin of *nie$_2$* in Afrikaans, provides some examples of bipartite negation with phrase-final *niet* from Middle Dutch and early Holland texts. Many of the examples in Ponelis (1993) are constituent negation, and thus not necessarily relevant to the transfer of a sentential negative particle. Indeed, Burridge (1993:187) suggests that "including instances of constituent negation [from corpora of written Middle Dutch] will lead to misleadingly high percentages of single post-verbal negation with *niet*."

We must therefore discount examples of constituent negation from Ponelis (1993). Several of Ponelis' sentential negation examples are intriguing, however. Consider the following.

(6) a. **Niements** gout ... begherdic **niet**. MIDDLE DUTCH
nobody's gold ... covet-I not
'I covet nobody's gold.'

b. Ick pratt met **niement niet**. EARLY 17TH CENTURY DUTCH
I speak to nobody not
'I don't speak to anybody.'

c. Alsulx **en** es hij ghenegen **niet**. DUTCH C. 1550
thus NEG is he disposed not
'He isn't disposed to this.' (Ponelis 1993:468)

Examples (6)a-c all show phrase-final negative particles *niet*, and at first glance appear to be ideal models for transfer of a final negative into Afrikaans. However, as suggested by Jacques Arends and Tonjes Veenstra (personal communications), I argue that *niet* in these environments is *accidentally final*, that is, final purely by virtue of the rather unique syntax of each sentence. In (6)a, the DP *niements gout* has been fronted, stranding the normally phrase-medial *niet* in final position. In (6)b, addition of an adverbial or prepositional phrase would alter the phrase-final status of *niet*, while in (6)a, the object has been fronted, again stranding *niet* in phrase-final position. Clearly, such structures are the rare exception, rather than the rule, in Middle and early Modern Dutch.

Ponelis (1993) documents what he terms "*nie*-spread," that is, the movement of the negative particle *nie(t)* to phrase-final position in Middle and early Modern Dutch. Yet this pattern of "*nie*-spread" is totally unattested in other works on Germanic sytax, for example Burridge's (1993) chapter on the development of negation in Middle Dutch – despite the fact that she considers data from northern and southern dialects. Furthermore, Burridge's (1993) detailed statistical studies of the rise and fall of bipartite negation in Dutch do not include reference to this pattern, suggesting that it was far from frequent.

In the next section, I consider Khoekhoe (Nama) as a possible influence on Afrikaans negation.

5.4.3 Negation in Khoekhoe

Khoekhoe (Nama/Damara) is a Central Khoesan which was spokend in and around the Cape colony throughout the period of colonial expansion (Elphick 1989), and continues to be spoken today in South Africa and Namibia. In a series of papers, den Besten (1977, 1985, 1989, 2002) argues that Khoekhoe and Cape Dutch/Afrikaans share several typological traits that made Khoekhoe an ideal source for syntactic borrowing into Afrikaans. He argues that features of Afrikaans including genitive marking, the object marker *vir*, and the phrase-final negative particle *nie*$_2$, are cases of transfer from Khoesan, and Khoekhoe in particular.[3] Consider the following data from Khoekhoe.

Khoekhoe has post-verbal negative particles, as illustrated below in (7). These particles normally appear in either phrase-final or near phrase-final position, depending on whether an aspect marker is present.

(7) a. horaga ti ũi hãb !na ta ge ‖na !ãsa mũ **tama** hã.   **KHOEKHOE**
    entire my life in I DECL that city seen NEG ASP
    'In my entire life, I have not seen that city.' (den Besten 1985:33)

   b. tsĩ gâreti ke ‖nuie ‖eiti lka uu **tama**.
      and foolish-ones PART oil them with take NEG
      'And the foolish ones didn't take oil with them.' (ibid.)

   c. sadu ge ‖eisa ma **tite.**
      you(pl) Decl her give NEG. FUT
      'You should/will not give (to) her.' (ibid.)

---

[3] For more on Khoekhoe syntax, see Hagman (1977), Washburn (2001), and Akasaka (2003).

d. tita ge ‖nâu **tite**.
   I PART hear NEG-FUT
   'I won't hear.' (Ponelis 1993:471)

The data in (7)a-d illustrate sentential negation in Khoekhoe. Of the two negative particles, *tama* is used in conjunction with the present-tense, while *tite* is used with future and conditional tenses. *Tama* can appear either directly preceding the aspect marker *hã*, as in (7)a, or in phrase-final position, as in (7)b. *Tite* normally occurs in phrase-final position, as in (7)c-d. *Tama/tite* is the only negative marker present in all of the sentences in (7), thus it is natural to assume that it is the locus of negation, i.e. carries an interpretable negative feature. Note the difference with Afrikaans, in which the locus of negation is the pre-verbal negative particle nie_1, or a pre-verbal N-word (see Chapter Two). Khoekhoe also has N-words, that is, words that carry inherent negative force. Consider the data in (8).

(8) a. k^hoi-xareĩ ge ‖nati mĩ **tama** hã   **KHOEKHOE**
       man-none DECL this say **NEG** ASP
       'No one says this.' (den Besten 1985:33)

   b. tatsets ge ‖kawa homi **tite**
      not-you DECL again lie **NEG**-FUT
      'Never again will you lie.' (ibid.)

Native-speaker judgments confirm that k^h*oi-xarei* in example (8)a and *tatsets* in (8)b have inherent negative force. For example, both can be single-word negative answers to questions. Note that in both cases the same final negative particles *tama* and *tite* are present, suggesting that Khoekhoe allows negative concord, and showing that Khoekhoe presents a model for final negatives even in the presence of N-words. A Khoekhoe consultant also confirms that the unmarked position for *tama* is post-verbal, even in sentences that apparently contain negative polarity items such as *tsina* 'even'. Consider example (9).

(9) tita ge ǀgui blom-i tsina ǁama **tama** hã. KHOEKHOE
    I   PART one flower-3sg even buy NEG ASP
    'I didn't buy any [lit. even one] flowers'

Example (9) shows an NPI *tsina* 'even', which is licensed by the presence of negation (*tama*). Interestingly, the licenser *tama* occurs to the right of the NPI, unlike English (cf. *Anyone didn't see me). This strongly suggests a movement analysis in which the DP 'even one flower' is initially c-commanded by *tama*, and then moves to some higher position. Example (9) is also further confirmation that the negative particle occurs in final or near-final position, even in cases when it licenses another element to its left in linear order.

Thus far, we have seen that Khoekhoe possesses phrase-final negative particles that could have served as the model for transfer of syntactic structure to Cape Dutch. However, there are several problematic issues with such an account. First, the negative particle in Khoekhoe is not always phrase-final. Both den Besten (1985) and Ponelis (1993) document cases in which a negative particle occurs higher in the clause, though final position is in general the unmarked position. Thus we must assume that negatives occurred in their unmarked position frequently enough to trigger transfer. Second, even when negation occurs in post-verbal position, it can be followed by aspect markers such as *hã*, although these markers did not transfer into Afrikaans. Thus, again, we must assume that aspect markers, when they occurred, did not block transfer of a final negative particle. Third, the interpretable negative feature in Khoekhoe is associated with the (normally final) single negative particle, while in Afrikaans the final negative has no interpretable negative feature. Valkhoff (1966) makes a similar, if non-theoretic, claim about transfer of nie_2 from Khoekhoe:

> When the Hottentots [i.e. the Khoekhoe] learned to speak Cape Dutch, they adopted the pre-verbal *nie(t)*, but at the same time they looked for a means to maintain their usual construction with a post-verbal negation. To fill this hiatus they introduced another *nie(t)* behind the verb. (Valkhoff 1966:17)

Despite the problems pointed out above, I follow Valkhoff (1966) and den Besten (1985) in arguing that Khoekhoe is the optimal source for transfer of a phrase-final negative particle into Afrikaans. However, there is a fourth problem which has received no attention in the literature to the best of my knowledge: Khoekhoe, while it allows negative concord as in examples (8)a-b above, does not employ two separate negative particles in simple sentential negation. Furthermore, it does not show any of the properties of BNF illustrated in chapters 3-4. It is not a BNF language. Indeed, as I have stated above, there are no available models for transfer of BNF from any of the language groups or languages in contact with Afrikaans, including Khoesan, Germanic, and Malay-Portuguese. How then did Afrikaans develop BNF? In the next section, I argue for a two-step process of borrowing (transfer) and expansion, based on the idea that the features of BNF are universally available, and triggered by the adoption of a final negative particle into a language.

5.4.4 Negation in !Korana

Further evidence of borrowing comes from a corpus of !Korana that I have recently analyzed. !Korana is a Central Khoisan language that became extinct around 1940. The corpus, gathered in the 1930s by the South African anthropologist Englebrecht, includes 14 short texts narrated by the last surviving speakers of !Korana, ‖hamarib (Benjamin Kats) and |gob (Andires Walter Bitterbos). It totals roughly 2250 words. Both speakers were bilingual in Afrikaans and !Korana, and Bitterbos, purportedly the best speaker of the language, provided the interlinear translations of the !Korana text into Afrikaans. Engelbrecht (1936:212) describes the translations as "fairly literal, but not wholly so." As we will see below, these interlinear translations are very revealing when considering the head-final postition of the functional negative marker *nie* in Afrikaans. Englebrecht goes on to describe the sociolinguistic situation of these !Korana speakers as follows.

> Owing to the prominent part Afrikaans, or some form of it, plays in the daily life of the Korana, it became the medium in which most of our conversations were carried on, and this has partly suggested the method of translation adopted here (Engelbrecht:1936 203).

This statement is revealing in several ways. First, Englebrecht suggests a difference in dialects for the !Korana speakers, calling their speech "some form of" Afrikaans. Secondly, we see that Afrikaans played a large role in the daily lives of the !Korana, whose language, we should recall, was eventually utterly subsumed by Afrikaans.

In the corpus itself, there are 25 negative sentences. A preliminary analysis reveals the distribution of the negative markers in Afrikaans and !Korana, and is given in Table 5.

Table 5. Negation in a corpus of !Korana texts

!Korana text	#	Afrikaans gloss	#
post-verbal *tama*	18	post-verbal *nie*	17
pre-verbal particle	7	pre-verbal *nie*	7
Neg. sentences (total)	25		24

As we can conclude from *Table* 5, there appears to be an almost one-to-one correlation with the placement of the negative marker in the two languages. Recalling that the Afrikaans is not a morpheme-by-morpheme gloss, but a "fairly literal" translation, this appears to be convincing evidence of the similarity of the underlying grammars of the two languages in these speakers, for this particular structure.

Examples (10) and (11) below are taken from the corpus. The top line is an English gloss of the !Korana. The middle line is !Korana, and the bottom line is the Afrikaans interlinear translation, which I have attempted to align exactly as it is on the page in the original document.

(10)   game   ASP   killed   (if)   FOC   men   **!KORANA**

        xamareb   ta   ⁿamhe   o ,   i tje   doroxaku

        As wild   sal   doodgemaak   word,   het   ingewyde-manne

DIM-game   eat   **NEG**   rabbit   FOC   eat   **NEG**

‖axamare   ɲ|ũ   **tama**   ⁿ!õas   tje   ɲ‖ũ   **tama,**

*kleine-wild   geëet   **nie**   haas   eet   hulle   **nie**,*

jackal   FOC   eat   NEG   cat   FOC   eat   **NEG**

‖eieb   tje   ɲ|ũ   **tama,**   ‖hõab   tje   ɲ|ũ   **tama**

*jakkals   eet   hulle   **nie**,   kat   eet   hulle   **nie***

"If game had been killed, the full-blooded men did not eat small game; they did not eat the hare, the jackal or (any kind of cat)." (Engelbrecht 1936:216)

(11)   Foc   water   touch   **NEG**   raw-meat   (it)(FOC)

        i tje   ɴama   ⁿxo   **tama,**   kx|ora̰kx|ob   tje

        *het   hy   aan water gevat   **nie**,   rou-vleis het*

AUX (fall)   house   in   enter   **NEG**

!na...   kx/umme   !na   ‖a   **tama**

*daardi   huis   in   ingegaan   **nie***

"He did not touch water, nor would raw meat enter that home." (ibid.:228)

In the above examples, I have attempted to maintain the relative spacing found in the original text. I refer the reader to Englebrecht (1936) for a complete version of the corpus. These data reveal, first, that Khoekhoe and !Korana have much the same negation strategy, at least on the surface. This is not surprising given their close historical and typological relationship. Secondly, and more importantly, they show the very close affinity between the position of negation in Afrikaans and the position of negation in !Korana. For the !Korana speakers of Afrikaans who provided the glosses of these texts, a post-verbal negation in !Korana triggers a post-verbal negation in the translation. Similarly, as shown in Table 5 above, instances of pre-verbal negation in !Korana trigger use of pre-verbal negation in Afrikaans. I propose that this reflects the tendency on the part of !Korana speakers of Afrikaans to associate negation with two separate positions: pre-verbal and a post-verbal, and, furthermore, to extend this possibility into Afrikaans. Let us see how this is possible from a structural point of view. In the next section, I develop a proposal for the syntax of negation in Khoekhoe and !Korana that can explain the elucidate the precise mechansim of transfer from these Central Khoisan languages into Afrikaans of a final negative particle.

5.4.5 The Syntax of Negation in Khoekhoe and !Korana

As we have seen in the data above, Khoekhoe and !Korana have very similar negation strategies on the surface. Given these similarities, I will assume that they employ parallel syntactic structures. Negation in Khoekhoe and !Korana is very often found in phrase-final or post-verbal position. However, there are also examples of pre-verbal negation in Khoekhoe (den Besten 1978, 1985). Thus I propose that Khoekhoe has a BNF structure identical to that of Afrikaans, Hausa, etc., but that spell-out of both particles is illicit in Khoekhoe (and !Korana). As we will see in Chapter 6 below, there are a number of CCLs in which spell-out of both particles is optional. Thus, Khoekhoe would represent the opposite end of the spectrum from Afrikaans: while it employs a BNF structure, only one particle may be spelled out at a time.

In my representation of Khoekhoe phrase-structure, I follow the basic template for focus and declaratives in Khoekhoe proposed in Washburn (2001). I propose that the expanded NegP in Khoekhoe selects *v*P, as in Afrikaans and other BNF languages. Consider the representation of the sentence in (12)a, as in (12)b.

(12) a. kʰoi-xareĩ ge   ‖nati mĩ **tama** hã ⁴   **KHOEKHOE**
       man-NEG DECL this say **NEG** ASP
       'No one says this'

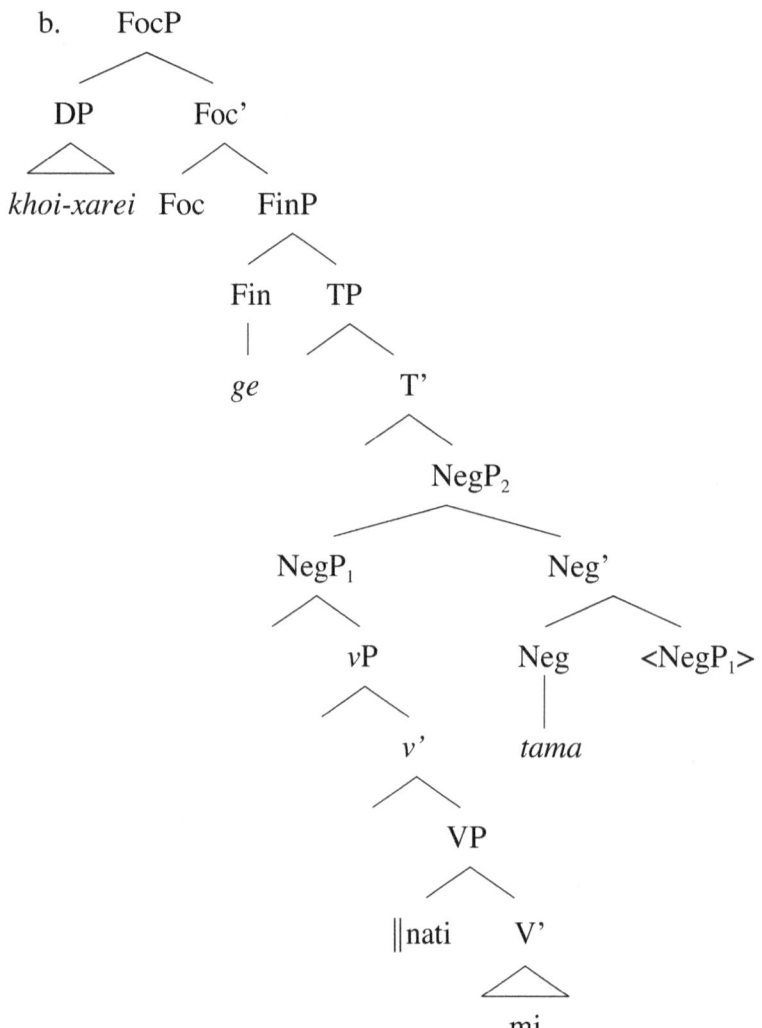

The representation in (49') shows the structure of sentential negation with an N-word in subject position in Khoekhoe. Following Washburn (2001), I place the

---

⁴ For ease of exposition, I ignore the aspect particle *hã* in my representation. It is possible that it occupies a position high in the left periphery, and that FocP moves into the Specifier of this position. Alternatively, it could cliticize to the negative *tama* via head movement or affix hopping, assuming it occupies a lower position in the tree.

focused subject and the declarative particle in the specifier positions of [FocP] and [FinP], respectively. I assume that negation, as in Afrikaans, licenses a [+Neg] feature on the verb, and that this feature triggers the projection of NegP$_2$ directly above VP. The specifier position of NegP is available as a landing site for V to move and check its strong [+Neg] feature against the head of NegP, *tama*. I assume a similar representation for the final future negation *tite*, with the possible added complication that Aspect moves and adjoins to the head of NegP, giving this marker of negation a future or conditional reading. Note that *tama* is not strictly phrase-final in Khoekhoe in case there is material in AspP. In this case, the verb alone moves, stranding its aspect marker under negation, which is precisely the word order we see on the surface in Khoekhoe. Below are the relevant syntactic structures as discussed in this section.

(13)   a. !Korana: [NP   [(Neg) [VP   [**Neg$_F$**   [Asp]]]]
       b. Khoekhoe: [NP   [(Neg) [VP   [**Neg$_F$**   [Asp]]]]
       c. Afrikaans: [NP   [Neg$_L$ [VP   [**Neg$_F$**]]]

Examples (13)a-c illustrate the exact match in negation typology between Afrikaans and Khoekhoe/!Korana. If one discounts the tense and aspect markers, which in some cases occur after the negation particle in Khoesan, the structures are completely analogous. This, coupled with the word-order facts, is a convincing argument for the partial role of structure transfer in adoption of a phrase-final negative particle in Afrikaans. However, the data from !Korana still leave open the question of how BNF languages developed the particular properties associated with this negation strategy. In the next section, I put forth a proposal of transfer coupled with UG-motivated internal development to explain the rise of BNF in Afrikaans.

5.5   Borrowing and Expansion: a UG-Based Account

I have argued that BNF is a negation strategy available under UG, with a well-defined set of properties and parameters, and can be captured with a unified syntactic analysis.

Afrikaans shares the core properties of BNF with other languages, such as Bukusu, Dagara, Hausa and Nweh. Unlike these languages, we have rich documentation on the history and development of Afrikaans showing that it has developed BNF only over the last 150 years. There are several plausible sources for the transfer of a final negative particle, the most viable of which is Khoekhoe. Yet no language in contact with Afrikaans exhibits BNF.

To resolve this apparent paradox, I propose the following five-stage developement process for BNF. Clearly, some of these stages may have overlapped to a greater or lesser degree. However, I believe that the model is sufficiently detailed so as to clarify the primary event at each stage.

Stage Zero is Dutch prior to colonization, up to the first moments of contact between Dutch speakers and Khoisan peoples, circa 1590. As we have seen above, there is some evidence of a final negative particle in Middle Dutch dialects, as well as some suggestion that a negative tag may have grammaticalized. However, I believe that the evidence for both of these is weak enough that we can essentially rule them out as prime movers in the development of BNF in Afrikaans. We can assume that the BNF parameter was set in the *off* position for the arriving speakers of Dutch.

Stage One is the period of first contact between Dutch colonists and speakers of Khoisan languages. Based on the historical documentation discussed in this chapter, we know that Khoisan peoples began, very early, to speak a variety of Dutch that is probably best described as a creole or a koine. We know that it sounded aberrant and "pitiful" to the ears of the Dutch colonists and Dutch travelers in southern Africa – a sure sign, although anecdotal, or burgeoning creolization. During this stage, which may have continued from 1590 through the early 1700s, the two parallel languages, Cape Dutch and Creole Dutch, began to develop. Although there are no data on negation available from this period, we can extrapolate back from the 1800s and deduce that, most likely, Cape Dutch had no second negative morpheme at this point: BNF was not yet activated. The Dutch pidgin, on the other hand, may have used a second negative particle on occasion, most likely with an emphatic sense (see the discussion of Palenquero and Vernacular Brazilian Portuguese in Chapter 6). However, it seems that the Dutch Creole did not develop full-blown BNF at this point – the second negative morpheme remain optional (as it still is today in some dialects of Afrikaans), and, presumably, the BNF morpho-sytnactic properties were not present.

Stage Two involved an extended period of contact and cross-feeding between Cape Dutch and Dutch Creole, from 1700 to roughly 1850. This is the period during which the Khoisan, now speakers of Creole Dutch, came to live in much closer proximity to the Dutch colonists, caring for their children, and often working as translators. This is the crucial period of transfer of the second negative morpheme from Creole Dutch to Cape Dutch. We know from the later part of this period that Cape Dutch speakers began to use nie_2, although far less frequently than their Khoisan counterparts. Again, I assume that nie_2 was at first used as an emphatic marker of negation, and was, in principle, not associated with the articulated NegP of BNF. Rather, it may have had the syntax of a negative tag, and perhaps the phonology of a tag as well – although the evidence here is of course lacking. In any case, it was not obligatory in either Cape Dutch or Dutch Creole at this point, and there is no indication from any historical documents that, for example, the position of nie_2 was used to disambiguate *because*-clauses.

Stage Three is the period of standardization. At some point in the late 19th and early 20th century, Afrikaaner nationalism, the growth in the South African economy and improving conditions in South African schools led to normative efforts on the part of Afrikaaner scholars and teachers. The language began to standardize, grammars and teaching manuals were produced, and a national Afrikaaner identity began to forge, primarily around the Afrikaans language. We know that by the early 1920s the use of *nie$_2$* was already completely obligatory in the standard language, according to Le Roux's (1923) Afrikaans grammar. In addition to normative pressurs, I assume that another pressure was at work as well. As I have already shown at several junctures above, several languages that use two negative particles, the second in phrase-final position, appear to have a small group of morpho-syntactic properties associated with negation. I argue that there is a universal pressure at work in the case of Afrikaans. As soon as Cape Dutch adopted a second, phrase-final negative particle, these properties began to develop. Because some of the properties involve the obligatory presence of *nie$_2$*, for example disambiguation, the pressure for *nie$_2$* to become an obligatory part of the grammar increases.

Stage Four is the current state of the standard language. *Nie$_2$* is obligatory in all negative sentences in Afrikaans, with a few exceptions such as simple intransitives. *Because*-clauses are disambiguated via the position of *nie$_2$*, and elements stranded to the right of *nie$_2$* fall outside the scope of negation – as illustrated with NPIs embedded in prepositional phrases, from Chapter 4. PPs and CPs can occur to the right or the left of *nie$_2$*, but DPs must move to receive case, and are subsequently frozen in situ while NegP$_1$ moves to [Spec,NegP$_2$], etc. As we saw in Chapter 3-4, there are a number of languages across the world that display a similar negation strategy, with a similar set of morpho-syntactic properties associated with negation. It would be instructive to do historical research on one or more of these languages to determine whether there are any parallels in the development of BNF across BNF languages. In the next chapter, I examine three languages that may be in the process of developing BNF.

Below, I lay out the steps in an organized fashion in Table 6, and show where each step falls in the Afrikaans genesis model, in Figure 2.

Table 6. Five Stages of Development of BNF in Afrikaans.

	PERIOD	**SOCIOLINGUISTICS**	**GRAMMAR**
Stage ⓪	*c. 1590*	First settlers arrive at the Cape Colony. Contact established.	No BNF in Dutch or Dutch dialects. Creole Dutch on the Cape did not exist.
Stage ❶	*1590-1700*	First contact between Dutch and Khoisan. Relations involve trade, and also some familial.	Cape Dutch remains close to European Dutch. Creole Dutch begins to form.
Stage ❷	*1700-1850*	Intense contact between colonizers and Khoisan, including co-habitation. Anecdotal reports of a "pitiful" Dutch being spoken on the Cape.	Creole Dutch begins to use a second, emphatic negative nie_2. Cape Dutch uses nie_2 infrequently, if at all, though use increases over the period. Nie_2 functions as emphatic or negative tag.
Stage ❸	*1850-1920*	Standardization of Afrikaans. Normative pressures begin, first grammars are written.	BNF parameter set to *on* at some point during this period. BNF properties begin to emerge. Nie_2 head $NegP_2$.
Stage ❹	*1920-now*	A more-or-less standard variety of Afrikaans is spoken by blacks and whites in South Africa. Afrikaans is the official language of at least one university.	BNF is fully-formed in Afrikaans, and functions as it does in other languages. Nie_2 is obligatory in the standard language.

In Table 6, I outline the proposed five-stage process of BNF development in Afrikaans. In Figure 2 below, I show how each of these stages aligns in the Afrikaans genesis model, adapted from Den Besten (1989). The stages are represented above the figure by their number.

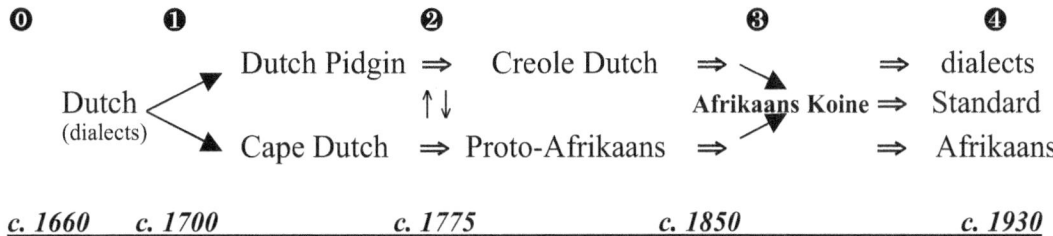

Figure 2. Model of Afrikaans genesis, with stages of BNF from Table 6 above.

If the above scenario is correct, then we might expect to find either historical or synchronic data on languages that are somewhere within one of the stages, but do not yet exhibit the (full set of) properties of BNF. Unfortunately, there is no historical data on the syntax of negation in any known BNF language, nor are there any early syntactic studies of negation in Afrikaans – for example from the late 19th century, when nie_2 was still optional and the properties of BNF presumably were not fully developed. However, as I will show in the next chapter, there are data from a number of Spanish- and Portuguese-lexified creoles and contact languages that have adopted an optional final negative particle, but that do not yet show full-blown BNF. I argue that these languages are missing links in the development of BNF proposed here.

In this chapter I have presented an extensive review of the literature on the development of Afrikaans, and, in particular, of the development of bipartite negation in Afrikaans. In Chapter Two above, I argued that negation in Afrikaans instantiates a particular (universal) strategy for sentential negation that I have labeled BNF. Here, based in part on the sociolinguistic data available, I have argued that BNF developed in Afrikaans over several hundred years. I proposed a five-stage development process that roughly reflects the critical phases in the growth of BNF in Afrikaans. Now, I turn to an examination of languages that are in the process of developing BNF.

CHAPTER SIX

THE SYNTAX AND DEVELOPMENT OF BNF IN CREOLES AND CONTACT LANGUAGES

In Chapter Five I argued that the development of BNF in Afrikaans was a five-stage process. After an initial contact period in Stage One, Cape Dutch began to adopt a second, phrase-final negative particle *nie$_2$*. At the outset this particle was used optionally, in conjunction with the pre-verbal negative marker. The BNF parameter was not yet activated, and *nie$_2$* may have had the syntax of a tag or an emphatic marker. In Stage Three, the particle became obligatory, and Afrikaans developed the core properties of BNF, which it shares with other BNF languages, as outlined in Chapters Two and Three. I further proposed that, while Stage Two (adoption of the particle) most likely occurred due to contact-induced borrowing, Stage Three is the result of both normative pressures and language universals.

As I outlined at the end of the previous chapter, the proposed five-stage process predicts that, either historically or at present, we might observe languages that have adopted a final negative particle but have not developed all the properties of BNF, or that have slightly different properties different from those already identified for BNF. In this chapter, I examine data from one creole and one contact language that appear to show exactly such intermediate stages.

The broad contours of the data are as follows: the languages in question, Palenquero and Vernacular Brazilian Portuguese (VBP), show mixed negation strategies using either a preverbal particle, a postverbal particle, or both. As we shall see, the distribution of the phrase-final particle is similar to the distribution of *nie$_2$* in Afrikaans. However, the phrase-final particle NEG$_2$ is not obligatory in Palenquero or VBP. At the same time, NEG$_2$ can appear alone as the sole overt marker of sentential negation. Thus we can state that spell-out of *both* negative particles in these two languages is optional; either NEG_1 or NEG_2 may be spelled out alone. In the case of Palenquero, optional spell-out of NEG_1 leads to certain ambiguities involving negative scope, while it appears that these ambiguities are filtered out in VBP via a requirement to spell-out NEG_1 in heavy clauses.

As I will show, Palenquero and VBP show certain properties of BNF, but also manifest the above-mentioned optionality of NEG particles, and certain scope ambiguities, not seen in BNF as defined in Chapters Two-Four. In addition, the use of the phrase-final negative, in conjunction with a preverbal negative, is often felt to be emphatic, or is used to deny a presupposition – much as we observed for West Flemish in Chapter Four. I account for these facts within an expanded NegP framework. Unlike standard BNF, the languages considered in this chapter allow the head of $NegP_2$, the higher negative projection, to be phonologically null. Furthermore, they also allow the head of $NegP_1$, which carries the interpretable negative feature, to be null. Essentially, only one head of the expanded NegP must be spelled out in these languages, while *both* must be spelled out in BNF, and the head of $NegP_1$ must be spelled out in West Flemish (*nie*) and French (*pas*). Finally, based on both syntactic and sociolinguistic evidence, I argue that negation in Palenquero and VBP exemplifies stage two development of BNF, in other words, adoption of the particle without all of the concomitant properties of BNF.

The chapter is organized as follows. In §6.1 I present the languages under discussion and the data that I will consider, and offer a brief comparison with data from Afrikaans. I explore in detail the negation strategies of Palenquero and Vernacular Brazilian Portuguese – both of which present important data for an accurate synchronic and historical account of BNF. Then, in §6.2, I move to a discussion of some broader issues related to BNF in diachronic perspective, as they relate to creole genesis. I argue that the development of BNF constitutes important evidence against the primacy of relexification across all areas of syntactic development in creoles. §6.3 explores the rather puzzling question of why certain creoles, such as Haitian Creole, did *not* develop BNF, and indeed why creoles in general, given the possibility of relexification, do not adopt certain syntactic properties of the substrate language. I offer conclusions of the chapter, and of the dissertation, in §6.4.

6.1 Creoles and Contact Languages with Mixed Systems

There are a number of creoles[1] and contact languages (CCLs) that show a bipartite negation strategy with a final negative particle. In addition to Afrikaans, they include: Columbian Chocó Spanish, Domincan Spanish, Palenquero, Santome, Angolar, and Vernacular Brazilian Portuguese (henceforth VBP). There are also many other Romance varieties (Spanish, Portuguese, and Italian dialects and contact languages) that employ a second, phrase-final NEG particle (Cf. Lipski 2001). For the purposes of this dissertation, I restrict myself to a close consideration of three languages: Palenquero, Santome, and Vernacular Brazilian Portuguese. First, however, let us consider a broader sample in (1)a-i.

(1) a. Piet het **nie** 'n appel by die mark geëet **nie**.　　　　**AFRIKAANS**
　　　　Peter has NEG an apple at the market eaten NEG
　　　　'Peter didn't eat an apple at the market.'

　　　b. Yo **no** aguanté el calor de allá **no**.　　　**Columbian Chocó SPANISH**
　　　　I NEG stand the heat of here NEG
　　　　'I can't stand the heat here.' (Schwegler 1991a)

　　　c. Yo **no** sé nada que se llama así **no**.　　　**Dominican SPANISH**
　　　　I NEG know nothing that REFL call this NEG
　　　　'I don't know anything that has this name.' (Lipski 2001)

---

[1] I follow the language-specific literature in classifying the languages in this section as *creoles* and *contact languages*. There is much debate as to the precise nature of a creole language, whether creoles are structurally identifiable as such, how creoles arise, etc. For excellent recent discussion, see DeGraff (1999, 2001).

d. **Nu** ten kumina **nu** ayá casa mi. PALENQUERO
 NEG have food NEG at house mine
 'There is no food in my house.' (Schwegler 1991b)

e. A **na** mêsê pa plôkô pali **fa**. SANTOME
 IMP NEG want that pork give-birth NEG
 'One doesn't want the pig to have piglets.' (Hagemeijer & Santos 2003)

f. Kolómbá **na** tá methé pa no tá zunto 'ne **wa**. ANGOLAR
 whites NEG TA want for us be near them NEG
 'The whites don't want us (living) near them.' (Dieck 2000)

g. **Não** sei se você está mentindo **não**. VBP
 NEG know if you are lying NEG
 'I don't know whether you are lying.' (Schwegler 1985-7:199)

h. **No** kredo ke pödia parlar kon elo **no**. CEMBRE
 NEG think-1SG COMP could speak with him NEG
 'I don't think that I could talk to him' (Zanuttini 1997:97-99)

i. **No** lagarlo davert **no**. LISIGNAGO
 NEG leave-it open NEG
 'Don't leave it open.' (ibid.)

In (1)a-i I illustrate examples of negation from a number of CCLs. (1)a is the familiar case of Afrikaans, with obligatory bipartite negation with a final negative particle. Example (1)b illustrates negation from a contact variety of Spanish spoken in the Chocó region of Columbia, near the Panamanian border. Note that in (1)b the final negative particle *no* follows both indirect and direct objects, as we would expect given the properties of BNF. The variety of Spanish spoken in the Dominican Republic also shows a bipartite strategy, as we observe in (1)c, where the final negative *no* follows an embedded clause, but is associated with the matrix negation. Example (1)d, from the Spanish-lexified creole Palenquero. Here, interestingly, we observe a post-posed PP *ayá casa mi* 'at my house', much as we have seen in Afrikaans (Cf. Chapter Two). Next, consider example (1)e from Santome, a Portuguese-based creole language spoken on the island of São Tomé, off the coast of

Gabon, and (1)f, from Angolar, another Portuguese-based creole spoken by an isolated community of Africans living on São Tomé. These data are unique in showing two phonologically distinct morphemes, *na* and *fa*. Example (1)g is a vernacular variety of Brazilian Portuguese. Here again we observe two homophonous particles bracketing the entire clause, with the final NEG following an *if*-clause, but clearly associated with the matrix negation. Finally, (1)h-i shows negation in two dialects of Italian. At first blush, the data in (1)b-i appear strikingly similar to Afrikaans (1)a, and to the other BNF languages we saw in Chapter Three. These surface similarities raise an obvious question: do these languages employ some form of BNF?

To answer this question, we must investigate the structural properties of the syntax of negation in the above languages. I will look in more detail at three of them: Santome, Vernacular Brazilian Portuguese, and Palenquero. As we shall see, these languages show a substantial amount of variation in their negation strategies. Santome appears to employ BNF in much the same form as seen in Chapter Three. Palenquero and VBP are mixed systems, by which I mean that they employ either a preverbal or a postverbal particle, or both. I begin by looking at the Portuguese-based creole Santome in §6.1.1. Then in §6.1.2, I look at negation data from Spanish-based creole Palenquero. In §6.1.3 I will present a more detailed discussion of Vernacular Brazilian Portuguese, a particularly interesting case for which there are considerably more data available, including field data that I have recently collected. Finally, I summarize the section and the relevant properties of each language in §6.1.4. I present syntactic analyses of relevant issues throughout the section.

6.1.1 Negation in Santome

Santome, a Portuguese-based creole spoken on the island nation of São Tomé and Principe, appears to show a BNF negation strategy. Let us briefly consider some of the core properties of negation in Santome. First, like Afrikaans and other BNF languages, both preverbal and phrase-final particles are obligatory in Santome – that is, in the framework developed here, both NEG heads must have a phonetic realization. Furthermore, the position of the phrase-final particle is quite restricted – constituents and phrases cannot normally scramble around NEG_2. Consider (2).

(2) A **na** mêsê (***fa**) pa plôkô pali *(**fa**). SANTOME
     IMP NEG want NEG that pork give-birth NEG
     'One doesn't want the pig to have piglettes.' (Hagemeijer & Santos 2003)

Sentence (2) contains the infinitival complement clause *pa plôkô pali* 'for the pig to have piglets'. Placing the second negative particle *fa* before this clause results in ungrammaticality. Moreover, a sentence without the particle *fa* in final position is also ungrammatical. These facts distinguish Santome from Afrikaans and, as we will see, from Palenquero as well. In the latter two languages, CPs and PPs can appear post-NEG_2, while in Santome they generally cannot (Cf. Hagemeijer & Santos 2003). In structural terms, the absence of post-posed PPs and CPs in Santome corresponds to absence of a position to which they can scramble. Recall that both Afrikaans and Hausa, the two BNF languages that allow post-NEG_2 scrambling, allow scrambling in a number of contexts. By contrast, Bukusu and Nweh appear much more restrictive in terms of word-order; scrambling is not generally observed in these languages (see Chapter Four). It seems that Santome patterns with these latter languages, suggesting that the expanded NegP in Santome does not contain an XP landing site for scrambling.

Not surprisingly, Santome shows *because*-clause facts similar to those found in other BNF languages. The position of NEG_2 triggers two distinct readings in *because*-clauses. Consider examples (3)a-b.

(3) a. Zon **na** ka fla **fa** plôvya migu dê.   SANTOME
João NEG ASP speak NEG because friend of-3SG
'John doesn't speak, because of his friend.'

   b. Zon **na** ka fla plôvya migu dê **fa**.
'It's not because of his friend that John doesn't speak.' (Hagemeijer & Santos 2003)
* 'John spoke not because of his friend.'

When the final negative particle *fa* appears before the *because*-clause, as in (3)a, the *because*-clause falls outside the scope of negation. Interestingly, in Santome both the matrix and the *because*-clause are interpreted as negative when *fa* appears sentence-finally. As pointed out by Hagemeijer (*to appear*), there is a similar effect in negated *because*-clauses in French, without the (overt) structural difference. The sentence in (6) can be interpreted with either a negative matrix clause, or with both clauses as negative, but, crucially, not with an affirmative matrix clause and a negative *because*-clause.

(4)   Jean **ne** parle **pas** à cause de son ami.   FRENCH
'It's because of his friend that Jean doesn't speak.'
or: 'It isn't because of his friend that John doesn't speak.' (Hagemeijer 2004)

The syntactic data in Santome are perfectly clear: the position of NEG_2 triggers a change in meaning. However, it appears that, as in French, some semantic fact allows for a double-negative reading when NEG_2 appears in final position, to the right of a *because*-clause. It is possible that NEG_2 in this case bears an interpretable negative feature, meaning that there are two per clause in this case. However, why this would be the case only in *because*-clauses is rather mysterious. Perhaps a more plausible explanation would be that the single negation extends over the matrix verb and the *because*-clause (which is non-finite in Santome). In either case, the issue is not directly relevant to the present discussion.

Based on the data available, it appears that the syntax of negation in Santome is relatively analogous to that in Bukusu and Nweh. The expanded NegP contains one intermediate position YP to which *because*-clauses move. There is no other position available for post-posed CPs or PPs; these never occur in Santome. Consider the phrase-structure in (5).

(5)
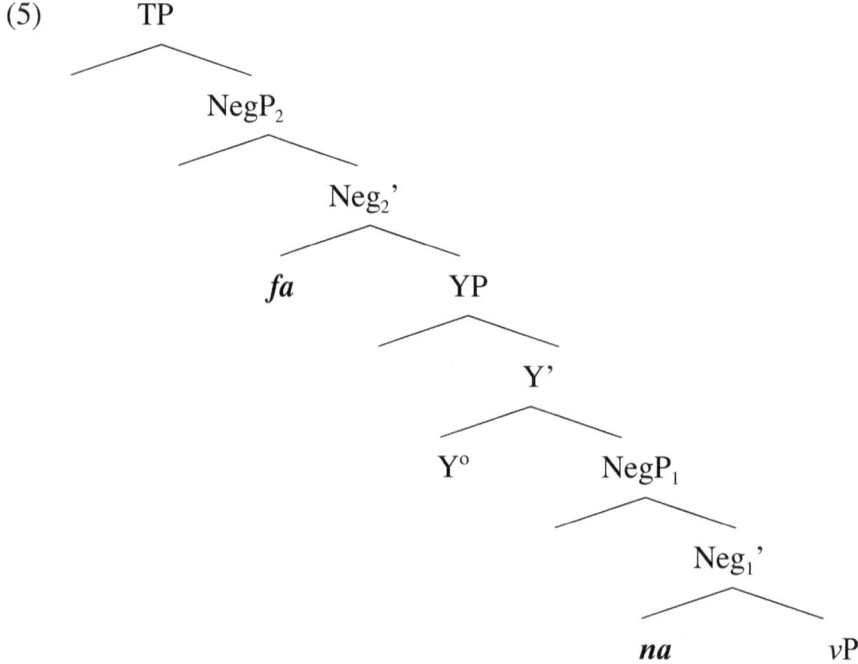

As I propose across BNF languages, TP selects the expanded NegP in Santome. NegP$_2$, headed by *fa*, dominates YP and NegP$_1$, the latter headed by *na*, which contains the interpretable [+neg] feature that gives a negative interpretation to the clause. *Because*-clauses post-posed after *fa* move to Spec-YP, followed by remnant movement of NegP$_1$ to Spec,NegP$_2$.[2]

Santome resembles Afrikaans in allowing N-words to occur alongside negation without triggering a double negative reading; i.e. Santome has negative concord. Consider example (6), where the DP *nya ngê* 'none person' appears to the right of the verb.

---

[2] Recall the other possibility, raised in Chapter 2, that *because*-clauses are base generated in Spec, YP. I do not pursue this possibility further here.

(6) Zon **na** bê nya ngê ni fesa **fa**. SANTOME
Zon NEG see none person at party NEG
'Zon didn't see anyone at the party.' (Hagemeijer, *to appear*)

Given the fact that aspect heads occur to the left of the verb (see example (3) above), it is probable that Santome verbs do not move to T. This in turn suggests that the negative DP *nya ngê* has remained in a relatively low position, and has not moved to Spec,NegP$_1$. Afrikaans requires N-words to move to Spec,NegP$_1$ due to an occurrence (OCC) feature on the NEG$_1$ head. Santome has no such requirement, and thus Santome NEG$_1$ does not possess an OCC feature.

Santome presents intriguing data suggesting that NEG$_2$ is some type of polarity head, as suggested for Afrikaans *nie$_2$* (Oosthuizen 1998) and West Flemish *en* (Haegeman 2002). Consider the data in example (7). The negative particle *fa* in (7)a alternates with the particle *an*, with slightly different presuppositions in questions.

(7) a. Bô **na** bê nadaxi di bisu ni kabêsa mu **fa**? (presupposes negative reply)
    b. Bô **na** bê nadaxi di bisu ni kabêsa mu **an**? (neutral presupposition)
       2SG NEG see nothing of animals in head 1SG fa/an
       'Didn't you see anything of the animals in my head?' (Hagemeijer 2004)

The presence of *fa* presupposes a negative response, while the presence of *an* presupposes either a positive or a negative response. These data do not conclusively show that NEG$_2$ is a polarity position in Santome. If there were a full-fledged polarity phrase in Santome, we would expect to encounter positive polarity items such as English *so* ("he is so a good person") co-occurring with the negative polarity across clause types (Cf. Laka's 1994 proposed Σ-phrase). However, the particle *an* is restricted mainly to questions (Hagemeijer, personal communication). It is possible that Santome is developing positive polarity items across other sentence types, perhaps from grammaticalized tags (Hagemeijer 2003, *to appear*). Overall, given the relatively small dataset from Santome, it appears that it displays a full-fledged BNF system, with two obligatory, non-homophonous negative particles, *because*-clause disambiguation, and an interesting alternation with a neutral (or positive) polarity item. In the next section, I look at negation in Palenquero.

6.1.2 Negation in Palenquero

Now, consider the negation strategy in the Spanish-based creole language Palenquero (also *Palenque* or *Lengua*), spoken by some 2,500 people in the village of San Basilio de Palenque in Columbia. Palenquero shows what I will term a mixed system of sentential negation. Depending on context, presupposition, speaker age and gender, and other discourse-related factors, one of the following strategies is employed.

(8)   a. S **NEG** V O
        b. S **NEG** V O **NEG**
        c. S   V O **NEG**

Palenquero can use a single preverbal particle (8)a, a bipartite structure with a final negative particle (8)b, or a single postverbal particle (8)c. According to both Schwegler (1991b) and Dieck (2000), (8)c represents the unmarked strategy in Palenquero.

Like Afrikaans and other BNF languages, Palenquero can employ two negative particles in simple sentential negation. Consider the data in (9).

(9)   a. Rikagdito **no** a kelé nda mi **nu**.   **PALENQUERO**
           Ricardito NEG TA want give me NEG
           'Ricardito didn't want to give it to me.' (Schwegler 1991b:177)

        b. I **nu**   kelé naa   **nu**.
           I NEG want nothing NEG
           'I don't want anything (at all).' (ibid.:196)

Note that in example (9)a, the preverbal negative is *no*, while the phrase-final particle is *nu*. As Schwegler (1991) points out, there is an alternation between *no* and *nu* in preverbal position, which may be due to Spanish influence. I return to this alternation in a moment. Although the bipartite construction in (9) is attested in declaratives, it is far more common in imperative constructions, as in (10)a-b.

(10) a. Yebá mi te! **Nu** dejá mi te **nu**!
    take me you NEG leave me you NEG
    'Take me along [to sell fish]! Don't leave me here!' (Schwegler 1991b:177)

   b. **No** ba a pie **nu**!
    NEG go by foot NEG
    'Don't go on foot!' (ibid.)

   c. **nu** mandá mi ele p'andi D. **nu** (...)
    NEG send me it to-where D. NEG
    'Don't send it to me at D.'s place.' (Dieck 2000:57)

Indeed, Schwegler (1991b) characterizes the bipartite[3] forms in (10) as occurring most frequently in imperatives, continuing:

> Double negation, most frequent in imperatives (cf. **nu** kumé ese pekao **nu**! 'don't eat this fish!'), serves to contradict statements or assumptions from the preceding discourse. NEG_2 constructions [those with bipartite negation] are often felt to be emphatic. (Schwegler 1991b:199)

Dieck (2000), in her corpus-based study of negation in Palenquero, identifies several environments where bipartite negation, and single preverbal negation, appear with greater frequency. Bipartite negation and single preverbal negation occur in imperatives, following *pa* 'so that' (11)a, in conditionals (11)b, in rhetorical questions (11)c, and following *lo ke* 'that (REL)'. Single preverbal negation, especially with *no* rather than *nu*, is found in other contexts as well, as in (11)d.

(11) a. p'i **nu** tené má monaisito.
    that-I NEG have more children
    '(..) so that I won't have more children.' (Dieck 2000:70)

---

[3] Throughout the discussion here "bipartite" refers specifically to a preverbal NEG plus a phrase-final NEG of the BNF type. I avoid using BNF at this point so as not to impose the theory on the data.

b. (...) si **nu** tené agua pa rregá **nu**, á sé mori.
   if NEG have water to irrigate NEG, TA REFL die
   'if there is no water to irrigate (with), they die.' (Dieck 2000:51)

c. **nu** ten ke pagao yo memo?
   NEG have REL pay-it I same
   'Don't I have to pay it myself?' (ibid.:47)

d. (...) pero **no** era así kumo agué
   but NEG was this like now
   'but it wasn't as it is now.' (ibid.:60)

The relative frequency of *no* in (single) preverbal negation leads both Schwegler (1991b) and Dieck (2000) to propose that this negation strategy is a Spanish influence. Although somewhat isolated geographically, Palenquero speakers are in constant contact with Columbian Spanish, which uses a single preverbal negator *no* in sentential negation, and the majority of speakers have some fluency in standard Spanish (Schwegler 1991b). This raises the question of whether Palenquero employs two separate negation strategies, one based on Spanish, and one that resembles BNF.

Employing two syntactically distinct negation strategies appears less than optimal from a learnability perspective. Rather, I will argue that, in languages such as Palenquero (and, as we will see, Vernacular Brazilian Portuguese), there is simply greater flexibility in spelling out one, or both, negative heads. Conceiving of negation in Palenquero in this manner, we can unify our analysis of BNF and mixed systems like Palenquero and VBP. BNF languages must spell out both negative heads. As we observed in Chapters Two and Three, omitting one negative particle results in ungrammaticality in BNF. This is not the case in Palenquero. Rather, it appears that *at least* one negative particle must be present in Palenquero, either NEG_1 or NEG_2. The unmarked negation strategy in Palenquero is a single phrase-final negator *nu*. This fact, asserted by Schwegler (1991b), is borne out in the statistical analysis of Dieck (2000:69), who finds phrase-final negation in 87.8% of negative sentences (a total of

296) across 5 speakers of different ages/genders. Of the remaining 12%, roughly one-third are bipartite negations, while the other two-thirds are preverbal occurrences of either *nu* or *no*. Consider the examples of phrase-final negation in (12).

(12) a. teneba   agua **nu**.
         have-PST water NEG
         'There was no water.' (Dieck 2000:38)

    b. no, ngombe mi ten ngombe **nu**.
         no, cow   mine has calf   NEG
         'No, my cow doesn't have a calf.' (ibid.:54)

As we saw above, the contexts in which bipartite and preverbal negation can occur – while interesting to note from a discourse perspective – do not have any unifying characteristics in syntactic terms. Therefore, it is important to account for the syntax of all three negation strategies in Palenquero. An expanded NegP with optional spell out of one or both negative particles straight-forwardly accounts for the data, while at the same time showing Palenquero to be maximally similar to BNF languages in its syntactic structure. As we will see, Palenquero differs from VBP in allowing ambiguities related to the use of NEG_2 in embedded clauses, where NEG_2 can be associated either with the matrix or the embedded clause. That these ambiguities are tolerated in Palenquero – and not in VBP, as we will see – may be a direct reflection of Palenquero's predilection for NEG_2 as the sole overt marker of sentential negation. I return to this below.

As we saw in example (1)d above, repeated below, prepositional phrases can scramble around the NEG_2 in Palenquero.[4] Consider (13)a-b.

---

[4] As pointed out by Schwegler (1991b), phrase-final *nu* can also be followed by the aspect marker *ba*, as in (i) below. I do not consider these data further here, however, note the interesting parallel with the position of the Khoekhoe aspect marker *hã*, which also appears following negation.

    i. E, ané asé- ba miní mucho **nu**-ba
       eh they T/A T/A come much NEG TA
       'Eh, they did not come [to Palenque] often.' (Schwegler 1991b:185)

(13) a. **nu** ten kumina **nu** ayá casa mi.   PALENQUERO
         NEG have food NEG at house mine
         'There is no food in my house.' (Schwegler 1991b)

   b. i bae konbedsá má **nu** por eso.
      I go converse more NEG of this
      'I'm not going to talk about this anymore.' (Dieck 2000:39)

The data in (13) closely resemble the BNF scrambling facts from Afrikaans and Hausa (see Chapters Two and Three). It is noteworthy that scrambling can occur whether following NEG_2 in a bipartite structure, as in (13)a, or when a single post-verbal NEG is present, as in (13)b. This suggests a structural parallel between the two negation strategies.[5] Again, this parallel is easily explained within an expanded NegP framework. Palenquero, like Afrikaans, allows a NegP-internal XP projection to serve as the landing site for scrambled/post-posed PPs. The same structure is available whether both negative particles are spelled out, as in (13)a, or whether uniquely the phrase-final particle is spelled out, as in (13)b. Presumably, the scrambling position would also be available when only NEG_1 is spelled out, however, movement to this position would be string vacuous and thus invisible on the surface.

Phrase-final negation can take scope over a matrix clause even when it appears following an embedded clause in Palenquero. Consider the data in (14).

(14) a. pero i sabé paké jue lo ke palenkero sigí por eso **nu**.
         but I know why is that Palenqueros continue with this NEG
      'but I don't know why the Palenqueros continue with this.' (Schwegler 1991b:191)

   b. pero i sabé **nu** paké jue lo ke palenkero sigí por eso.
      but I know NEG why is that Palenqueros continue with this
      'but I don't know why the Palenqueros continue with this.' (Schwegler 1991b:193)

---

[5] Dieck (2000:39) qualifies the scrambled PP in (13)b as representing "a kind of afterthought," and further states that "the position of *nu*, thus, is basically phrase-final ('postoracional'), but it is possible to find variations in this structure" (her emphasis, my translation).

The sentences in (14)a-b are truth-conditionally identical. The phrase-final negation in (14)a is associated with the matrix clause, as it is in (14)b. Dieck (2000) also cites numerous examples of this phenomenon. Consider the examples in (15).

(15)   a. kuchá bo, bo (á) aprendé brujería lo ke abuelo sí á sabeba **nu**?
          hey you, you TA learn witchcraft that grandfather your TA know NEG
          'Hey you, you didn't learn the witchcraft that your grandfather knew?'
                                                (Dieck 2000:59)

    b. pogke ané á seba usá kusa lo ke bo á ten aí oleja **nu**.
          because they TA TA use thing that you TA have here ear NEG
          'because they don't use the thing that you have here in your ear.' (ibid.)

Unlike the distinction between bipartite/preverbal and phrase-final negation, neither Schwegler (1991b) nor Dieck (2000) find any discourse-related factors influencing the use of (14)a over (14)b: "we have not been able to detect any meaningful semantic or stylistic differences between these variant patterns" (Schwegler 1991b:193). However, it is noteworthy that a single phrase-final negation following an embedded clause can be associated with the matrix clause in examples (14) and (15) above. According to Schwegler (1991b) and Dieck (2000), context serves to disambiguate sentences such as (14) and (15), although the readings in which negation takes scope over the embedded clause are also available. These data show that very heavy movements are allowed in Palenquero. Consider the derivation of example (15), repeated below in (16)a.

(16)   a. bo (á) aprendé brujería lo ke abuelo sí á sabeba **nu**?
          you TA learn witchcraft that grandfather your TA know NEG
          'You didn't learn the witchcraft that your grandfather knew?' (Dieck 2000:59)

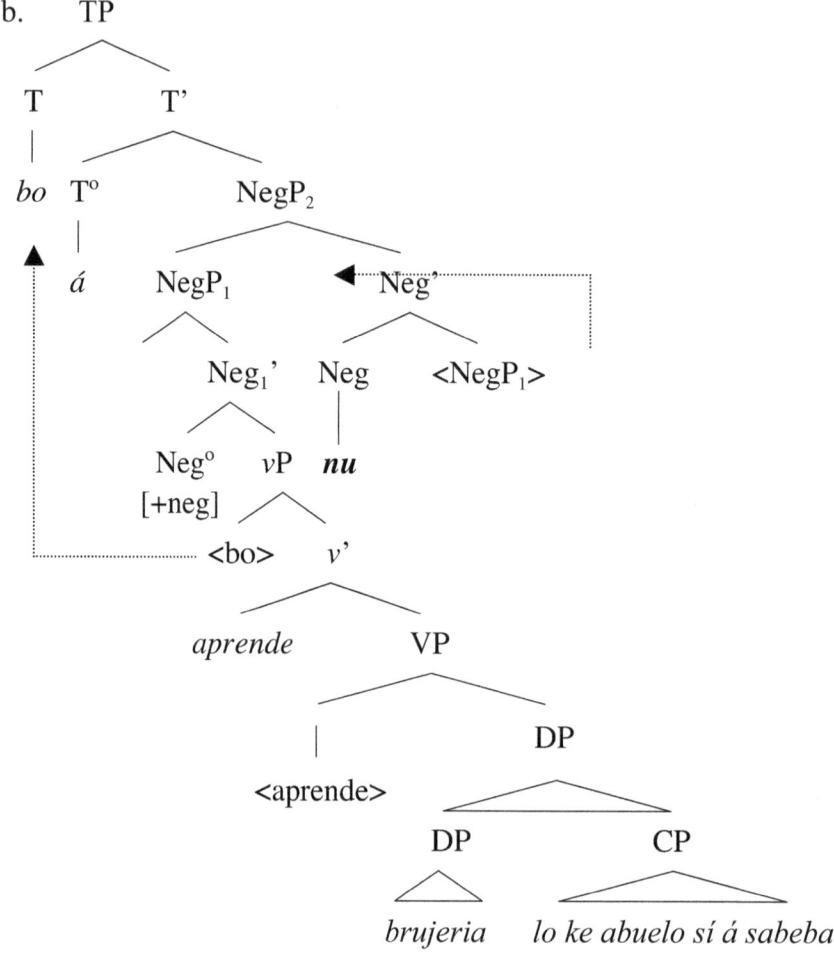

Negation in (16)a takes scope over the matrix clause, meaning that the interpretable negative feature [+neg] is located in the matrix clause. Unlike Santome, and other BNF languages, Palenquero can optionally spell out only one head of the expanded NegP. In the case of example (16)a, the head of $NegP_2$, *nu*, is spelled out. The [+neg] feature does not have an overt phonetic realization, but is associated with the head of $NegP_1$. I make standard assumptions about subject movement to Spec,TP, and local verb movement to $v°$. Palenquero negative sentences allow very heavy pied-piping of $NegP_1$ and everything contained in it, including the embedded CP, to Spec,$NegP_2$ in the matrix clause. As we shall see in a moment, other languages with mixed systems, such as Vernacular Brazilian Portuguese, also allow heavy pied-piping of this type.

Not surprisingly, there are ambiguities that arise as a result of the availability of phrase-final negation being the sole marker in embedded contexts. Consider the data in (17).

(17) a. I **nu** dudá **nu** ke bo a-ten plata.   **PALENQUERO**
I NEG doubt NEG that you TA-have money
'I don't doubt that you have money.'

b. I **nu** dudá ke bo a-ten plata **nu**.
'I don't doubt that you have money.'
or: 'I don't doubt that you don't have money.' (Schwegler 1991:199)

Example (17)a is unambiguous. When negation brackets the main clause, it can only take scope over the matrix verb. However, in (17)b, the phrase-final negation can either be associated with the main clause, or with the embedded clause, yielding a scopal ambiguity and two possible readings. A similar ambiguity exists in (18).

(18)   Miná ke i polé jablá to ma kusa di lengua suto sin meté un palabra español **nu**
 look that I can say all PL thing of Palenquero our without put one word spanish NEG
    'Look! I **can** say everything in Palenquero without putting in a Spanish word.'
or: 'Look! I **cannot** say everything in Palenquero without putting in a Spanish word.'
(Schwegler 1991b:192)

Schwegler (1991b:192) summarizes the issue of ambiguity in negative scope as follows:

> When the negative particle is in sentence-final position, interpretation of the utterance may be entirely context dependent. The reason for potential ambiguity is obvious. Since the predicate negator does not travel with the negated verb in clauses containing two or more verbal complexes, it becomes unclear which verb is being negated.

Again, the context-dependent ambiguities illustrated in (17)-(18) are in fact structural ambiguities, easily captured within the expanded-NegP analysis developed above for BNF. Example (17)a is unambiguous, since it only corresponds to (19)b.

(19) a. I **nu** dudá **nu** ke bo a-ten plata.
       I NEG doubt NEG that you TA-have money
       'I don't doubt that you have money.'

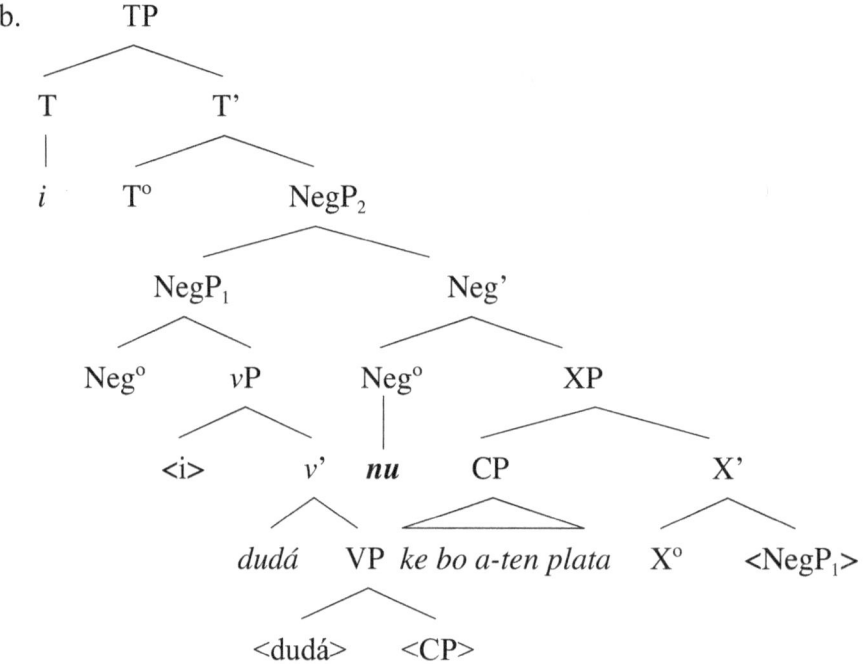

Unlike Santome, Palenquero allows CPs to be post-posed following NEG_2. CP moves to the intermediate projection XP within the expanded NegP, after which $NegP_1$ undergoes remnant movement to Spec,$NegP_2$. The particle *nu* associated with the matrix $NegP_2$ can also appear in final position, meaning that CP-movement to Spec,XP is optional in Palenquero. However, unlike BNF, phrase-final *nu* in (17)b can also be the unique spell-out of a second NegP in the embedded clause, yielding the ambiguity suggested by the gloss. This is a purely structural ambiguity; the interpretation in which both clauses are negative corresponds to the structure in (20)b.

(20)   a. I **nu** dudá ke bo a-ten plata **nu**.
       'I don't doubt that you don't have money.'   (Schwegler 1991:199)

b.
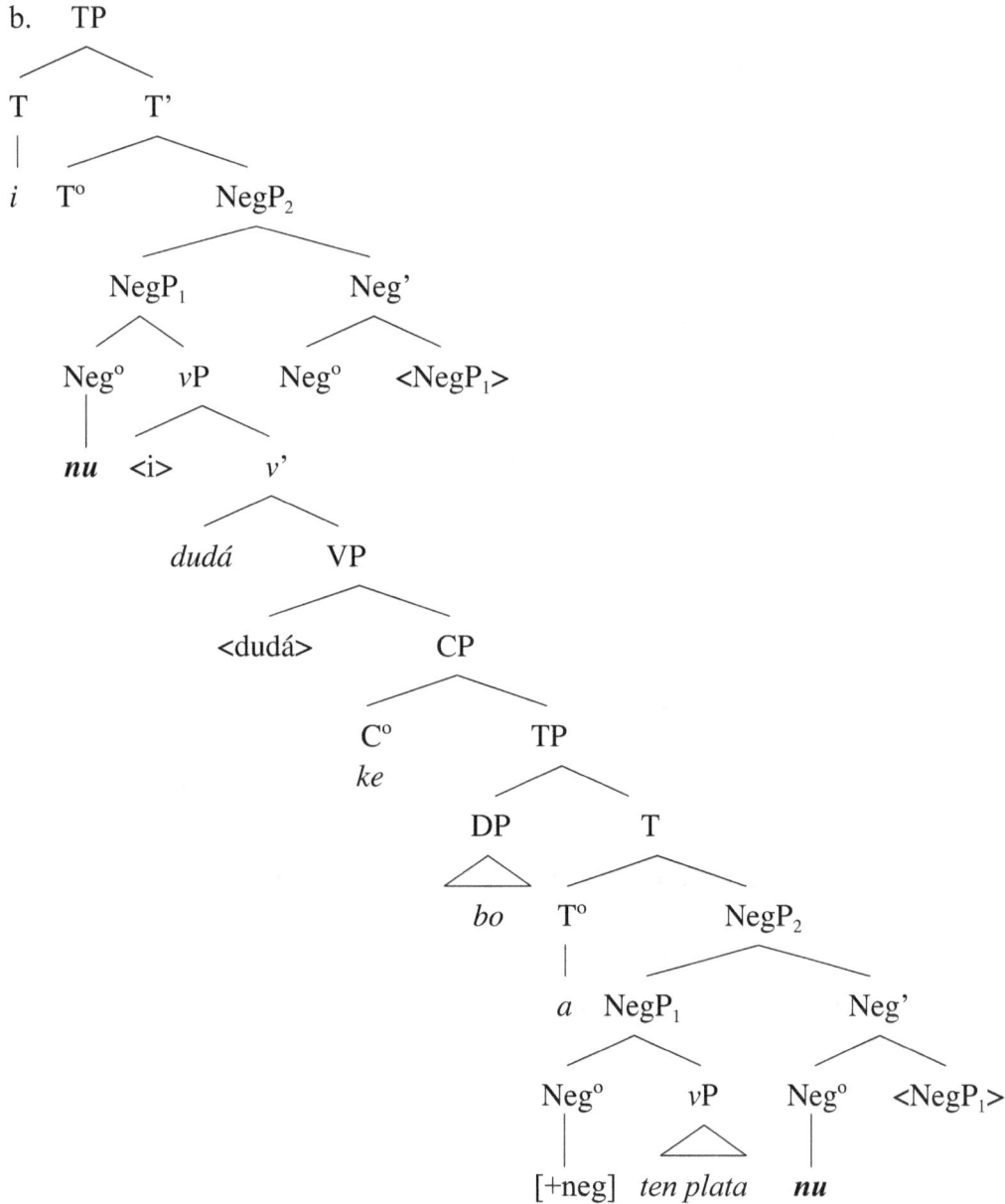

The structure in (20)b yields a reading in which both clauses are interpreted as negative. Spell out of both negative particles is optional in Palenquero. In the case of (20)a, NEG_1 has been spelled out in the matrix clause, while NEG_2 has been spelled out in the embedded clause, meaning that NEG_1 in the embedded clause has no phonetic form. A structural ambiguity exists, since the phrase-final *nu* may either be associated with NegP$_2$ of the embedded clause, or with NegP$_2$ of the matrix clause.

Given such ambiguities, it comes as little surprise that *because*-clauses are not disambiguated via the position of NEG$_2$ in Palenquero. (Armin Schwegler, personal communication). Indeed, the phrase-final NEG following a *because*-clause can be associated with that clause, as in example (21).

(21) I saká ané tuabía **nu** pogké i sabé si ané ba rreklamá mi el **nu**.
I take out them yet   NEG because I know if they go ask-from me it NEG
'I don't take them out yet because I don't know whether they will want it back
   from me.' (Schwegler 1991b:191)

Furthermore, a single instance of phrase-final negation may appear after the matrix clause, as in example (22). Here only the matrix clause is negated.

(22)   Pasá mi **nu** pogké y- a- sabé p ande hu i tando.
happen me NEG because I T/A know to where it is I going
'It won't happen to me, because I know where I am going.'
(Schwegler 1991b:191)

Recall that similar examples are ungrammatical in Afrikaans, where both NEG$_1$ and NEG$_2$ must be present. The position of NEG$_2$ determines the scope of negation in *because*-clauses in full-fledged BNF.

(23)   a. Piet   het   *(**nie**) vertrek *(**nie**), omdat dit gereën het.　　**AFRIKAANS**
Peter AUX NEG leave NEG because it rain AUX
'Peter didn't leave, because it was raining.'

   b. Piet   het   *(**nie**) vertrek omdat dit gereën het *(**nie**).
Peter AUX NEG leave because it rain AUX NEG
'Peter left not because it was raining.'

In the next section, I will look at data from Vernacular Brazilian Portuguese, the third language in our brief survey of CCLs with (partial) BNF.

6.1.3 Negation in Vernacular Brazilian Portuguese (VBP)

Next, consider the negation strategy of the vernacular Brazilian Portuguese (VBP) spoken in the north-east of the country, and in some urban centers such as Rio de Janeiro. Like Palenquero, VBP negation is characterized by three distinct patterns. Consider the data in (24)a-c.

(24) a. A Cláudia **não** veio à festa.   VBP
         DET Claudia NEG come to-the party
         'Claudia didn't come to the party.'

     b. A Cláudia **não** veio à festa **não**.
         DET Claudia NEG come to-the party NEG
         'Claudia didn't come to the party.'

     c. A Cláudia veio à festa **não**.
         DET Claudia come to-the party NEG
         'Cláudia didn't come to the party.' (Schwenter 2002)

As in Palenquero, the three negation strategies in (24) are attested in various sentence types. However, while truth-conditionally equivalent, the distribution of the three distinct patterns of negation illustrated in (24) is governed by a complex set of discourse-related properties which I do not consider here. For a detailed examination of these facts, I refer the reader to the excellent discussions in Schwegler (1985-87) and Schwenter (2002). Based on my own recent work with a native speaker consultant from northern Brazil (Bahia state), the three constructions are judged as equally grammatical across a wide variety of sentence types, though there are undoubtedly discourse-related properties associated with each.

Like Palenquero, VBP allows spell out of one negative particle. Alternatively, both particles can be spelled out. Consider the examples in (25) below.

(25) a. A Luísa **não** veio à festa **não**.   VBP
         DET Luísa NEG came to-the party NEG
         'Luísa didn't come to the party.'

b. ?? A Luísa **não** veio **não** à festa.
   DET Luísa NEG came NEG to-the party

c. A Luísa **não** comeu o bolo **não**.
   DET Luísa NEG came to-the party NEG
   'Luísa didn't eat the cake.'

d. ??/* A Luísa **não** comeu **não** o bolo.
   DET Luísa NEG came NEG to-the party

e. Ele **não** fala a mesma coisa que fala o baiano **não**.
   he NEG speaks the same thing that speaks the Bahian
   'they REALLY don't speak the same way as Bahians do.' (Schwenter 2002)

f, *Ele **não** fala a mesma coisa **não** que fala o baiano.
   he NEG speaks the same thing NEG that speaks the Bahian

The unmarked position for NEG$_2$ in VBP is phrase-final, following, PPs (25)a, direct objects (25)c, and relative clauses (25)e. Note the subject-verb inversion typical of complement clauses in both Brazilian and European Portuguese, as in (25)e. Scrambling around NEG$_2$ is generally dispreferred in VBP. My consultant judged PP-scrambling as in (25)b to be quite degraded. Only slightly worse was indirect object scrambling, as in (25)d. However, both of these were judged as clearly better than the utterly impossible (25)f, in which a CP is scrambled around NEG$_2$. The VBP data at this point resemble those from Bukusu, for example, as being highly restrictive in placement of constituents and phrases relative to the NEG morphemes. As I discuss below, the gradations in grammaticality judgments may be related to a heaviness constraint on scrambling, and perhaps a signal of a change-in-progress. These examples immediately distinguish VBP from Palenquero, since the latter allows scrambling around NEG$_2$. As in Bukusu and Santome, it seems there is no position to which PPs and CPs can scramble in VBP.

As in other cases of BNF, it is impossible to stress NEG$_2$, nor can a pause be inserted prior to NEG$_2$. Note that VBP and Palenquero are similar in using bipartite structures such as (25)e to add emphasis, at least in certain contexts. This is in stark contrast to standard BNF systems, in which NEG$_1$ and NEG$_2$ are obligatorily present and do not bring any special emphasis to a negative sentence.

Example (25)e above, from Schwenter's (2002) corpus of spoken VBP, is glossed based on the context as having an emphatic interpretation. However, my consultant judged this sentence to be either emphatic or non-emphatic, depending on the intonational contour and stress pattern. As in Palenquero, there is some tendency to interpret negative sentences in which both particles are overtly realized as emphatic. Such sentences can also have different presuppositions from sentences with a single negative. Consider the examples in (26).

(26)   a. Eu **não** gosto do meu professor (#***não***), eu adoro ele!   **VBP**
          I NEG like of my teacher NEG I adore him.
          'I don't like my professor, I adore him!'

      b. Eu **não** gosto do meu professor (***não***), eu odeio ele!
          I NEG like of my teacher NEG I adore him.
          'I don't like my professor, I hate him!' (Schwenter 2002)

Spelling out NEG$_2$ in (26)a is pragmatically anomalous given that the speaker intends a negative assessment of his/her professor. By contrast, spelling out NEG$_2$ in (26)b is licensed, since the speaker fully intends to convey a negative presupposition.

Recall the general paradigm for the double-NEG filter in BNF, repeated below.

(27)   a. Ek het **nie** geweet dat hy **nie** sou kom **nie**.   **AFRIKAANS**
          I AUX *nie*$_1$ know that he *nie*$_1$ would come *nie*$_2$
          'I didn't know that he wouldn't come.' (Donaldson 1993)

      b. *Ek het **nie** geweet dat hy **nie** sou kom **nie nie**.
          I AUX *nie*$_1$ know that he *nie*$_1$ would come *nie*$_2$ *nie*$_2$ (ibid.)

The double-NEG filter is also in effect in VBP. Consider the following data.

(28)   a. ?Eu **não** imagino que você **não** tem dinheiro **não**.   **VBP**
           I NEG imagine that you NEG have money NEG
           'I can't imagine that you don't have any money.'

       b. *Eu **não** imagino que você **não** tem dinheiro **não não**.
                                                    (Schwegler 1985-7:199)

Sentence (28)a was judged as slightly degraded by Schwegler's consultant, perhaps owing to the odd semantic effect of the double negative. My consultant also found this sentence somewhat semantically anomalous, but otherwise grammatically well-formed.

Unlike Palenquero, VBP can disambiguate *because*-clauses via the position of NEG$_2$. Compare (29)a-b to (30)a-b respectively. My VBP consultant immediately judged the meaning of (30)b as different from (30)a, as reflected in the glosses.

(29)   a. Piet   het **nie** vertrek **nie**, omdat dit gereën het.   **AFRIKAANS**
           Peter AUX NEG leave NEG because it rain AUX
           'Peter didn't leave, because it was raining.'

      b. Piet   het **nie** vertrek omdat dit gereën het **nie**
          Peter AUX NEG leave because it rain AUX NEG
          'Peter left not because it was raining.'

(30)   a. Pedro **não** foi embora **não**, porque estava chovendo.   **VBP**
           Peter NEG went away NEG because was raining
           'Peter didn't leave, because it was raining.'

      b. Pedro **não** foi embora porque estava chovendo **não**.
         Peter NEG went away because was raining NEG
         'Peter left not because it was raining.'
         *'Peter didn't leave because it wasn't raining.'

Recall that in Palenquero, a phrase-final NEG gives rise to scopal ambiguities. No such ambiguity exists in VBP. Example (30)b has a single interpretation. In other words, NEG$_2$ in the *because*-clause cannot be interpreted as signaling the presence of NegP, that is to say an interpretable [+neg] feature, in the *because*-clause.

The absence of scopal ambiguities with NEG$_2$ in VBP is further confirmed by the data in (31) below. A phrase-final NEG in a matrix clause gives a negative reading to the clause, as in (31)a. Embedded conditional clauses can use either a single preverbal negator, as in (31)b, or a bipartite strategy, as in (31)c. However, a single phrase-final negative following an embedded conditional clause cannot be associated with the embedded clause, as in (31)d-e.

(31)   a. Eles vão ganhar este jogo **não**.   **VBP**
              they go win   this game NEG
              'They are not going to win this game.' (Schwegler 1985-7:191)

       b. Eu vou sozinho se você **não** quiser ir.
          I   go   alone if you NEG want to-go
          'I'll go alone if you don't want.COND to go.'   (ibid.:195)

       c. Eu vou sozinho se você **não** quiser ir **não**.
          I   go   alone if you NEG want.COND to-go NEG
          'I'll go alone if you don't want to go.'   (ibid.)

       d. *Eu vou sozinho se você quiser ir **não**.
          I   go   alone if you want.COND to-go NEG (ibid.)

       e. *Eu imagino que você tem dinheiro **não**. (=19c)
          I   imagine that you have money NEG
          'I imagine that you don't have any money.'   (195)

There is a general restriction in VBP against the association of a phrase-final negative following an embedded clause with the embedded clause. Schwegler (1985-7) indicates that (31)d-e are ungrammatical. Consultation with a native speaker confirms that, in (31)d-e, the phrase-final negation cannot be associated with either the matrix clause or the embedded clause. This is in sharp contrast to Palenquero, in which a phrase-final negation following an embedded clause can be associated with either the matrix or the embedded clause, depending on the context (cf. (15)a above). In Palenquero, certain ambiguities arise as a result – ambiguities which I have argued to be purely structural. These ambiguities do not arise in VBP simply because one of the structures is blocked.

Compare (32)a and (32)b below. In VBP (32)a, the presence of two negative particles triggers a negative interpretation only in the matrix clause. The reading in which both clauses are negative is not available. In contrast, consider Palenquero, in which the phrase-final negative can be associated either with the matrix clause, or as a separate negator in the embedded clause. In this respect and others, VBP appears to function much more like Bukusu and other 'restrictive' BNF languages: the position of the phrase-final negative particle is highly restricted. Palenquero, on the other hand, allows phrase-final negatives to function as the overt marker of sentential negation.

(32)   a. Eu **não** vou se você estiver a fim de ir com a gente **não**.   **VBP**
I   NEG go if you are   at end to go with the people NEG
'*I won't go if you don't want to go with us.'
'√ I won't go if you want to go with us.' (Schwegler 1985-7:195)

    b. I **nu** dudá ke bo a-ten plata **nu**.   **PALENQUERO**
I NEG doubt that you TA-have money NEG
'I don't doubt that you have money.'
or: 'I don't doubt that you don't have money.' (Schwegler 1991:199)

Based on (32) and the analysis in §6.1.2 above, it appears that both VBP and Palenquero allow heavy pied-piping of embedded clauses with $NegP_1$ to Spec,$NegP_2$. However, in VBP NEG_2 cannot be the only particle spelled out in an embedded clause. Essentially, we may view this as an ambiguity filter. For an embedded clause to be interpreted as negative, NEG_1 – the morpheme that carries the interpretable feature – must be spelled out, either in the matrix clause or the embedded clause, depending on which clause is negated. The ambiguity filter may be formalized in terms of heaviness, as in (33).

(33) **NEG₁ Filter**: In heavy clauses, all instances of NEG₁ – the morpheme bearing the interpretable negative feature – must have a phonetic realization.

The NEG₁ filter in (33) blocks heavy clauses from having a covert negative particle with an interpretable [+neg] feature, the net effect being to filter out potential ambiguities relating to negative scope – such as those in Palenquero. The notion of *heaviness* in the case of VBP negation and NEG₁ spell-out refers in general to the presence of an embedded clause. (31)d-e violate the NEG₁ filter, since NEG₁ is not overtly spelled-out in the presence of a heavy CP-complement clause. An interpretation of (32)a where both clauses are negative is also blocked. If the phrase-final NEG₂ in (32)a were associated with a NegP in the embedded clause, then NEG₁ in the embedded clause would have to be realized.

The NEG₁ Filter applies freely to both matrix and embedded clauses in heavy contexts. Consider the paradigm in (34).

(34) a. * Eu sei se você tem dinheiro **não**. **VBP**
          I   know if you have money NEG

   b. * Eu sei **não** se você tem dinheiro **não**.

   c. * Eu sei **não** se você tem dinheiro.

   d. * Eu **não** sei se voce tem dinheiro **não não**. (Schwegler 1985-7:200)

   e. Eu sei **não**.
      I know NEG
      'I don't know.'

   f. Você tem dinheiro **não**.
      you have money NEG
      'You don't have money.'

   g. Eu **não** sei se você tem dinheiro **não**.
      I   NEG know if you have money NEG

Example (34)a is ruled out by the NEG$_1$ Filter; a single instance of NEG$_2$ cannot appear in a heavy context. (34)b shows that two occurrences of phrase-final NEG$_2$ in a heavy context are ungrammatical, as is a single instance of NEG$_2$ in (34)c. The latter case is of interest, since it appears to show an over-application of the filter. Clearly an occurrence of NEG$_2$ preceding the embedded clause can only be associated with the matrix clause. However, (34)c is blocked, as is (34)a, since NEG$_1$ is not overtly realized. Finally, (34)d is blocked by the double-NEG$_2$ filter, as seen above in other BNF languages.

As in Afrikaans, the presence of NEG$_1$ in VBP is optional in the presence of N-words. However, if NEG$_1$ is not spelled out in the presence of an N-word, then NEG$_2$ must be spelled out; that is, there must be at least one overt NEG particle to license N-words. Consider the data in (35).

(35) a. * Eu vi **ninguém**.   **VBP**
         I saw nobody

      b. Eu **não** vi **ninguém não**.
         I NEG saw nobody NEG
         'I didn't see anybody.'

      c. Eu **não** tenho **nenhuma** ideia disso **não**.
         I NEG have none   idea of-this NEG
         'I didn't know anything about this.'

      d. Eu tenho **nenhuma** ideia disso **não**. (Schwegler 1985-7)
         I have none   idea of-this NEG
         'I didn't know anything about this.'

Both NEG particles can be spelled out in the presence of an N-word such as *ninguém* 'nobody' or a negative DP such as *nenhuma ideia* 'no idea', as in (35)b-c. Not surprisingly, and similar to standard Brazilian and European Portuguese, N-words must occur in the presence of some marker of sentential negation. (35)a is ungrammatical since neither NEG particle is spelled out. Example (35)d is grammatical, since the N-expression is licensed by the presence of NEG$_2$, which c-commands the N-expression early in the derivation. Consider the structure in (36), which represents the derivation of sentence (35)c above.

(36)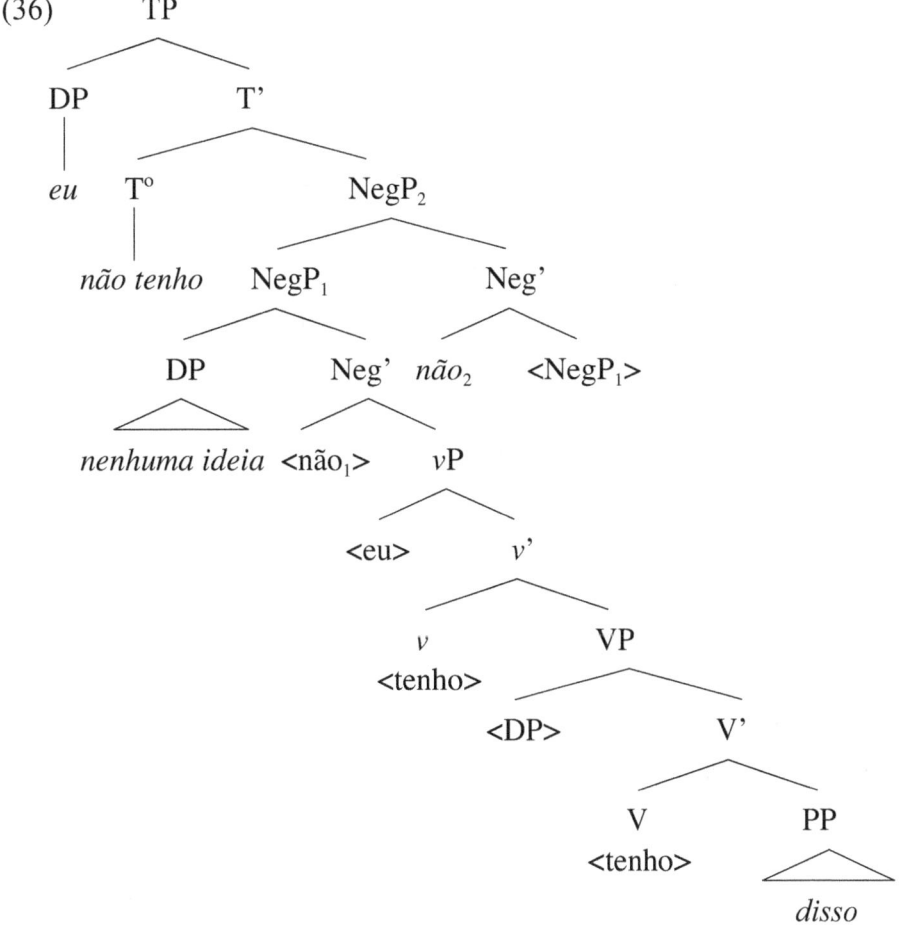

As I stated above, VBP and Palenquero always employ an expanded NegP in sentential negation. In (36), both NEG particles are spelled out. NegP$_1$ moves to Spec,NegP$_2$, accounting for the phrase-final position of NEG$_2$. As in Afrikaans, I assume that N-words and N-expressions in VBP move to Spec,NegP$_1$ to eliminate the OCC feature on NEG$_1$. However, note that in this particular case the N-expression could also remain *in situ* and yield the correct word order, ignoring the question of case checking. I follow Zanuttini (1997) in assuming a close relationship between

NEG_1 and tense in VBP, as in Romance in general. I assume that NEG_1 undergoes local head movement to adjoin with the verb in T, accounting for its preverbal position.

6.1.4 Summary of Shared Properties and Parametric Variation

Above we have seen three examples of creoles and CLs that employ two negative particles in sentential negation. All allow the second negative particle to occur in phrase-final position, following complements and adjuncts. I argue that these three languages can be captured within the BNF/expanded NegP analysis proposed for Afrikaans, Bukusu, Dagara, Hausa and Nweh. Of the three, Santome most closely embodies all the properties of BNF observed in Chapters Two and Three. It obligatorily employs two separate NEG particles in non-emphatic sentential negation. VBP and Palenquero can also employ two overt NEG particles. Unlike Santome, however, spelling out both particles is optional in VBP and Palenquero, and often adds emphasis, or leads to somewhat distinct presuppositional effects in comparison with spelling out a single NEG.

There is also some variation within the 'mixed' systems found in VBP and Palenquero. VBP is much less flexible in allowing scrambling of PPs and CPs around NEG_2 than Palenquero, where NEG_2 can occur before or after PP and CP complements. Also, VBP has a requirement that the interpretable negative feature [+neg] have an overt phonetic realization in heavy clauses; that is, NEG_1 must be spelled out if the clause is heavy. Palenquero has no such requirement, resulting in ambiguities of negative scope. I summarized the properties of the three languages, as compared to Afrikaans, in *Table 7* below.

Table 7. Properties of BNF Languages

Property ↓ Language→	Afrikaans	Santome	Palenquero	VBP
Optional spell-out of NEG$_1$ or NEG$_2$	*no*	*no*	*yes*	*yes*
NEG$_1$ Filter	*n/a*	*n/a*	*no*	*yes*
Double-NEG$_2$ Filter	*yes*	*yes*	*yes*	*yes*
NEG$_1$ precedes verb	*yes*	*yes*	*yes*	*yes*
NEG$_2$ can follow DOs, IOs, PPs, Adverbs	*yes*	*yes*	*yes*	*yes*
NEG$_2$ can follow CP complements	*yes*	*yes*	*yes*	*yes*
Scrambling around NEG$_2$	*yes*	*no*	*yes*	*no*
NEG$_2$ *Because*-clause disambig.	*yes*	*yes*	*no*	*yes*
Haplology of final NEG-NEG	*yes*	*yes*	*yes*	*yes*
2 NEGs are morphologically distinct	*no*	*yes*	*no*	*no*

As shown in *Table 7*, Santome patterns by and large with Afrikaans, and by extension with other BNF languages. Indeed, Santome in some ways more closely resembles other BNF languages; for example, it employs non-homophonous negative particles, and is much more restrictive than Afrikaans in terms of what constituents can scramble around NEG$_1$. This concludes the synchronic analysis and discussion of negation in Santome, VBP, and Palenquero. In the next section, I discuss the historical development of BNF in these three languages. I argue that the negation systems of VBP and Palenquero represent intermediate stages in the development of BNF.

6.2 Diachrony of Negation in VBP, Palenquero & Santome

Dahl's (1979) broad cross-linguistic survey of negation reveals a marked tendency for languages using a negative particle to place this particle in preverbal position, while recognizing that sentence-final NEG is also relatively common in SVO languages of West Africa. The majority of creole languages employ a single, preverbal particle. Dieck (2000:121) points out that, of the 53 creoles with European lexifiers cited in Holm (1989), all use a preverbal particle, while 7 use either a final particle in combination with a preverbal particle (e.g. Palenquero), or a BNF strategy (e.g. Santome). In this section, I will investigate the theories of how creole and contact languages developed BNF negation strategies.

Both Palenquero and (especially) Santome are easily identified as creole languages by the broadest measures. While the bulk of their lexicons can be traced to Spanish and Portuguese, respectively, they are unintelligible to speakers of these languages, due to large-scale syntactic and phonological differences. VBP, as a contact language, is largely intelligible to speakers of Standard Brazilian and even European Portuguese, while still exhibiting a number of novel structures vis-à-vis the standard language. Under some theories of creolization, then, conflating the development of Santome and Palenquero on the one hand with VBP on the other is an inherently flawed enterprise, since VBP is not a creole. However, as outlined in the introduction, I assume here, following DeGraff (1999, 2001, 2003), that the process known as creolization reduces to (universal) processes of language acquisition and language change. I have argued above that Santome, Palenquero and VBP have identical underlying negation structures: all employ an expanded NegP. They differ from each other in some expected ways, given the BNF parameters described in Chapter Four above. Negation in VBP and Palenquero also differs from negation in (other) BNF languages in allowing optional spell-out of one NEG particle, yielding scopal ambiguities in Palenquero – ambiguities which are blocked in VBP by a filter requiring NEG_1 to be spelled out in heavy clauses. In this section I argue that this difference is not merely another parameter of BNF, but that Palenquero and VBP represent a distinct stage in the development of full-fledged BNF, such as that observed in Afrikaans and Santome, for example.

As is the case for Afrikaans, there is some controversy surrounding the origins of bipartite negation with a final NEG particle in Spanish and Portuguese dialects and creoles. The possibilities are analogous to those discussed for Afrikaans in Chapter Five: i) internal development; ii) transfer/borrowing from the lexifier(s), or; iii) transfer/borrowing from the substrate(s). Given the relatively short time-frame involved in the genesis of Santome and Palenquero, and the development of unique features in VBP, scenario (i) can be reliably discounted. Scenario (ii) is also unlikely in the case of Spanish and Portuguese lexifiers, neither of which show bipartite or post-verbal negation during the period under consideration, from roughly the 16th to the 18th century (Cf. Schwegler 1996). The main focus in the creolistics literature on negation is thus scenario (iii), the controversy being twofold. First, what African languages can be identified as substrates in a transfer/borrowing scenario? Second, what role did UG play in the growth of the properties associated with BNF? I will address these questions in turn in the next two sub-sections.

6.2.1 African Substrates

Schwegler (1996) argues for a monogenetic origin of bipartite negation with a final NEG particle across Spanish and Portuguese creoles. He hypothesizes the existence of an Afro-Portuguese pidgin or (semi-) creole with phrase-final negation that, working in concert with the preverbal negation of the lexifier (Spanish or Portuguese), yielded the *bozal* (= African slaves recently imported to Spanish/Portuguese colonies) negation strategy observed across a number of languages in the Caribbean, South

America, and the Atlantic. The strength of Schwegler's (1996) proposal lies in its ability to explain the similarities in negation strategies across geographically diverse areas (Brazil, Columbia, Dominican Republic, São Tomé, etc.) with similar sociolinguistic histories involving slavery and colonialism. The main weakness is the absence of data on the precise structure of the proposed Afro-Portuguese pidgin that spread phrase-final negation throughout the Spanish- and Portuguese-speaking colonies. The proposed Afro-Portuguese pidgin may have employed phrase-final negation due to the influence of African languages. Alternatively, it is possible, under a polygenetic account, that African substrates directly influenced the development of negation across Spanish and Portuguese CCLs.

In a recent paper on negation across Spanish and Portuguese CCLs, Lipski (2001) considers the substrate hypothesis. Among the strongest candidates, also mentioned in Schwegler (1991b, 1996) and Dieck (2000), is Kikongo. Consider some example of Kikongo negation in (37).

(37) a. **ke** be kuenda malembe **ko**.   **KIKONGO**
        NEG 3PL walk slowly NEG
        'They don't walk slowly.' (Lipski 2001)

      b. **ke** tu-kwe-ndanga lumbu yawaonso **ko**.
         NEG 3PL-ASP-go each day NEG
         'We do not go every day.' (ibid.)

The data in (37)a-b appear virtually identical to those seen in Hausa in Chapter Three. Note that NEG_1 precedes the weak subject pronouns. It is well-known that slaves from the Congo basin, where Kikongo is spoken, were forcibly removed to at least some of the Spanish and Portuguese colonies where we find bipartite negation with final NEG today, especially São Tomé and Columbia. However, Kikongo is only one of the numerous languages spoken in the region from which slaves were drawn. Many other languages of the area do not have a phrase-final negative particle. Moreover, there are no convincing demographic data showing how many Kikongo speakers were present (presumably a greater number than other speakers if the substrate borrowing hypothesis holds), nor socio-historical data revealing Kikongo speakers attaining positions of relative importance in the burgeoning slave community (meaning their speech would be socially valued). Lipski (2001) concludes with a negative assessment of the role of African languages as the (unique) explanation for the development of BNF across Portuguese and Spanish CCLs:

> Negative structures among African languages exhibit so much diversity that there is little hope for the discovery of a unified 'African' negation pattern in *bozal* Spanish and Portuguese. Most non-Bantu African languages contain a single negative particle, whose placement in the sentence varies somewhat, but which is functionally homologous to Spanish *no*/Portuguese *não* (Lipski 2001:14).

The problems encountered by both the monogenesis hypothesis and the substrate hypothesis are very reminiscent of the problems encountered in the transfer scenario from Khoekhoe to Afrikaans. In particular, the sociolinguistic evidence for direct borrowing is at most inconclusive, and the syntactic evidence, lacking in the case of the Afro-Portuguese creole, is also not conclusive for the transfer scenario. The strongest hypothesis we can advance, it seems, is the following. An Afro-Portuguese pidgin and/or African substrates *may* have triggered the adoption of a phrase-final negative particle in Spanish and Portuguese CCLs. However, both Palenquero and VBP exhibit properties of negation that are not attested in Kikongo (optional spell-out of both NEGs, NEG_1 Filter). Therefore, I will argue in the next section that, like Afrikaans, the negation strategies of VBP and Palenquero underwent a UG-based development, and, furthermore, are part of a Jespersen-like cycle in the development of BNF.

6.2.2 A UG-based Scenario

As I suggested at the end of Chapter Five, the development of BNF in Afrikaans can be described in terms of a five-stage model. In Stage Two, after an initial contact period, Afrikaans adopted an optional phrase-final negative particle. Structurally this particle may have been used as am emphatic or negative tag, much as the leftmost NEG appears to be used in Palenquero today. In Stage Three, the negative particle *nie$_2$* was fully encorporated into the grammar. Its structural position was as the clausal functional head of a second negative phrase NegP$_2$. Possessing uninterpretable [uNeg] features, it triggered NegP$_1$ movement to its Specifier, accounting for its phrase-final position. The particle was most likely adopted due to the influence of Khoekhoe negation. In Stage Three, the use of the particle became obligatory, most likely under normative and standardization pressures. Concomitantly, Afrikaans developed the general properties associated with BNF identified in Chapter Three.

Given this five-stage process, we would predict the existence of languages currently in one of the intermittent stages. I propose that Palenquero and VBP are examples of such languages. This implies that there is a Jespersen-like process at work in the development of BNF. First, a language adopts a second negative word, either through contact or, presumably, via internal means. Unlike the French case, however, the unmarked position of this second negative word is phrase-final. The presence of the second negative word then triggers development of other universally-available BNF properties. As I have shown above, the syntactic evidence that Palenquero and VBP share the use of an expanded NegP with Afrikaans and other BNF languages is fairly strong. Interestingly, we have seen that, in both Palenquero and VBP, there are pragmatic distinctions between the use of a preverbal particle, a phrase-final particle, or both. Part of the process of moving from Stage One to Stage Four of BNF development clearly must involve the loss of these pragmatic distinctions; as spell-out of the final NEG particle becomes obligatory, and emphatic or presuppositional effects engendered by its use are necessarily lost. Schwegler (1991b) remarks that this process of overgeneralization of the phrase-final particle is occurring in present-day Palenquero:

> [...] there seem to exist only minimal differences in the use of negation strategies between older and younger Palenqueros, [although] there is some indication that some of the younger, less fully bilingual speakers at times fail to capture the (admittedly) subtle pragmatic distinctions between preverbal and postverbal negation, thereby overextending NEG_2 [double negation] and NEG_3 [phrase-final negation] into environments previously dominated by NEG_1 [preverbal negation]. (Schwegler 1991b:184)

These are exactly the type of sociolinguistic data we would expect to see given a change-in-progress from single preverbal negation to BNF. Of course, this is not to say that Palenquero and VBP will necessarily resemble Afrikaans or other BNF languages at some future point. However, given the syntactic and sociolinguistic evidence, it appears fairly certain that Palenquero and VBP represent the intermediate stage in the development of BNF.

Before concluding the dissertation, I wish to explore one final question. We have seen that certain creoles have developed BNF, at least partially due to substrate influence. However, recalling Holm's (1989) statistics, most creoles with European lexifiers employ a single preverbal negative particle. At the same time, many of these creoles have as their main substrate(s) a language/languages that use either a final negative particle or a BNF strategy. Why did these creoles not develop BNF, as Afrikaans, Palenquero and VBP did?

6.3   Creoles without BNF

Why did some creoles *not* adopt certain features from their substrate, for example bipartite negation with a final NEG particle? This is a perplexing question for creole studies in general and relexification theories in particular – as pointed out recently in

Ingo Plag's (2002) review of Lefebvfre (1998), and Chris Collins' (2001) review of Veenstra (1997). Collins, for example, points out that logophoric pronouns are ubiquitous in West African languages – including Kwa languages, presumably the substrates of many creoles – yet, curiously, no known creole has logophoric pronouns. In regards to negation, consider the particular case of Haitian Creole (HC) and its (purported) substrate, Fongbe. According to Lefebvre (1998), HC is essentially relexified Fongbe. However, the two languages have somewhat different negation strategies, as illustrated below in (38).

(38) a. Jan **pa** t' av- ale nan mache. **HAITIAN CREOLE**
John NEG ANT IND-FUT go in market
'John would not have gone to the market.' (DeGraff 1993)

b. Kɔ̀kú **mà** nĭ wá àxì mɛ̀. **FONGBE**
Koku NEG SUB come market in
'Koku does not have to come to the market.' (Lefebvre and Brousseau 2002:121)

c. (Nĭ) Kɔ̀kú **mà** xɔ̀ àsɔ́n lɛ́ **ǎ**, é ná yĭ.
if Koku NEG buy crab PL NEG 3sg DEF.FUT leave
'If Koku does not buy the crabs, (s)he will leave.' (ibid.)

d. Kɔ̀kú xɔ̀ àsɔ́n lɛ́ **ǎ**.
Koku buy crab PL NEG
'Koku did not buy the crabs.'
('It is not the case that Koku bought the crabs.') (ibid.:128)

(39) a. Kɔ̀fí mú plé àvɔ́ ó **GENGBE**
Kofi NEG buy cloth NEG
'Kofi did not buy a cloth.'

b. Kɔ̀fí me fle gasɔ o **EWEGBE**
Kofi NEG buy-Perf bicycle NEG
'Kofi did not buy a bicycle.' (Aboh 2004:47)

As both DeGraff (1993) and Lefebvre (1998) point out, the negation patterns in Haitian Creole (38)a and Fongbe (38)b possess some striking similarities. For example, note that in both languages TMA markers follow negation. However, both (38)c and (38)d illustrate negation patterns in Fongbe that are not attested in Haitian Creole. Bipartite negation in Fongbe (38)c occurs in conditional clauses, while the final-negative morpheme ǎ is employed when a speaker disagrees with the content of a proposition. Under Lefebvre and Brousseau's (2002) analysis, the negation marker ǎ in Fongbe is part of a larger class of phrase-final particles that express a speaker's point of view with respect to a proposition. Lefebvre (1998) argues that one of these particles, the emphatic marker *o*, is relexified into Haitian, and housed in a SigmaP projection along the lines of Laka's (1990) analysis of Basque. Lefebvre (1998) argues that Fongbe ǎ did not relexify into Haitian "because there were no available forms in the superstratum language to provide them with a phonetic matrix." However, this raises an interesting question about creole and contact languages with BNF: what forms in the Dutch, Spanish, and Portuguese (not so different from French after all) provided the phonetic matrices for the final negative marker in Afrikaans, Palenquero, Vernacular Brazilian Portuguese, etc.? In fact, it is clear that there *was* phonetic material available, and it was quite simply the identical material used for the first NEG marker. This neatly explains why in most cases of creole and contact languages with (stages of) BNF, we find two homophonous particles. It also is strong counter-evidence to the claim that no phonetic material was available for a second negative marker in HC. Why not /pa/? Thus we return to the original question of why HC did not develop the same negation strategies as Fongbe. It seems a possible explanation for the absence bipartite negation in Haitian conditionals, and the final NEG correlate to Fongbe ǎ, would be analogous to the explanation for the absence of logophoric pronouns in creole languages.

6.4 Chapter Conclusions

In this chapter I present data from two creole languages, Palenquero and Santome, and one contact language, Vernacular Brazilian Portuguese. I propose that Santome has developed a full-fledged BNF system. Palenquero and VBP, on the other hand, appear in some sense to be 'mixed' systems. For example, it is not obligatory to use both negative particles in either of these languages, as it is in all other examples of BNF that we have seen throughout the dissertation. Also, it appears that Palenquero does not disambiguate *because*-clauses via the position of NEG_2, owing perhaps to scopal ambiguities that arise in the context of embedded clause negation. However, Palenquero does allow post-NEG_2 scrambling of PPs, which is reminiscent of Afrikaans. I argue that, in historical terms, Palenquero and VBP represent intermediate stages in the development of BNF.

In the next and final chapter, I delve briefly into the wider applicability of the theory of negation proposed here. In particular, I examine whether the BNF system can accommodate French. I also offer conclusions from the dissertation.

CHAPTER SEVEN
EXTENDING THE PROPOSAL

In Chapters 2 through 4 of the dissertation, I develop an analysis of the syntax of negation based on data from a number of languages, including Afrikaans, Bukusu, Hausa, and Nweh. On the surface, these languages have very similar negation strategies. They all use a pre-verbal negative particle in conjunction with a phrase-final negative particle. I have argued that standard accounts of the syntax of negation, and in particular Haegeman's (1995) NEG Criterion, cannot accommodate these languages. I develop a new analysis based on an articulated NegP, with two separate head positions containing the two negative heads, and one or more intermediate positions that serve as landing sites for stranded PPs, *because*-clauses, and so forth. I show that, in addition to the surface similarities, languages that employ bipartite negation with final NEG (BNF) share a small group of morphosyntactic properties.

In this chapter, I wish to explore the possibility that the BNF system can be extended to other bipartite languages such as French. Thus far, I have proposed an analysis that can account for negation in the languages mentioned above, that is, languages that employ a bipartite negation strategy *and* use a phrase-final particle. However, a stronger hypothesis would argue that *all* bipartite negation languages are in fact instances of BNF as I have developed it above. In this case, the difference between French, for example, and (some dialects of) Hausa would simply be based on the availability of intermediate landing sites within the expanded NegP. I will develop this strong hypothesis over the next three sections. I should also state that, by necessity, the proposal outlined below is far more speculative than the fully developed analysis of Chapters 2-4. I view the following sections, in part, as an outline for future research on the topic of bipartite negation.

The chapter is organized as follows. First, in §7.1, I present some data from French, and discuss the standard analysis of Pollock (1989), Ouhalla (1990), Zanuttini (1997) and others. Then, in §7.2, I develop a BNF analysis of French. Finally, in §7.3, I discuss a few of the empirical advantages of adopting such an analysis of French. I conclude the chapter, and the dissertation, in §7.4.

7.1   Negation in French

Negation in French differs from the languages mentioned above in two central ways. First, modern French does not obligatorily employ two negative particles. Indeed, French looks much more like West Flemish, in that the negative particle *ne* is optional – indeed, dispreferred – in most spoken dialects of French today (Ashby 1981). Compare this to West Flemish *en*, which is also optional (Haegeman 2002). Throughout the discussion, I work under the assumption that, although it is optional, the syntactic position of French *ne* must still be accounted for. Modern French, especially written French, still employs the discontinuous *ne...pas* very frequently. Thus we must have a syntactic analysis of discontinuous *ne...pas* in French. Second, French does not employ a phrase-final negative marker like BNF languages. Rather, the two negatives in French bracket the verbal complex. The only elements that may occur between *ne* and *pas* in finite clauses are the finite verb, and a few clitic pronouns. Consider the data in (1).

(1)   a.   Jean (**ne**) voit **pas** Marie.   **FRENCH**
                John *ne* sees *pas* Mary
                'John doesn't see Mary.'

         b.   Jean (**ne**) la voit **pas**.
                John *ne* her sees *pas*
                'John doesn't see her.'

         c.   De   **ne pas** voir   Marie est très difficile pour Jean.
                INF *ne pas* to-see Mary is very difficult for John
                'To not see Mary is very difficult for John.'

The sentences in (1) illustrate negation in French. Recall that *ne* is optional in finite clauses such as (1)a-b. Interestingly, *ne* is obligatory in most dialects in infinitival clauses such as (1)c. I will return to this fact below in §7.3.

A third important difference between most dialects of French, and a BNF language such as Afrikaans, is the interaction of negation with N-words such as *personne* 'no one' and *rien* 'nothing.' French allows negative concord. More than one N-word can appear in a sentence without yielding a 'double negative' reading. However, the negative particle *pas* cannot co-occur with N-words in most dialects of French. Consider the following data.

(2)   a. Jean (**ne**) voit pas Marie.   **FRENCH**
           John *ne*-see NEG the car
           'John haven't seen Mary.'

        b. Jean (**ne**) voit **personne**.
           John *ne*-see no one
           'John haven't seen anyone.'

        c. *Jean (**ne**) voit **pas personne**.
           John *ne*-see NEG no one seen

Many French speakers find sentence (2)c to be entirely ungrammatical. Others find that it has a double negative interpretation equivalent to 'John doesn't ***not*** see nobody' in standard English (i.e. 'it is not the case that John saw nobody'). The important fact is that *pas* and N-words cannot co-occur in the dialect of French described in (2). Recall that this is not the case in Afrikaans, as I show below in (3).

(3)   a. Ek sal jou **nooit (nie)** vergeet ***nie.***   **AFRIKAANS**
           I will you never *nie$_1$* forget *nie$_2$*
           'I will never forget you.' (Oosthuizen 1998)

        b. Dit blyk dat sy absoluut **niks** (**nie**) het opgedaag **nie**.
           it seems that she absolutely nothing *nie$_1$* can remember nie$_2$
           'It seems that she can remember absolutely nothing.' (ibid.)

Unlike French, Afrikaans allows N-words to co-occur with both negative particles $nie_1...nie_2$. While the sentences in (3) are not accepted by all speakers, many find them well-formed or, at worst, slightly degraded.

Given the facts about French outlined above, it is easy to see that the attractiveness of a single NegP analysis of French, such as we find in Pollock (1989), Ouhalla (1990), and elsewhere. Recall the basic outline of the analysis, as described by Ouhalla (1990:191).

> [...] sentence negation is expressed in terms of a NegP category which consists of a head element and a specifier. Variation among languages is restricted to whether both or either of the two elements of NegP is realized lexically. In languages like Turkish and Berber the head is realized lexically while the specifier is realized as an empty operator. In languages like German, Swedish and Colloquial French it is the specifier which is realized lexically, while the head is realized as an abstract morpheme. Finally, in languages like Standard French both the head and the specifier are realized lexically.

The approach outlined by Ouhalla (1990) nicely captures some of the cross-linguistic differences in negation seen in Romance and beyond, using a single NegP analysis. Following Pollock (1989), Ouhalla (1990) proposes to account for cross-linguistic (and indeed dialectal) variation in negation strategies based on the overt realization of either the head, the specifier, or both head and specifier of the NegP. I give he corresponding structure, from Pollock (1989), in (4).

(4)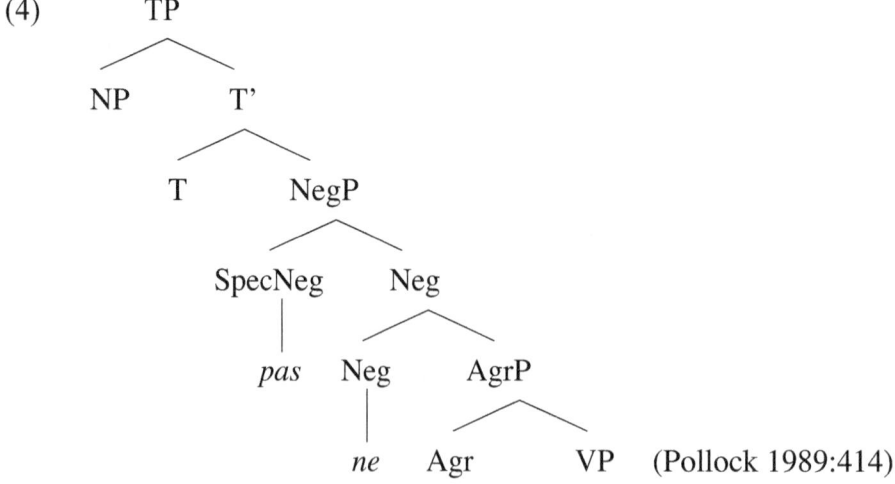

(Pollock 1989:414)

To account for the position of *ne*, Pollock (1989) argues that, as a clitic, *ne* must move to a tense position, *viz* T°. When *ne* moves to T°, it is left-adjoined to the verb in T°, yielding the surface word order in French. Updating Pollock's (1989) account to conform with the NEG Criterion (Haegeman 1995), we see that it has another advantage. It clearly explains why *pas* and N-words cannot co-occur in French, as in (2)c above. The NEG Criterion states that N-words must be in a spec-head relation with a negative head: in the case of French, the particle *ne*. However, in (2)c, under Pollock's (1989) analysis, *pas* is already occupying [Spec,NegP], blocking N-words from landing in this position, thereby violating the NEG Criterion. This further explains the surface phenomenon of certain N-words such as *rien* 'nothing' and *pas* occurring in complementary distribution. On the whole, the single NegP analysis of French appears to have several empirical advantages.

In the chapters above, I have proposed that a certain group of bipartite negation languages provide evidence for an expanded NegP, with multiple projections, two of which house negative heads. I have shown that this analysis has distinct advantages, at least for these languages, over a single NegP analysis along the lines of Pollock (1989), Haegeman (1995), and others. In the next section, I will show that the BNF analysis can be adapted to account for the data in French. Then, in §7.3, I will argue that adopting such an analysis has some clear empirical advantages.

7.2 A BNF Analysis of French

As we observed above, French differs from BNF languages such as Afrikaans and Hausa in several respects. The most important and obvious of these is that the rightmost negative particle in French, *pas* does not occur phrase-finally except in intrasitives or clauses with pronominal objects. It must precede DPs, PPs, and CPs. In other words, it occurs in an entirely different position from NEG_2 in BNF languages. However, we have seen in Chapters 2 - 4 and Chapter 6 that several BNF languages allow certain elements to follow NEG_2. In Afrikaans, for example, both PPs and CPs can follow NEG_2 in many contexts. Bukusu is more restrictive, but still allows *because*-clauses to appear to the right of NEG_2. Finally, we have observed that Hausa allows CPs to appear to the right of NEG_2, especially when they are heavy. In addition, recall that certain dialects of Hausa also allow DPs to appear to the right of NEG_2 – something unattested in any other BNF language in the dataset. Consider the data in (5).

(5)   a. **bà** mù kāmà ɓàrāwòn **ba**   **HAUSA**
            NEG we catch thief NEG
            'We didn't catch the thief.'   (Newman 2000:358)

       b. **bà** mù kāmà **ba** ɓàrāwòn   **NORTHERN HAUSA**
            NEG we catch NEG thief
            'We didn't catch the thief.'   (Newman 2000:358)

       c. Nous **n'**avons **pas** arrêté le voleur.   **FRENCH**
            we *ne* have NEG stopped the thief
            'We didn't stop (apprehend) the thief.'

While the standard dialect of Hausa described in Newman (2000) does not allow DPs to occur to the right of NEG_2, certain Northern dialects do allow this, as we see in (5)a-b. As I pointed out in Chapter 4, the sentence from Northern Hausa in (5)b bears a striking resemblance to the French sentence in (5)c. To account for the Hausa dialect described in (5)b, we may simply propose that, unlike standard Hausa, Northern Hausa allows DPs to occur to the right of NEG_2. Indeed, this would be a very minor change to the BNF architecture, especially considering the amount of variation already attested across BNF languages concerning the nature of the categories allowed to appear to the right of NEG_2.

An account of Northern Hausa along these lines opens the door to a similar account of French. First, assume that French *pas* corresponds to NEG_1 in the BNF system, and French *ne* corresponds to NEG_2. This equates *pas* with West Flemish *nie*, and *ne* with West Flemish *en* (Cf. Chapter 4 above, and Haegeman 1995). Both *ne* and *pas* are syntactic heads within the expanded NegP, as developed above. Like Afrikaans, French allows both PPs and CPs to appear to the right of negation – indeed, this is the obligatory position for complements of NegP in French. Additionally, like Northern Hausa, French allows DPs to appear to the right of negation – in fact, this is again the required position in French. Given these preliminary assumptions, the difference between French and the BNF languages described above reduces to a simple question of movement. In BNF, we have seen that XP-movement (of PPs, CPs, etc) to an intermediate position within the expanded NegP is optional. In French, such movement is obligatory. Furthermore, French has obligatory head movement of NEG_2 *ne* to $T°$, and obligatory verb movement to $T°$, as in Pollock (1989). This again equates French to West Flemish, which has clitic movement of NEG_2 *en* in finite clauses. Consider the following derivation.

(6) a. Jean (**ne**) voit **pas** Marie.   **FRENCH**
John *ne* sees *pas* Mary
'John doesn't see Mary.'

b.
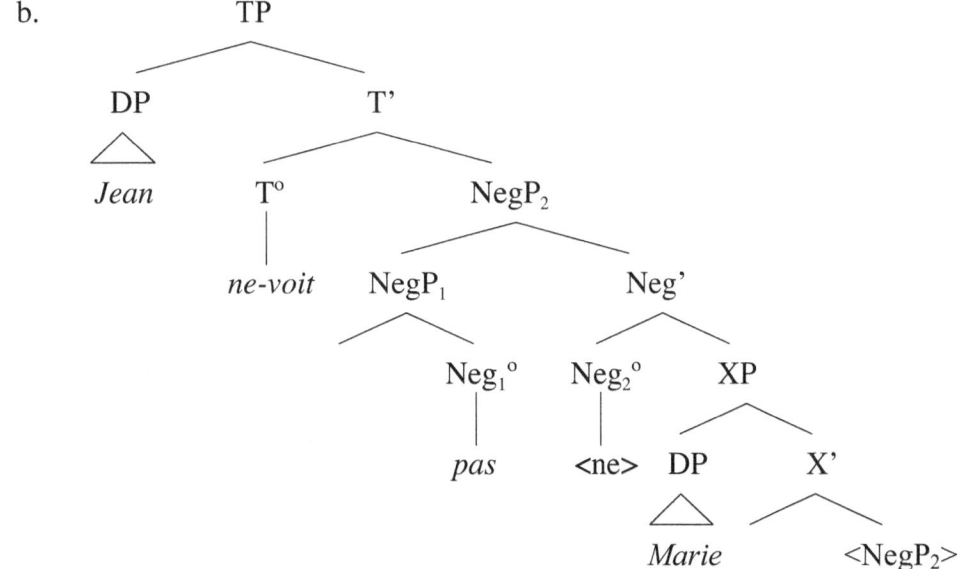

The derivation in (6)b operates under identical mechanisms to the derivation of negative sentences in Afrikaans proposed in Chapter 2. As in Afrikaans, the expanded NegP in French has at least one intermediate position inside the expanded NegP, labeled above as XP, available as a landing site for XP-movement. In Afrikaans, PPs and CPs optionally move to XP, and are thereby stranded to the right of negation. In French (and also in Northern Hausa, for example), all post-NegP constituents can move to this intermediate position. And, in French, they must move to this position. For example, in the sentence in (6)a, the DP *Marie* moves to XP, effectively stranding it to the right of negation, and yielding the surface word order observed in French. After the structure below the NegP complex is evacuated, $NegP_1$ undergoes (remnant) movement to the specifier of $NegP_2$. I take this operation, $NegP_1$ movement to [Spec,$NegP_2$] to be universal across BNF languages. Given the line of argumentation pursued here, this operation may also play a crucial role in BN languages such as French.

In the next section, I consider some of the theoretical and empirical advantages to the proposal outlined above.

7.3 Advantages of the Analysis

In §7.1 above, I discussed several advantages to the 'single NegP' analysis of negation in French, proposed by Pollock (1989) and adopted by Ouhalla (1990), Haegeman (1995), and others. However, as I show in Chapters 2-4, the 'single NegP' approach cannot account for what I have labeled BNF languages. Data from these languages strongly suggest that the basic structure of bipartite negation involves two separate syntactic heads, and thus two separate negative projections. As I show above, we can account for the surface word order as well as the underlying morpho-syntactic properties of BNF languages by adopting an articulated NegP structure.

The 'single NegP' approach accounts for French, a number of other Romance languages, West Flemish, and Berber. However, as I illustrated in §7.2, it is in principle possible to adapt the BNF system to accommodate BN languages such as French – and, by extension, other BN languages. We must simply assume, in the case of BN languages like French, that *all* material to the right of the NegP complex must be evacuated prior to $NegP_1$ movement. Furthermore, in the specific case of French, we must assume that NEG_2 *ne* undergoes obligatory head movement to $T°$ in finite clauses. Note that this latter assumption is key to either theory in accounting for the position of *ne*. Given the relative ease with which the BNF system can be adapted to account for French, I argue that it is preferable from a theoretical standpoint, since it can account for a larger number of languages. However, the BNF analysis also has at least two clear empirical advantages over the 'single NegP' approach.

First, recall the data on infinitival clauses from (1)c above, repeated in (7)a below, with another example given in (7)b.

(7) a. De **ne pas** voir   Marie est très difficile pour Jean.   **FRENCH**
INF *ne pas* to-see Mary is very difficult for John
'To not see Mary is very difficult for John.'

b. De **ne pas**   manger est mauvais pour la santé.
INF *ne* NEG eat   is bad   for   the health
'To not eat is bad for your health.'

c. *De **ne** manger **pas** est mauvais pour la santé.

Note the order of the discontinuous negatives *ne...pas*. In finite clauses such as (1)a-b above, we observed that only the verb and certain pronominal clitics can appear between *ne* and *pas*. In infinitivals, nothing can appear between *ne...pas*. The verb, which has no tense marking to pick up and thus does not move to $T°$, remains *in situ* to the right of negation. We may in fact assume, following much recent work, that there is no TP present in infinitivals, but rather an infinitival phrase InfP (Cf. Koopman &

Szabolsci 2000). We may even posit that French *de* in (7)a-b is the head of InfP. Adapting the 'single NegP' account to incorporate an infinitival phrase, we have the following structure.

(8)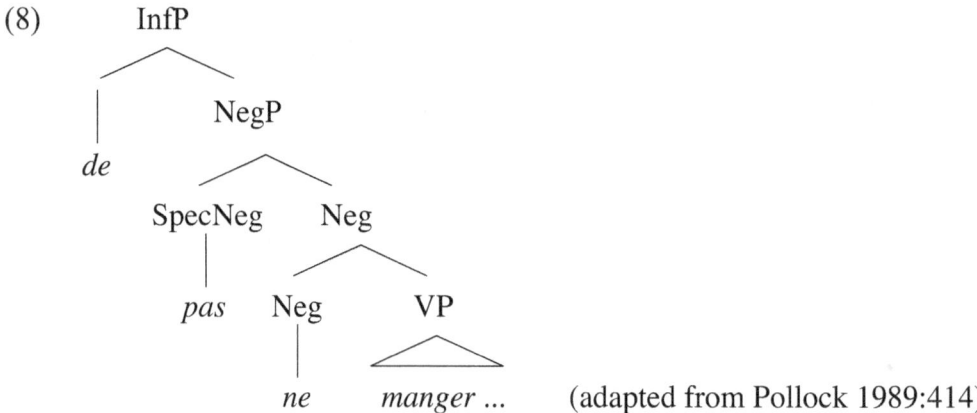

(adapted from Pollock 1989:414)

If we adopt the 'single NegP' approach, as represented by the structure in (8), we are faced with an immediate problem: how to account for the order *ne...pas* in infinitival clauses. The structure in (8) predicts the order 'de **pas ne** manger', which is ungrammatical in every dialect of French known to me. In finite clauses, *ne* moves to T° and left-adjoins to the verb. There is no such movement in infinitivals. We could propose movement of *ne* to left-adjoin with *pas*, but the motivation for such a a movement is far from obvious. We could also propose that *ne* moves to Inf°; however, this predicts the order '**ne** de **pas** manger,' which is even worse than *pas...ne*.[1]

Under the expanded NegP analysis, the infinitival facts fall out for free. First, assume that, as above, infinitival clauses contain InfP, which selects NegP. Second, assume that there is no verb movement in infinitivals in French, and, crucially, that there is no $NegP_1$ movement. The latter is a natural assumption if we agree that negation and tense have a close syntactic relationship. Also assume that the basic

---

[1] See Benmamoun (2001) for interesting discussion and analysis of this point.

BNF architecture remains the same in infinitivals: there is an expanded NegP that licensed by the two negative heads *ne* and *pas*. Now consider the structure in (9).

(9)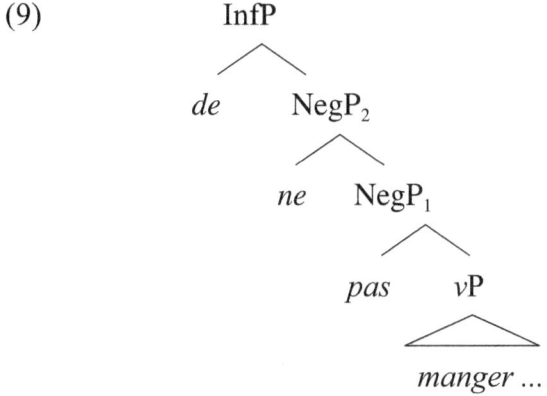

As we can observe in the structure in (9), the expanded NegP approach yields the correct word order for infinitivals in French with no further stipulations or movement operations. This constitutes a clear empirical advantage over the 'single NegP' approach, which predicts the wrong ordering of negative particles in infinitivals.

Second, recall the data on the distribution of *pas* and N-words in French from above. In many dialects of French, *pas* and N-words such as *rien* 'nothing' occur in complementary distribution, immediately following the finite verb. Other N-words such as the negative quantifier *personne* 'no one' appear in the same position as DPs, that is, following both the finite verb and the main verb. However, *pas* is not licensed in these cases either. Consider the data in (10).

(10) a. Jean (**ne**) voit **pas** Marie.   **FRENCH**
      John *ne*-see   NEG the car
      'John haven't seen Mary.'

    b. Jean (**ne**) voit **personne**.
      John   *ne*-see   no one
      'John haven't seen anyone.'

    c. *Jean (**ne**) voit **pas**   **personne**.

As I stated above in §7.1, the data in (10) are easily captured under a NEG Criterion account within the 'single NegP' framework. The negator *pas* and the N-word *personne* cannot co-occur, since *personne* must at some point move into the specifier of NegP.[2] Now consider the following data, from the dialect of French spoken in the Quebec region of Canada.

(11) a. J'ai **pas** vu **parsonne**.　　　　　　　　　　　**QUEBECOIS FRENCH**
　　　　I-have NEG seen no one
　　　　'I haven't seen anyone.'

　　　b. J'ai **pas** parlé à **parsonne**.
　　　　I-have NEG spoken to no one
　　　　'I haven't spoken to anyone.'

　　　c. On va s'retrouver dans un d'ce maudits pays communisses ousque
　　　　one go REFL-find in　one of-these damned countries communist where

　　　　parsonne a　**pas**　le droit de **rien**　faire.
　　　　no one　has NEG the right of nothing do

　　　'We'll end up in one of these bloody Communist countries where no one can do anything.' (Déprez 1999:383)

The data in (11), from Quebecois French, show that *pas* and N-words can co-occur in some dialects of French. To account for these data under the 'single NegP' approach, we would be forced to adopt a multiple specifier analysis of NegP, providing a landing site for the N-word (at LF), in order to satisfy the NEG Criterion and, in the case of N-words such as *rien*, derive the surface word order. Again, no such steps are necessary if we adopt the expanded NegP. The specifier position of NegP$_1$ is available as a landing site for N-words, since NEG$_1$ *pas* is a syntactic head.

---

[2] Note that *personne* moves to [Spec,NegP$_2$] at LF, on a NEG Criterion account, while N-words such as *rien* move prior to Spell-out. I overlook this difference for ease of presentation.

Having discussed one theoretical and two empirical advantages to adopting an expanded NegP analysis of French, I now conclude the dissertation in the following section.

7.4 Conclusions

This dissertation presents an analysis of the syntax of negation within the Minimalist framework. I argue that the need to eliminate uninterpretable negative features drives movement and accounts for word order in negative sentences across a number of languages, obviating the need for criterion-based approaches such as Haegeman (1995). I further propose that the negative phrase has an articulated structure, at least in languages that employ more than one negative particle. I propose that negative particles are syntactic heads across these languages. I also argue that the 'expanded NegP' contains intermediate projections that are landing sites for XP-movement.

I have argued for a unified analysis of a particular negation strategy found in a number of languages. I have dubbed this strategy bipartite negation with final NEG, or BNF, and have developed an analysis of the strategy based on data from Afrikaans (Chapter 2). I have shown that BNF has a number of core properties that are constant across languages (Chapter 3). Furthermore, I have illustrated that BNF languages can vary in their negation patterns in a number of ways, which I attribute to parametric variation (Chapter 4). I have investigated the historical development of BNF negation in Afrikaans (Chapter 5), and argued for the existence of a universal component in the development of BNF. I have also explored the structure and historical development of negation in a number of creole and contact languages, and argued that these languages represent intermediate stages in the development of BNF (Chapter 6). Finally, in this chapter, I have extended the proposed 'expanded NegP' analysis of BNF to French. I argue that the 'expanded NegP' can easily account for negation in French, giving it a clear theoretical advantage over the 'single NegP' approach.

REFERENCES

Aboh, Enoch. 2003. The Morphosyntax of Complement Head Sequences: Clause Structure and Word Order Patterns in Kwa. Oxford University Press.

Akasaka, Yukiko. 2003. Antisymmetry and Declaratives in Khoekhoe. Ms. Cornell University.

Aldridge, Edith. 2003. Remnant Movement in Taglog Relative Clause Formation. *Linguistic Inquiry*. **34**:3.

Bayer, J. 1990. What Bavarian negative concord reveals about the syntactic structure of German. In: Mascaró, J. and M. Nespor (eds.), *Grammar in Progress*. Dordrecht, Foris. 13-23.

Bell, Arthur. 2004. How N-words Move: Bipartite Negation and the Split-NegP Hypothesis. *Proceedings of the Conference on Triggers*. Berlin. Mouton de Gruyter.

Bell, Arthur and Aggrey Wasike. 2004. Negation in Bukusu. Paper presented at the 35th Annual Conference on African Linguistics. Boston, MA.

Benmamoun, Elabbas. 2000. *The feature structure of functional categories: a comparative study of Arabic dialects*: Oxford studies in comparative syntax. New York. Oxford University Press.

Bickerton, Derek. 1981. *Roots of language*. Ann Arbor. Karoma.

Chomsky, Noam. 1994. Bare phrase structure: MIT occasional papers in linguistics **5**. Cambridge, MA.

Chomsky, Noam. 1995. *The minimalist program*. Cambridge, Mass. The MIT Press.

Chomsky, Noam. 1998. Minimalist inquiries: the framework. MIT occasional papers in linguistics **15**. Cambridge, MA.

Chomsky, Noam. 1999. Derivation by phase. Cambridge, MA. MIT Working Papers in Linguistics.

Chomsky, Noam. 2001. Beyond explanatory adequacy. MIT occasional papers in linguistics **20**. Cambridge, MA.

Chomsky, Noam. 2004. Three factors in language design: Background and prospects. Plenary Address given at the 78th annual meeting of the Linguistic Society of America. Boston, MA.

Cinque, Guglielmo. 1999. *Adverbs and functional heads: A cross-linguistic perspective*. Oxford Studies in Comparative Syntax. Oxford University Press.

Collins, Chris. 1997. *Local economy*: Linguistic inquiry monographs . 29. Cambridge, Mass. MIT Press.

Collins, Chris. 1997. Argument Sharing in Serial Verb Constructions. Linguistic Inquiry 28. 461-497.

Collins, Chris. 2003. The internal structure of vP in Jul'hoansi and ǂHoan [1-25]. Studia Linguistica 57.

Collins, Chris. 2004. A Smuggling Approach to the Passive in English. Ms. Cornell University.'

Culicover, Peter. 1991. Polarity, Inversion, and Focus in English. *ESCOL '91*. 46-68.

DeGraff, Michel. 1999. *Language creation and language change: creolization, diachrony, and development: Learning, development, and conceptual change*. Cambridge, Mass. MIT Press.

DeGraff, Michel. 2001. Morphology in Creole Genesis: Linguistics and Ideology. In *Ken Hale: A Life in Language*, ed. Michael Kenstowicz, 53-121. Cambridge. MIT Press.

DeGraff, Michel. 2003. Creolization is Acquisition. Paper presented at the Summer Meeting of the Society for Pidgin and Creole Linguistics. Honolulu, Hawai'i.

Delplanque, Alain. 1990. Assertion et Mode en Dagara. Linguistique Africaine 4. 47-63.

den Besten, Hans. 1978. Cases of possible syntactic interference in the development of Afrikaans. *Amsterdam Creole Studies (Publikaties van het Instituut voor Algemene Taalwetenschap)*. 2. 5-56.

den Besten, Hans den. 1985. Die doppelte Negation im Afrikaans und ihre Herkunft. *Acten des 1 Essener Kolloquiums über "Kreolesprachen und Spachkontakte."* 26, 1. Bochen. Thiebes.

den Besten, Hans. 1989. *Studies in West Germanic syntax*, Katholieke Universiteit Brabant. Ph.D. dissertation.

den Besten, Hans. 2000. The Slaves' Languages in the Dutch Cape Colony and Afrikaans vir. In Institut Algemene Taalwetenschap, 949-971. Amsterdam.

den Besten, Hans. 2002. Khoekhoe Syntax and L2 Acquisition of Dutch and Afrikaans. Jounal of Germanic Linguistics 14:3-56.

den Besten, Hans & Gert Webelhuth. 1990. Stranding. In Scrambling and Barriers, ed. Günter Grewendorf & Wolfgang Sternefeld, 77-92. Amsterdam/Philadelphia. John Benjamins.

Déprez, Vivianne. 1999. Roots of Negative Concord in French and French-Lexicon Creoles. In Language Creation and Language Change, ed. Michel DeGraff, 375-427. Cambridge. MIT Press.

Dieck, Marianne. 2000. *La negación en palenquero*. Frankfurt. Iberoamericana.

Donaldson, B. C. 1993. *A grammar of Afrikaans: Mouton grammar library* 8. New York. Mouton de Gruyter.

Donaldson, B. C. 2000. *Colloquial Afrikaans: the complete course for beginners*. London. Routledge.

Elphick, Richard. 1977. *Kraal and castle: Khoikhoi and the founding of white South Africa*. New Haven. Yale University Press.

Elphick, Richard, and Giliomee, Hermann Buhr. 1989. *The Shaping of South African society, 1652-1840*. Middletown, Conn. Wesleyan University Press.

Engelbrecht, J. A. 1936. *The Korana. an account of their customs and their history, with texts*. Cape Town. M. Miller limited.

Fox, Danny. 2000. Antecedent Contained Deletion and the Copy Theory of Movement. Linguistic Inquiry.

Haegeman, Liliane M. V. 1995a. *The syntax of negation*: Cambridge studies in linguistics 75. Cambridge. Cambridge University Press.

Haegeman, Liliane M.V. 1995b. The Syntax of N-words and the NEG Criterion. *Negation and Polarity*. CILT 155. 113-137.

Haegeman, Liliane M. V. 2002. West Flemish Negation and the Derivation of SOV Order in West Germanic. *Journal of Nordic Linguistics*. 25:2.

Haegeman, Liliane and Raffaella Zanuttini. 1991. Negative Heads and the Neg Criterion. *The Linguistic Review* 8. 223-251.

Hagemeijer, Tjerk. 2004. Aspects of Discontinuous Negation in Santome. Ms. University of Lisbon.

Hagemeijer, Tjerk and Ana Lucia Santos. 2003. Elementos polares na periferia direita: negaçao aparentemente discontinua, afirmaçao enfatica e tags. Paper presented at XIX Encontro Nacional da Associaçao Portuguesa de Linguistica, Lisbon.

Hagman, Roy S. 1977. *Nama Hottentot grammar*. Bloomington. Indiana University.

Hajdu, Peter. 1963. *The Samoyed peoples and languages*. Bloomington. Indiana University.

Harris, Alice C., and Campbell, Lyle. 1995. *Historical syntax in cross-linguistic perspective*. Cambridge studies in linguistics. New York. Cambridge University Press.

Hesseling, D. C. 1899. *Het afrikaansch. bijdrage tot de geschiedenis der nederlandsche taal in Zuid-Afrika*. Leiden. Boekhandel en drukkerij voorheen E.J. Brill.

Hill, Clifford Alden. 1976. Negation in Hausa and Principles of Information Processing: Secondary Signalling and Surface Bracketing. Columbia University Working Papers in Linguistics 3:59-74.

Hopper, Paul J., and Traugott, Elizabeth Closs. 1993. *Grammaticalization*. Cambridge textbooks in linguistics. New York. Cambridge University Press.

Hornstein, Norbert, Jairo Nunes and Kleanthes K. Grohmann. 2004. *Understanding Minimalism: An Introduction to Minimalist Syntax*. Ms.

Jaggar, Philip J. 2001. *Hausa*. London Oriental and African language library, v. 7. Philadelphia. J. Benjamins.

Jespersen, Otto. 1917. Negation in English and Other Languages. World Press.

Kato, Yasuhiko. 1994. Negative Polarity and Movement. MIT Working Papers in Linguistics 24:101-120.

Kato, Yasuhiko. 1999. Local Negation. Sophia Linguistica 44-45. 33-41.

Kayne, Richard S. 1994. *The antisymmetry of syntax*. Linguistic inquiry monographs . 25. Cambridge, Mass. MIT Press.

Kishimoto, Hideiki. 2003. Negative Head Raising in Japanese. Paper presented at The Cornell Linguistics Colloquium, Cornell University.

Kitahara, Hisatsugu. 1997. *Elementary operations and optimal derivations. Linguistic inquiry monographs*. 31. Cambridge, MA. MIT Press.

Koopman, Hilda and Ana Szabolcsi. 2000. Verbal Complexes. MIT Press.

Koster, Jan. Predicate Incorporation and the Word Order of Dutch. G. Cinque, et al. (eds.) *Paths Towards Universal Grammar: Studies in Honor of Richard S. Kayne.* Georgetown University Press. 255-276.

Kouwenberg, Silvia. 1994. *A grammar of Berbice Dutch Creole.* Mouton grammar library. 12. Berlin . New York. Mouton de Gruyter.

Laka, Itziar. 1990. *Negation in Syntax. On the nature of functional categories and projections.* Ph.D. dissertation. MIT.

Laka, Itziar. 1994. On the Syntax of Negation. New York. Garland Publishing

Le Roux, Jacobus Johannes. 1923. *Oor die Afrikaanse sintaksis.* Amsterdam. Swets & Zeitlinger.

Lefebvre, Claire. 1998. *Creole genesis and the acquisition of grammar: the case of Haitian creole*: Cambridge studies in linguistics **88**. New York. Cambridge University Press.

Lefebvre, Claire, and Brousseau, Anne-Marie. 2002. *A grammar of Fongbe.* Mouton grammar library **25**. New York. Mouton de Gruyter.

Lightfoot, David. 1991. *How to set parameters*: *arguments from language change.* Cambridge, Mass. MIT Press.

Maingard, L. F. 1962. *Korana folktales: grammar and texts.* Johannesburg. Witwatersrand University Press.

McWhorter, John H. 1997. Towards a new model of creole genesis: Studies in ethnolinguistics, vol. 3. New York. P. Lang.

McWhorter, John H. 1998. *The word on the street: fact and fable about American English.* New York. Plenum Trade.

McWhorter, John H. 2000. *The missing Spanish creoles: recovering the birth of plantation contact languages.* Berkeley. University of California Press.

Molnárfi, László. 2002. Die Negationsklammer im Afrikaans: Mehrfachnegation aus formaler und funktionaler Sicht. In Issues in Formal German(ic) Typology., ed. Werner Abraham and C. Jan-Wouter Zwart, 223-261. Amsterdam. John Benjamins.

Moritz, L. and D. Valois. 1994. Pied-piping and specifier-head agreement. Linguistic Inquiry 25:667-707.

Mufwene, Salikoko S. 2001. *The ecology of language evolution: Cambridge approaches to language contact.* New York. Cambridge University Press.

Müller, Gereon. 2000. Shape Conservation and Remnant Movement. Paper presented at NELS 30.

Ndayiragije, Juvenal. 1999. Checking Economy. Linguistic Inquiry 30:3. 399-444.

Ndayiragije, Juvenal. 2003. Eliminating the Phase Impenitrability Condition. Paper presented at The Cornell Linguistics Circle Thursday Colloquium.

Newman, Paul. 2000. The Hausa language: an encyclopedic reference grammar. New Haven. Yale University Press.

Newman, Paul. 1971. The Hausa negative markers. Studies-in-African-Linguistics. 2, 3. New Haven. Yale University Press. 183-195.

Newman, Paul. 2002. *Chadic and Hausa linguistics.* Kèoln. Kèoppe.

Oosthuizen, Johan. 1998. Afrikaans *nie*-2. Stellenbosch Papers in Linguistics 29.

Nkemnji, Michael. 1995. *Heavy Pied-Piping in Nweh.* Ph.D. dissertation. UCLA.

Oosthuizen, Johan. 1998. Final NIE in Afrikaans. Stellenbosch Papers in Linguistics. Cape Town.

Ouali, Hamid. 2002. Sentential Negation in Berber. Paper presented at ACAL 34.

Ouhalla, Jamal. 1990. Sentential Negation, Relativized Minimality and the Aspectual Status of Auxiliaries. *Linguistic Review* 7. 183:231.

Picoche, Jacqueline, and Marchello-Nizia, Christiane. 1989. Histoire de la langue française. Collection Nathan-université. Série "Etudes linguistiques et littéraires". Paris. Nathan.

Pollock, Jean-Yves. 1989. Verb Movement, Universal Grammar, and the Structure of IP. Linguistic Inquiry 20. 365-424.

Ponelis, Fritz. 1993. *The development of Afrikaans*. New York. Peter Lang.

Rizzi, Luigi. 1991. Residual verb second and the wh-criterion. Ms. Université de Genève.

Rizzi, Luigi. 1997. The Fine Structure of the Left Periphery. In Elements of Grammar, ed. Liliane M. V. Haegeman. Boston. Kluwer Academic Press.

Robbers, Karin Barbera Maria. 1997. *Non-finite verbal complements in Afrikaans: a comparative approach*. HIL dissertations . 33. The Hague. Holland Academic Graphics.

Roberge, Paul T. 1992. Afrikaans and the Ontongenetic Myth. *Language & Communication* 12:31-52.

Roberge, Paul T. 1999. On Reconstructing Variation in Cape Dutch (1710-1840). Stellenbosch Papers in Linguistics 32.

Roberge, Paul T. 2002a. Afrikaans: considering origins. In Language in South Africa, ed. Rajend Mesthrie, 79-103. Cambridge. Cambridge University Press.

Roberge, Paul T. 2002b. Convergence and the Formation of Afrikaans. Jounal of Germanic Linguistics 14:57-93.

Schwegler, Armin. 1985-87. Predicate negation in contemporary Brazilian Portuguese: a change in progress. *Orbis* 34. 187-214.

Schwegler, Armin. 1991a. El espanol de Choco. *America Negra* 2. 85-119.

Schwegler, Armin. 1991b. Negation in Palenquero: synchrony. Journal of Pidgin and Creole Languages 6. 165-214.

Smith, Johannes Jacobus. 1952. *Theories about the origin of Afrikaans*. Johannesburg. Witwatersrand University Press.

Thomason, Sarah Grey, and Kaufman, Terrence. 1988. *Language contact, creolization, and genetic linguistics*. Berkeley. University of California Press.

Valkhoff, Marius François. 1966. *Studies in Portuguese and Creole, with special reference to South Africa*. Johannesburg. Witwatersrand University Press.

Valkhoff, Marius François. 1972. New light on Afrikaans and Malayo-Portuguese. Louvain. Editions Peeters Impr. Orientaliste.

Veenstra, Tonjes. 1996. *Serial verbs in Saramaccan: predication and creole genesis*. Holland Academic Graphics.

Veld, Jacob Hendrik. 1993. Postverbal constituents in Dutch and Turkish. Holland Academic Graphics.

Washburn, Paul. 2001. A Minimalist Approach to Khoekhoe Declaratives. Cornell Working Papers in Linguistics 18. 28-56.

Watanabe, Akira. 2004. The Genesis of Negative Concord: Syntax and Morphology of Negative Doubling. Ms.

Zanuttini, Raffaella. 1997. *Negation and clausal structure: a comparative study of Romance languages*. Oxford studies in comparative syntax. New York. Oxford University Press.

Zanuttini, Raffaella. 2001. Sentential Negation. In Baltin, M. and C. Collins (eds.) *The Handbook of Contemporary Syntactic Theory*. Blackwell. 511–535.

Zwart, C. Jan-Wouter. 1997. *Morphosyntax of verb movement: a minimalist approach to the syntax of Dutch*. Boston. Kluwer Academic Publishers.